D0215464

THE NEGRO AND HIS SONGS

THE NEGRO AND HIS SONGS

A STUDY OF TYPICAL NEGRO SONGS
IN THE SOUTH

BY

HOWARD W. ODUM, Ph.D.

KENAN PROFESSOR OF SOCIOLOGY AND DIRECTOR OF THE
SCHOOL OF PUBLIC WELFARE, UNIVERSITY
OF NORTH CAROLINA

AND

GUY B. JOHNSON, A.M.

INSTITUTE FOR RESEARCH IN SOCIAL SCIENCE
UNIVERSITY OF NORTH CAROLINA

NEGRO UNIVERSITIES PRESS
WESTPORT, CONNECTICUT

Odum, Howard Washington, 1884–1954.
 The Negro and his songs; a study of typical Negro songs
in the South, by Howard W. Odum and Guy B. Johnson.
New York, Negro Universities Press ₍1968, ᶜ1925₎

 vii, 306 p. 22 cm.

 Bibliography: p. ₍297₎–300. Bibliographical footnotes.

 1. Negro songs—History and criticism. 2. Negro songs.   ɪ. Johnson, Guy Benton, 1901–   joint author. ɪɪ. Title.

 ML3556.O3 1968   784.7′56   68–55902
                                                    MARC

 Library of Congress   ₍5₎   MN

Originally published in 1925 by University of North
Carolina Press

Reprinted in 1968 by Negro Universities Press, a division
of Greenwood Press, Inc., 88 Post Road West, Westport,
Conn. 06881

Library of Congress catalog card number 68-55902

ISBN 0-8371-0596-X

Printed in the United States of America

10 9 8 7 6 5

PREFACE

This volume is presented simply as a part of the story of the Negro. Other volumes are planned to follow: another collection of songs brought more nearly up to date; a presentation of song and story centered around case studies; a series of efforts to portray objectively the story of race progress in the United States in the last half dozen decades. In each case the material will be presented simply for what it is and not for cosmic generalizations or ethnic interpretation. In the present volume the use of the term Negro refers only to the Negro singer and to that which he represents. The term folk song is used in this collection in a general way and for comparative reference. In neither case are the terms employed with an all-inclusive and technically comprehensive meaning. The Negroes in this book are real Negroes, but they do not represent all the Negro race; the songs are real songs, but many of them are not folk songs in the accurate sense of the word.

The volume will be found to abound in paradoxes and contradictions. The songs are not alike; the dialect is not consistent. There are lyrics of power and appeal, and there are verses crude and sordid. There are lines of elegance and inelegance. There are ballads of worth and disjointed, inconsequential lines of trash. There is sorrow and there is joy; pathos stands alongside humor. If, as W. T. Dawson says, the secret of true poetry is to see and to feel, then there is poetry in the Negro songs. If images and allegories are better than material things, then the Negro singer is good. But if one is to find poetry, like some Richard

Jeffries, dwelling on the mystery and beauty of the flesh, on the sensitive elegance of nature and the soul, or like Wordsworth's man-to-man poet, there will be many who dissent from such a judgment of crude creative effort. For there abounds much coarseness. Well it is that this collection has no duty to evaluate overweening physical expression alongside spiritual aspiration, to judge whether buttercups are grazing grass or the substance of sun-spilt immortal gold! Other contrasts there are: stately measures and broken rhythm, forced triseme and ragged trochee, illogical asyndeton and mixed meters, and such other untamed technique as will undoubtedly do justice to the singer of the songs.

But here are the songs as they were found with something of their setting. Some of them have been published in *The Journal of American Folklore*, and some in *The American Journal of Religious Psychology*. Acknowledgment of previous publication in these journals is here rendered. Considerable material could not be included in this collection but will follow in the next. This material includes a group of songs collected in Tennessee by Anna Kranz Odum, to whom we are indebted for much help in the utilization of the material in this volume; new songs recently collected in North Carolina and other localities; and a miscellaneous collection of rhymes, games, improvisations, original compositions and riddles.

The songs in this volume were collected in Northern Mississippi, counties of Pontotoc and LaFayette, and in Northern Georgia, counties of Newton and Rockdale. A few other songs and fragments, chiefly from North Carolina and Tennessee, have been used here and there for comparative purposes.

Whatever of special merit the present volume may have besides the inherent value of the collection, is due to the work of Mr. Guy B. Johnson, who has taken the entire original collection, rearranged and reclassified many of the songs, eliminated much duplication, made comparative studies of other collections, and added generally to the effectiveness of the presentation. Special thanks are due Dr. L. R. Wilson, Director of the University of North Carolina Press, for his valuable suggestions in working out many important details, and to Dean J. F. Royster for his kindness in going over most of the original manuscript and making helpful suggestions.

CHAPEL HILL, N. C.   H. W. O.
   February, 1925.

CONTENTS

THE NEGRO AND HIS SONGS

CHAPTER I

PRESENTING THE SINGER AND HIS SONG

"I'm a worker, a pick and shovel man—what I want is an outlet to express what I can say besides work," wrote Pascal D'Angelo, Son of Italy, with the hardihood of a worker-poet trying to express his "living sufferings."[1] Nevertheless the poetic "cry of a soul stranded on the shores of darkness" had its counterpart in a "certain air almost of jollity, a smiling friendliness, without any trace of bitterness, that woke one's wonder," and in his own verses he represents the soul of a whistling, plodding farm lad as a bright blue sky, while the souls of many who speed faster through the valley "are dim with storms." So come the mixed messages of one worker, ethnic representative of a large group whose picks and shovels have contributed much to this golden age of industry.

"Law', cap'n, I's not a singin', I's jes a hollerin' to he'p me wid my wu'k," smiled a cheerful pick and shovel man, Watrous, Son of Africa, gathering himself and his song at dayspring. And, "You mus' be stringin' me to call that singin'." Yet what singing! Any one hearing him sing day in and day out, together with thousands of others like him, must agree, in all good will, with the oft-repeated song claim of the "musicianer," "music-physicianer" and "songster," that "All don't see me goin' to hear me sing." Not only does he sing, but he sings much and sings long, with such richness and variety as may be understood

[1] See Carl Van Doren's Introduction to *Pascal D'Angelo, Son of Italy*, New York, The Macmillan Co., 1924.

only by those who hear often and listen well to an
enviable range that calls forth the verdict,

> Well, he sets my soul on high,
> Makes me laugh and makes me cry.

Thus come the mixed songs of another group, basic
in the agricultural and industrial development of the
Nation.   Has the Negro succeeded more in his work
and song than other peoples?

And what vast amount and variety of things "besides work" the Negro singer can say and does say
with art, humor, pathos, spontaneity.   This volume
is a part of the story; a small part, it is true, but nevertheless a very real and vivid part, rich in examples of
the Negro's creative effort within the limitations of
the collection, vivid in the visualization of his imagin-
ings and the technique of his song.   What skill and
pride are found in the improvisation of the song leader
whose song had been sought by a university dean who
had listened with growing interest to the road gang
singing as they worked in front of his house.   This
dean accordingly sat himself down on his rock wall to
see if perchance he might not take down some of the
songs which he heard, the singing of which he so much
enjoyed.   He was thinking how oblivious the workers
were to his presence and to all things else save their
work.   He marveled that the words of the song he
could not gather; nevertheless he would be persistent,
he would get them.   And so he did, with the somewhat
startling effect, approximately versed to meet the
workman's technique:

White man settin' on wall,
White man settin' on wall,
White man settin' on wall all day long,
Wastin' his time, wastin' his time.

That the "white man" immediately moved on need not
be taken as evidence that he appreciated the song any
the less, but perhaps the incident reminded him of
other times when the words he sought were indistinct,
or it may recall to others with vividness similar Negro
songs about the white man.

Something of the Negro singer's imagery, style, and
creative effort will be set forth in detail in a later
chapter. But it seems only fair at the beginning to
introduce the Negro singer and his song by pointing
out some of the outstanding characteristics which
promise the reader a measure of pleasure as well as of
information concerning the important aspect of Negro
life and labor. What more appropriate mechanism,
for instance, for the Negro laborer on a hot day, under
the broiling sun, than the following song?

Well, she ask me—whuk—in de parler—whuk,
An' she cooled me—whuk—wid her fan,—whuk,
An' she whispered—whuk—to her mother—whuk,
Mamma, I love that—whuk—dark-eyed man—whuk.

Well, I ask her—whuk—mother for her—whuk,
An' she said she—whuk—wus too young—whuk,
Lord, I wish'd I'd—whuk—never seen her—whuk,
An' I wish'd she—whuk—never bin bohn—whuk.

Well, I led her—huh—to the altar—huh,
An' de preacher—huch—giv' his comman'—huch,
An' she swore by—huch—God that made her—huch,
That she'd never—huch—love 'nother man—huch.

The details of the meter of this and similar songs will be discussed in the chapter on Work Songs; the reader, however, will already have seen the rhythm, with the nasal caesural pause, long enough for the singer to catch his breath and start another stroke. If one wants to find scansion here, the triseme and trochee will serve him well, but that matters little in the imagery of the song and the swing of the pick.

Reviewers of Mr. Kennedy's delightful *Black Cameos* have complained that it concerned itself only with the Negro in his lighter vein. "Has the Negro," asks one, "no tale of true sorrow and tragedy to tell— tragedy ennobled by the simplicity and directness with which he can recount other stories? Must the Negro's sorrows forever be expressed only in his music, in the minor cadences of those spirituals which stir listeners to tears? Not far from the cabin door there must be more than has yet been written."[1] Of course, there is; and, of course, it has its expression outside the ordinary range of the white man. In the introductory part of the later chapter on Social Songs it is pointed out that, contrary to common opinion, the current secular songs of the Negro show as much sadness as the original spirituals, although slavery has been gone these several decades. It is left for the reader and student to interpret these, keeping them alongside the greater number of joyous and humorous songs, and not ascribing too much to the significance of whatever emotional mechanisms may result. But whatever else may be said about both the lighter and sadder songs, there can be no doubt that they represent, with rare distinctiveness, the Negro singer as nothing else

[1] See *The Saturday Review of Literature*, Jan. 3, 1925, and *The New York Evening Post Literary Review*, November 22, 1924.

does or can. They are the essence of his genius and his spirit and, whatever their defects, they most certainly reach the realm of art, and they interpret life. There is besides the sadder strains much that tends to bitterness. The singer is not only

> Po' boy 'long way from home
> Got no where to lay my weary head,

but also

> Got de blues but too damn mean to cry.

He used to sing

> You hurt my feelin's but I won't let on,

but now he sets forth

> Me'n my pad'nah an' three-fo' mo',
> Goin' raise hell 'roun' pay cah do'.

And in that remarkable work song in Chapter VIII, where the singer complains to his "captain" of his cold feet, cold hands, work in the rain, night work, long hours, little food, he exclaims,

> Well, if I had my weight in lime,
> I'd whip my captain 'til he went stoneblin'.

But even here with all his complaints the singer tells a story on himself, what the captain says and does, how the "fohty-fo's" or field peas are all gone, how the captain licked the neighboring boss, and ends with

> Well, I got up on level, look as far as I seen,
> Nuthin' wus a comin' but a big capteen,

who is so "dam' mean, musta come from New Orleans,

haw-haw." And although he would much rather be a Negro than a cheap white man, he realizes that the Negro has his own characteristics, among which is a sense of humor:

> Nigger be nigger whatever he do,
> Tie red ribbon 'round toe of his shoe,
> Jerk his vest on over his coat,
> Snatch his britches up 'round his throat,
> Singin' high stepper, Lawd, you shall be free,
> Yes, when de good Lawd done set you free.

With the singing of which, in his best moments, the Negro singer can defy imitation, banish ill feeling from himself and the white man, and project himself beyond the realism of human limitations into the land of the spirit, where after all

> 'Way up in de Rock of Ages
> In God's bosom gwin' be my pillah.

Listening in on the singers at camp, on the roads, in field and construction gangs and hearing the jollity of their morning and evening conversations as well as the humor of their daily talk, one must still recognize in the Negro common man a rare type who has not lost the art of cheerfulness of the practice of gayety. Good will and good wishes for the race follow the singer.

Recently a number of writers have pointed out something of the dual personality of the American Negro— one personality for himself and his race and one for the white folk with whom he comes in contact.[1] This situation is not new to Southern whites who have observed discriminatingly and have been frankly

---

[1] See, for instance, "Homo Africanus" in the December, 1924, *American Mercury*.

willing to see the situation; it is the merest common-place to the Negro, a situation about which he has had his fun all along, albeit also his very serious disposition of the matter. Much more artistically expressed is this attitude in his songs than in the bolder talk of individuals or groups or even in written fiction or essay now constituting an important part of Negro literature. All the more artistic is the Negro singer's effort if he now hides and now reveals his feeling-attitude toward the white man. "Ain't it hard to be a nigger?" com-plains the singer, "for you can't git yo' money when it's due."

> Well, it makes no dif'unce how you make out yo' time,
> White man sho bring nigger out behin'.
> If you work all the week, an' work all the time,
> White man sho to bring nigger out behin'.

And again the plaintive humor and protest:

> Nigger and white man playin' seven-up,
> Nigger win de money, skeered to pick 'em up.

This may be well balanced, however, according to the singer who affirms that

> When he gits old, old and gray,
> When he gits old, old and gray,
> Then white folk looks like monkeys,
> When dey gits old, old an' gray.

These examples showing some of the lighter aspects of the Negro and his song are presented to indicate the great variety and contrast found in the Negro songs in this collection. The more serious religious songs and spirituals are presented in Chapters II and

III.   No one who knows of the vast amount, seemingly unlimited, of native material, descriptive of the folk, the life, the regional civilization of the Negro can fail to regret its neglect.   Here are language, literature, and if poetry be the product of feeling and seeing, then poetry of unusual charm and simplicity.   They are parts of the story of the race.   And to preserve and interpret the contributions of a people to their own development and to civilization is to add to the science of folk-history.   Posterity has often judged peoples without having so much as a passing knowledge of their inner life, while treasures of folklore and song, the psychic, religious, and social expression of the race, have been permitted to remain in complete obscurity. Likewise peoples have lived, contemporaneously side by side, but ignorant of the treasures of folk-gems that lay hidden and wasting all about them.   The heart and soul of the real people are unknown, science is deprived of a needed contribution, and the world is hindered in its effort to discover the full significance of psychological, religious, social and political history of mankind.   That which is distinctly the product of racial life and development deserves a better fate than to be blown away with a changing environment, and not even remain to enrich the soil from which it sprang. The scientific spirit and fairness to the race demand the preservation of all interesting and valuable additions to the knowledge of folk life.   The successful study of the common development of the human intellect and primitive thought are advanced, while the exact form of expression itself constitutes a contribution to knowledge and literature.

In this collection of songs there are certain specific

values and certain obvious defects. It has been pointed out in the preface that the volume reflects much that is paradoxical and contradictory. There is likewise much that is incomplete. It would be a fine thing if Negro writers of ability today would set themselves the task of collecting and presenting the great body of folk material, in the abundance of which they would find rare opportunity. They could enrich the literature and heritage of the race and find in these songs and poetry media not only for the development of their own capacities, but for a more effective literary expression, and experience in meeting evolving, changing situations. This collection is suggestive of that larger body of material which can be gathered only through the devotion and ability of Negro writers and students.[1] This collection is of value and is presented as found, but it has all the shortcomings of work done from the outside, although with great care, with sympathetic interest, and at some length and expense.

This volume may be said also to be an effort toward good will and good wishes. From this viewpoint the objective presentation has its advantages. If the musical nature and potential of the race can be emphasized again and again; if the good nature, the resourcefulness and adaptability of the Negro may be studied from varying viewpoints; if the Negro's skill and art may be presented in this way; if his hypocrisy and two-faced survival mechanisms may be suggested along with his good manners, his diplomacy, his artistic expression and rare harmony, then added values may be found in the volume.

Explanatory and introductory material will be found

[1] See Bibliographical Notes for a statement concerning other collections of Negro songs.

in connection with each division of the songs. The manner of singing, the type of song, the environment of the singer—these and other important aspects must be interpreted with the song. The plan of this volume provides for a presentation of the Negro's religious folk songs and spirituals, preceded by an analysis of some of the chief subjects: heaven, hell, the judgment, Jehovah, Christ, the Lord, Scriptural characters and others. In this analysis not only the songs in this collection but those in former collections have been untilized so as to give an adequate picture of the Negro's religious imagery as expressed in his song.

Following the religious songs, the social songs are presented with analysis, examples and typical songs. Then follow the work songs and phrases. Finally, a chapter on the technique and creative effort of the Negro singer is presented.

Little attempt has been made at consistency in writing the dialect of the songs because there is no regular usage for any word in the Negro's vocabulary. The common and average dialect was copied in so far as it obtains in the easy and careless speech of the Negroes. In their rhymed words of the common verses they show a decided habit of making all final consonants silent. Thus mind, round, surround, hand, understand, land, sold, told, long, friend, wind, world, kind, and found are very common examples; they are most generally pronounced without the final consonant, though not always. While "d" is most commonly silenced, others are thus muted in proportion to their frequency of occurrence. Thus the final "g" in running, dropping, hanging, and all present participles is not sounded at all; the same is true of nouns and adjectives ending in this letter. More, before, door, floor, and sure are pronounced *mo'*, *befo'*, *do'*, *flo'*, *sho'*. Fire is *fier*, like is *lak*, from is *frum*, last and past are *las'* and *pas'*, don't is often *doan*, Lord is *Lawd* and *Loyrd*, dead is often *daid*, and is usually *an'*, to is often *ter*, of is *uv*, *uf*, *o'*, for is often *fer*, this is *dis*, with is *wid*, been is *bin*, there is often *dere*, them is *dem*, these sometimes *dese*, the is *de*, just is *jus'* and *jes*, because is often *'cause*, declare is *'clare*, enough is *'nuf*, about is *'bout*, your is *yo'*, unbelieving is *onbelievin'*, was is often *wus*. Besides these and many other similar words, the usual colloquial forms of verbs are used: *you'd, you're, he'll, they'll, I'll, I'm, can't, ain't, wouldn't, couldn't, don't* and so on. "Have" in the perfect tense with would, should and could is usually *a*: "I would *a done* this," "I would *a come through*." But it is sometimes *er*, as in "If I had *er died* when I wus young, I never would *a had* dis risk to run." So before the present participle and in qualifying words to make a simple rhythm, "a" is not infrequently inserted. "My father died *a-shoutin'* an' I'm goin' to die *a-shoutin'*, too." "Ezekiel said he spied the train *a-comin'*." The use of the double negative is too general to call for examples. The above illustrations will serve to indicate the principal characteristics of the dialect; others may be seen from the study of the songs themselves.

The reader must needs employ a vivid imagination like that which is reflected in the songs themselves if he would comprehend their essential qualities. The chief characteristics are often found in an improvised arrangement of words which makes the dominant feeling that of mingling successfully words and cadences. The meaningless phrases and refrains do not hinder the expression of feeling. Simple emotion, inherent melody, and colloquial language are combined with fine and differentiating imagery and humor in an under-meaning common to the folk song. An element of melancholy may be felt underlying many of the songs. But with all alike, vigor of expression, concreteness and naturalness of mental imagery, and simplicity of language and thought are combined with striking folk art. The Negro's projective mental imagery assumes that the hearer's comprehension can easily grasp the full picture of description, moral maxims, and dramatic dialogues, all combined into a single verse, and that he can do it without confusion. Here may be seen much of the naked essence of poetry with unrefined language which reaches for the Negro a power of expression far beyond that which modern refinement of language and thought may ordinarily approach. Rhythm, rhyme, and the feeling of satisfaction are inherent qualities.

The aim throughout the work has been to portray objectively the song life of the Negro. Consequently little has been ventured in the way of interpretation or evaluation. This collection of songs is but a fraction of the whole. For every song in this volume there are twenty that have never reached the ears of one who realizes the unexplored value for the sociologist and social psychologist as materials for the objective study of race problems. But this wealth of song will not continue indefinitely. Already the processes of civilization are operating to make the Negro ashamed of his old spirituals and to relegate the more naive of his social songs to a rapidly diminishing lower class.

Slowly but surely the folk creative urge will be dulled and this great body of folk song, perhaps the last of its kind, will pass away. It is to be hoped that sufficient research ability will be centered upon the songs of the Negro to preserve them for science and for posterity before it is too late.

CHAPTER II

THE RELIGIOUS SONGS OF THE NEGRO

Charteristic of the Race. The religious songs of
the Negro have commonly been accepted as characteristic music of the race. The name "spirituals"
given them long years ago is still current and many
songs still retain their former qualities. The publication of the old spirituals and the appearance of the
Jubilee Singers brought out the emotional beauty and
simplicity of expression which won for the Negro a
definite place in the hearts of those who had not hither-
to known him. He was often judged by these songs
alone, reported imperfectly, rendered artistically outside of the environment of the native folk. Forthwith
came expressions of delight and enthusiasm—expressions which indicate the power and the inherent
appeal of the plaintive melodies. Whatever may be
the relative place they hold in the life, history, and
nature of the Negro, there will scarcely be any doubt
as to the power of their appeal, then or now. Keeping
in mind the later presentation of secular and social
songs, and the present tendency to abandon the
spirituals, we do well to review some of the descriptive statements that came from persons first hearing
the old Negro songs. Said one,[1] "The hymns of a
congregation of impassioned and impressible worshipers have been full of unpremeditated and irresist-

[1] See *Atlantic Monthly,* Volume XIX, pp. 685, *seq.*
Scribners, Volume XX, pp. 425, *seq.*
Lippincott's, Volume II, pp. 617, *seq.*, and notes and introductions to
various volumes referred to in this work.

ible power." Sung "with the weirdest intonations," they have indeed appeared "weird and intensely sad." Or again, "such music, touching and pathetic as I have never heard elsewhere," "with a mystical effect and passionate striving throughout the whole." Or still again, "Never, it seems to me, since man first lived and suffered, was his infinite, longing and suffering uttered more plaintively." Besides being relaxation and solace to the Negroes such religious songs were "a stimulus to courage and a tie to heaven." And again: "I remember that this minor-keyed pathos used to seem to me almost too sad to dwell upon, while slavery seemed destined to last for generations; but now that their patience has had its perfect work, history cannot afford to lose this portion of the record. There is no parallel instance of an oppressed race thus sustained by the religious sentiment alone. These songs are but the vocal expression of the simplicity of their faith and the sublimity of their long resignation." Such songs "are all valuable as an expression of the character and life of the race which is playing such a conspicuous part in our history. The wild, sad strains tell, as the sufferers themselves could, of crushed hope, keen sorrow and a dull, daily misery, which covered them as hopelessly as the fog from the rice swamps. On the other hand the words breathe a trusting faith in rest for the future to which their eyes seem constantly turned. The attitude is always the same, and, as a comment on the life of the race, is pathetic. Nothing but patience for this life—nothing but triumph for the next." "One can but feel that these quaint old spirituals with their peculiar melodies, having served their time with effectiveness, deserve a better fate than to sink into oblivion as unvalued and unrecorded examples of a bygone civilization." Many have thought that these songs would pass away immediately with the passing of slavery and that the old system of words and songs "could not be perpetuated without perpetuating slavery as it existed, and with the fall of slavery its days were numbered." And "if they be found neither touching in sentiment, graceful in expression, nor well balanced in rhythm, they may at least possess interest as peculiarities of a system now no more forever in this country."

Satisfaction in Singing. The Negro found satisfaction in singing, not only at church, but perhaps even more while he performed his daily tasks. Those who heard the old slaves sing will never forget the scenes that accompanied the songs. After the lighter songs and brisk melodies of the day were over the Negroes turned toward eventide to more weird and plaintive notes. The impressions of such singing have been expressed: "Then the melancholy that tinges every Negro's soul would begin to assert itself in dreamy, sad and plaintive airs, and in words that described the most sorrowful pictures of slave life—the parting of loved ones, the separation of mother and child, of husband and wife, or the death of those whom the heart cherishes. As he drove his lumbering ox-cart homeward, sitting listlessly upon the heavy tongue behind the patient brutes, the creaking wheels and rough-hewn yokes exhibiting perhaps his own rude handiwork, the Negro slave rarely failed to sing his song of longing. What if its words were rude and its music ill-constructed? Great poets like Schiller have essayed the same theme, and mighty musicians like Beethoven have striven to give it musical form. What their splendid genius failed adequately to express, the humble slave could scarce accomplish; yet they but wrought in the same direction as the poor Negro, whose eyes unwittingly swam in tears, and whose heart, he scarce knew why, dissolved in tenderness as he sang in plaintive minor key one or another of his songs."

Booker T. Washington's Estimate. The above quotations suffice to give the general attitude toward the songs of the Negroes in the antebellum days and since. One other will be added, giving the expression of a distinguished Negro leader toward the songs of the slave, as perhaps the best interpretation that has come from within the race. In his introduction to *Twenty-four Negro Melodies* by Coleridge-Taylor in *The Musician's Library*, Booker Washington said: "The Negro folk song has for the Negro race the same value that the folk song of any other people has for that people. It reminds the race of the 'rock whence it was hewn,' it fosters race pride, and in the days of slavery it furnished an outlet for the anguish of smitten hearts. The plantation song in America, although an outgrowth of oppression and bondage, contains surprisingly few references to slavery. No race has ever sung so sweetly or with such perfect charity, while looking forward to the 'year of Jubilee.' The songs abound in Scriptural allusions, and in many instances are unique interpretations of standard hymns. The plantation songs known as the 'spirituals' are the spontaneous outbursts of intense religious fervor, and had their origin chiefly in the camp-meetings, the

2

revivals and in other religious exercises. They breathe a childlike faith in a personal Father, and glow with the hope that the children of bondage will ultimately pass out of the wilderness of slavery into the land of freedom. In singing of a deliverance which they believed would surely come, with bodies swaying, with enthusiasm born of a common experience and of a common hope, they lost sight for the moment of the auction block, of the separation of mother and child, of sister and brother. There is in the plantation songs a pathos and a beauty that appeals to a wide range of tastes, and their harmony makes abiding impression upon persons of the highest culture. The music of these songs goes to the heart because it comes from the heart."[1]

Effectiveness of Spirituals. It will thus be seen that emphasis has been placed almost entirely upon the emotional beauty of the Negro songs. They have been portrayed as the exponent of sadness in the race, and the feelings of the black folk have been described with no little skill. Observation for the most part has been made by those who have heard the Negro songs but have not studied them. No careful analysis has been attempted. Perhaps casual observers have been mistaken as to the intensity of the emotions expressed and have given undue emphasis to its practical relation and effect upon the individual and upon the race. The judgment of those who have not known the Negro and to whom his singing is a revelation, leads to sweeping generalizations. On the other hand, those who have known the Negro in many

---

[1] See also Du Bois, *Souls of Black Folk* and *The Gift of Black Folk;* James Weldon Johnson, *Book of American Negro Poetry,* B. G. Brawley, *Negro in Literature and Art.*

walks of life, and have come to know him better than any others have often emphasized a single phase of the Negro folk song. There can be no doubt as to the beauty and weirdness of the Negro singing, but a careful analysis of the general emotional feeling predominating, together with careful interpretation of all things concerned, makes comparisons less dangerous and expressions less extravagant. Slavery has passed, six decades of liberty for the slave people have signalized the better civilization, and there still remains among the Negroes the same emotional nature, the same sad, plaintive, beautiful, rhythmic sorrow-feeling in their songs.

Some of the qualities of the Negro's emotions as seen in his singing will be noted subsequently. Omitting for the present this feature of his songs, and qualifying the statement by interpreting his nature and environment, it may be affirmed that all that has been said of the spirituals is true. They are beautiful, childlike, simple and plaintive. They are the Negro's own songs and are the peculiar expression of his own being. Many of the spirituals are still popular among the Negroes, and often take the place of the regular church hymns. Ministers of all denominations take advantage of their peculiar power to sway the feelings of the Negroes into accustomed channels. Many of the old spirituals that were common in slavery are still current and are sung with but little modification; others are greatly modified and enlarged or shortened. Traces of the slave songs may be found in the more modern spirituals that have sprung up since the Civil War. The majority of the songs have several versions, differing according to localities, and affected by continual modifications as they have been used for many years. Some have been so blended with other songs, and filled with new ideas, as to be scarcely recognizable, but are clearly the product of the Negro singers. Besides the old and the mixed songs, there are many that are entirely new, arising out of various circumstances and developing with successive renditions.

Present-day Songs. The spirituals current among the Southern Negroes today are very much like those that were sung three or four decades ago. The differences may be seen in the comparisons that follow in the examples given. There are more rhymed words in the present-day Negro song than there were in the earlier ones; consequently there is often less meaning in a line or stanza. The tendency seems to be more toward satisfactory sound impression than for spontaneous feeling expression as in the older spirituals. Meaning and words in general are often sacrificed in the effort to make rhyme, to make the song fit into a desired tune, to bring about a satisfying rhythm, or to give prominent place to a single well-sounding word or phrase. It would thus seem that the religious songs composed in the usual way by the Negroes of the present generation have less conviction, and more purposive features in their composition. The dialect of the older songs is purer than that of the present-day Negro song. One finds little consistency in the use of dialect in the songs that are sung now; rarely does one hear the lines repeated in exactly the same form. Dialect or the common form of the word, it would seem, is used according as feeling, the occasion, and the necessity for rhyme or rhythm permit or demand.

Many of the Negro songs that are the most beautiful in their expression would appear expressionless were they robbed of their dialect and vividness of word portrayal. The imagery and dialect give the songs their peculiar charm; the more mechanical production that is apparently on the increase may be sung to the same melody, but the song itself has little beauty. However, the Negroes themselves prefer the old songs, and the older Negroes almost invariably return to the singing of the more primitive ones that have become a part of their heritage.

In those cases where the tunes differ from the old melodies the song has assumed a characteristic nature, either from its origin and composition, from constant usage by the Negroes, from local qualities, or from unusual combinations. And in these original creations of the Negro religion are found the truest expression of nature and life as it is reflected in the Negro of today; it is not the expression of complex life, but of simple longing. In the outbursts of joyous song and melody the note of victory is predominant; in the sadder-toned songs, sung in "plaintive, rhythmic melody," the prevailing note is that of appeal. In either case there is some sort of conviction back of the song, and it becomes the expression of primitive human life. They set forth the more simple thoughts of an emotional and imaginative worship. They magnify the personal and the spectacular in religion. They satisfy the love of melody, rude poetry, and sonorous language. Simple thought is expressed in simple rhyming phrases. Repetition of similar thoughts and a single chorus, with simple and pleasing music which lends itself easily to harmonious expression, are characteristic. The music is specially adapted to the chorus-like singing which is produced by the clever and informal carrying of many parts by the singers. The song often requires a single leader, and a swelling chorus of voices takes up the refrain. It is but natural that these songs should be suited to protracted services as good "shoutin' songs" or "runnin' speerichils." The same rhythm makes them pleasing to the toilers who are disposed to sing religious songs while they work, and promotes a spirit of good fellowship as well as being conducive to general "good feelin'." The united singing of children is also beautiful. Throughout these characteristic songs of the Negro the narrative style, the inconsequential, disjointed statements, the simple thought and the fastidious rhymes are all expressive of the Negro's mental operations.

Church Singing. All of the Negro's church music tends to take into it the qualities of his native expression—strains minor and sad in their general character. The religious "tone" is a part of the song, and both words and music are characterized by a peculiar plaintiveness. The Negroes delight in song that gives stress and swell to special words or phrases that for one reason or another have peculiar meanings to them. For the most part, all religious songs are "spirituals" and easily merge into satisfying melodies when occasion demands. With the idea gained from the music of the songs must be joined the church scene and its personalities freely mingled with the music. The preaching, praying, singing, and with it shouting, and unity of Negro worship—perfection of rhythmic sing-song—these, with the throbbing instinct of the people, make the Negro music what it is. The Negroes often sing their regular denominational hymns with the same feeling as they do the spirituals, and while mention must be made of their church hymns as such they often reach in singing them a climax similar to their most fervent outbursts, and freely mingle them with the old songs. In addition to the tune in which the hymn is written the Negro puts his own music into the singing, and his own interpretation into the words. This, together with the "feeling-attitude" which is unconsciously his, and the satisfaction which he gets from his singing, places Negro church music in a class of its own. A glance at the part which singing plays in the Negro's church services will aid in the interpretation of his songs.

Church services are opened with song; a leader may occupy his place at a central table or chair, select a song and begin to sing. Or they may wait for the "speerit" and a leader from the pews may begin to sing, others joining in the song, while the congregation begins to gather in the church. The leader often lines his song aloud, reading sometimes one, sometimes two lines, then singing. He often puts as much music-appeal into the lining of the song as he does in the singing. The rhythmical swinging tone of the reader adds zest to the singing which follows. Most of the Negroes who sing know a great many songs—in fact, all of their regular songs—if they are given a start by the leader. On the other hand, the congregation often gives the leader a start when he lags, and together they keep the song going until they are ready to stop singing or to begin another song.

If the service is prayer meeting or a class meeting the leader usually continues the songs throughout the singing part of the exercises; at regular preaching services the preacher reads the regular hymns and leaves the beginning and the final songs to the leaders. In the class meeting, the general congregation, led by song-leaders, sings, as a rule, while the class leaders are engaged with their classes. Now a woman on this side, now a man or woman on the other side of the church begins the song and others join in the doleful tunes; so too, while collections are being made the singing is kept up continuously. The process is the same; a leader begins to sing, another joins in the singing, then another and another until the majority of those present are singing. Most Negroes who attend church participate in the singing, although many will not do so regularly, preferring to remain quiet for a time, then to burst out into song. The Negroes have been proverbial for their good singing and undoubtedly they have won a deserved reputation. A group of five or ten Negroes singing at a mid-week prayer meeting will often create a volume of song equivalent to that of many times their number of white people singing. The comparison, however, is not a fair one, for the music is entirely different. One can scarcely appreciate the singing of the Negroes until he has heard them on various occasions and in different capacities. Let him listen on a quiet Sunday evening from a position on a hill to the singing of four Negro congregations, each clearly audible. It would appear to be the rhythmical expression of deep human feeling and longing in an unrestrained outburst of ten thousand souls. Inside the church one may watch the leaders as they line the songs and listen to their rich, tremulous voices; he may see the others respond and listen to the music of each peculiar voice. The voice of the leader seems to betray great emotion as he reads the lines and begins to sing. He appears literally to drink in inspiration from the songs while his soul seems to be overflowing as he sings the words telling of grace and redemption. However, he manifests the same kind of emotion when he sings one song as when singing another, the same emotion when he reads the words wrongly as when he has read them correctly; it makes little difference to him. He is consumed with the music and with the state of feeling which singing brings to him. After all, perhaps, one feeling dominates his whole being while he sings, and there can be no song to him which does not accord with this.

A complete analysis of the Negro church music in its detail is worthy of the efforts of any one who could describe it. And while the folk song is of more importance in the present work than the music of these songs, a few further details that are apparently characteristic of the Negroes will not be amiss. The singing begins slowly and with time-honored regularity, but is followed by the agreeable and satisfying effect made by the joining in of varied voices. Many times the singers begin as if they would sing a simple subdued song, or a hymn with its written music. But in a short while, apparently not being able to resist the impulse to give their feelings full sway, their voices fall into that rhythmical swing peculiar in a large degree to the Negro; all measures alike become stately. The average Negro is proud of his stylish choir because it represents a step towards a model which the Negroes wish to follow; but he does not like the choir's singing as well as his own informal song. In general the Negro's song will characterize his natural self wherever he sings or hears it sung; he is loath to give it up. And while some pastors have testified that there were no members in their church who would not sing the church songs, it is very evident that many of the younger Negroes do not enter fully into the spirit of the old songs, and they must necessarily undergo radical changes and rapidly pass away.

Standard Hymns. Before coming to the further study of the Negro spirituals, it will be well to inquire into the nature of the favorite standard church hymns commonly used by the Negroes in their church services. A comparison may then be made with the popular folk songs. The favorite songs and most common themes sung by the Negroes may best be seen at their prayer meetings or class meetings, or at such gatherings as require no formality. One may attend week after week and hear the same songs and feel the same pathos emanating from the songs which the worshipers have learned to sing and love. They enjoy singing of heaven and rest and luxury where ease abounds and where Sabbaths have no end. They love to sing the praises of the Deliverer who shall free them from life's toils. They have chosen the "good old" songs that have vividness and concrete imagery in them; they have placed a new feeling into them and a different interpretation. The meaning of the words and the sentiment of the song are transcended by the expression in the singing. The accustomed manner, together with their responsive feeling, absorbs whatever of pure devotion might have existed in their attitude—the singing itself becoming devotion. The Negro looks always to some future state for happiness and sings often:

> This earth, he cries, is not my place;
> I seek my place in heaven.

The Negroes sing with a peculiar faith the common stanzas of their hymns: "We've seen our foes before us flee," "We've seen the timid lose their fears," "We've seen the prisoners burst their chains," "We've seen the guilty lose their stains." So, too, they conceive, as of old, of the eternal rest, and sing, with its full stanzas:

> How sweet a Sabbath thus to spend,
> In hope of one that ne'er shall end.

The singing of these hymns is beautiful and impressive, testifying to the truth that their favorites appeal to the fitness of worship and accord with the ideal of rhythmical perfection as expressed in the feeling of the worshiper.

Satisfying Services. The general state of feeling which accompanies the song thus has much to do with the song itself. The singing with its results is the most satisfying and agreeable part of the worship to the Negro's nature. It satisfies his social wants and relieves to some extent his childlike psycho-physical cravings. His worship is music to his soul, whether it be in the word-music of the sermon and prayer, or in the natural outburst of his song, or in the rhythm of all combined. It is all freedom from restraint and the gratification of impulse and the experience of sustained

languor. Although the Negro expends a great deal of
energy in his singing, it is nevertheless rest for him as
he feels it.   Unrestrained expression goes far toward
relieving him of his troubles, sometimes real, sometimes imaginary. What the Negro imagines to be
total confession and contrite submission has a very
soothing effect upon him; the songs reach the climax
of this state of feeling. Many Negroes may be seen,
with their heads resting backward and eyes closed,
singing vigorously their favorite songs; often they
lean forward, sway back and forth, apparently in a
complete state of passivity. Tears and shouts of joy
are not inconsistent with the saddest strains of pathos.
Their senses are all turned toward the perception of
one attitude, and besides a wonderful tranquillity of
feeling, they also feel and see visions. At such a time
the Negro is at ease and is at liberty to give full expression to his feelings among his own people, without
incentive to action and without interruption. Is it
surprising that after a day's work, while he has passed
the hours away in emptiness of thought or in mis-
guided thinking and with perverted notions, he finds
sweet rest in some melodious songs and rhythmic
verses as he rests his body in the pew? Is it surprising
that he is unwilling to leave the church until a late
hour or that he does not tire of singing? For what
has he to attract him at home where he unwillingly
begins to think of work again? It is a little surprising,
after the outburst of song and shouts which reveal
so much of the Negro's nature that his attitude is one
of listlessness and apathy when he has finished.

This revelation of emotions which the Negro shows
in his singing but manifests the reality of his religion.
And although the greater part of his feeling in religion

is pleasurable excitement, it is, nevertheless, for this very reason the one reality in life to him. A study of the emotional element does not, then, detract from the beauty and value of the Negro's song; it does aid in interpreting those songs that arise spontaneously and also shows something of their origin and growth. Indeed, without a knowledge of the Negro's nature and environment, one would scarcely realize the fullest appreciation of his folk songs. In proportion as the investigator becomes acquainted with the people and circumstances which have furnished unique folk songs, to that degree will he be eager to search out their origin and be able to interpret them intelligently.

Source Material. The Negro has found much material upon which to base his songs and many sources from which he has selected a wide range of subject-matter. His religion is often synonymous with his song, and he has sung with little restraint the various experiences common to such a religion. The sermon and prayers, even the songs themselves, suggest new themes for an imaginative and religious being to sing. So, too, the church, the Christian and the "world" have furnished themes for his song. Sin, evil and the devil are ever-present subjects for religious thought. The scenes of everyday life form continous allegories to be imaged with the assistance of the Negro's definite self-feeling. But perhaps nowhere has the Negro found more acceptable subject-matter for his song than in the Scriptures; his songs abound in references to Scriptural characters and often portray individuals and scenes with unusual concreteness. A perusal of the Negro's song thus reveals the most common themes, but it is more difficult to locate the accidental circumstances which gave rise to particular forms of a song, or to ascertain the temperamental nature which originated many of the best known spirituals. In general, it may be said that the folk song of the Negroes has found its rise in every phase of Negro life. It is scarcely possible to trace the origin of the first spirituals and plantation songs. The American Negroes appear to have had their own songs from the earliest days of slavery. And while their first songs were undoubtedly founded upon the African songs as a basis, both in form and meaning, little trace of them can be found in the present song: Negro folk produce spontaneous song. The linguist and the anthropologist are able to find the parallel and apparent origin among the peoples of Africa of many words that have been used by the Southern Negroes in their lore and song, but there is now no practical relation between these words and the meaning of the words in their present usage. The origin of folk song has always been an interesting theme, proving full of fascination for him who finds it, nymphlike, vanishing from his grasp. Still the song of a people is ever present and appears, almost like myths, to have sprung into life in some way and at some time which no one can exactly tell. Many a bard of the common life has intensified their meaning and made them a part of that life.

However, many of the Negro folk songs may be explained when one has observed the Negro in many walks of life, or has found the conditions from which they arose. Many of the old spirituals were composed in their first forms by the Negro preachers for their congregations; others were composed by the slaves in the various walks of life, while still others were first sung by the "mammies" as they passed the time in imaginative melody-making and sought harmony of words and music. A great many of these songs never became current because they lacked the pleasurable features that appealed most to the Negroes. Those that proved satisfactory were seized upon and their growth and popularity dated from the moment they were heard. With the Negroes of today songs have arisen in much the same way. The difference of environment must necessarily make a difference in the nature of the songs; at the same time the coloring of present-day life is much in evidence in some of the old songs composed by the slaves but sung by the Negroes of the present generation. Some suggestions as to the natural origin and growth of Negro songs may be interesting and valuable.

Typical Origins. The Negroes have always been judged as full of feeling and very expressive. Their natures demand not only some expression of their emotions, but this expression must be easy and rhythmic at the same time that it is intense and continuous. The Negro's musical nature easily turns these expressions into melody, and a word, phrase or exclamation becomes a song in itself. The song is completed by the imaginative mind and the sense of fitness in sound. Worshipers often follow the preacher through his sermon in a mental state of song and when he has finished they burst out into song, singing no other than an elaborate sentence which the preacher has used in his sermon. When this is joined to a familiar chorus and tune, and then varied, a song has originated. Sometimes the song is remembered and sung again;

sometimes, like the words of the preacher, it simply becomes a part of the satisfaction of the hour and is forgotten. A Negro preacher recently reached a climax in his discourse in the phrase, "Oh, with the wings of the morning, I'd fly to that heavenly land." He repeated this a number of times and made gestures with his arms suggestive of flying. His black robe added to the forcefulness of the suggestion, and the impression became a part of the song of that church. So with praying, the pathetic appeal and word-music of a "p-l-e-a-s-e, my Lo-rd" is often the inspiration for a long song when a happy phrase from the prayer becomes an addition to a song that follows. Even more than preaching and praying, shouting gives rise to song among the Negroes; during exciting times in worship the Negroes often sing unheard-of songs, which they never recall again. It is indeed a mixed scene of song and motion, each contributing largely to the other, while the spectator looks on in wonderment at the astonishing inventiveness of the worshipers. The general motion, expressions of the face, words and harmonies, rests and rhythm, sense of fitness and even of humor, repetition—these make an occasion that defies limitation to its expression. If a single person- ality dominates the whole in an expression that appeals to the present sense of fitness, he is the author of a new song. For example, a visiting minister once shouted out during such a scene: "Oh, the hearse-wheel a-rollin' an' the graveyard opening—ha, ha," but got no further, for his refrain was taken up by the chorus, and the next day was a new version of the well-known song.

Such occasions might be cited in great numbers. Not infrequently a Negro who has assumed the posi-

tion of song leader sings a line while the others join
in with a chorus of singing and shouting. When the
leader has given all the lines that he knows, he will
often continue in the simplest manner possible, as if
he had known them for a long time, to improvise
lines, which often have little meaning, but which fit
into the tune and sound well. This process may be
continued indèfinitely, sometimes with repetition of
lines already uttered but slightly varied and the emphasis placed on the variation. It thus happens that
the songs need not have a limit. The necessity of the
occasion becomes the cause for the invention of the
song. Itinerant worshipers are often thus gratified to
sing to new congregations. As a rule the Negroes
always give attention and respect to strangers, so that
the man or woman who comes to them is at liberty
to sing old or new songs, and they often become skilled
in improvising songs. The new songs are then learned
and begin their history as folk song. Again, Negroes
often feel themselves called upon to introduce new
features into some of their songs and conceive of various novelties. The Negro's feeling toward leadership
puts a premium upon such a practice. In this effort,
a song that is little known among the Negroes will be
changed in some particulars, printed on a sheet of paper
and distributed as the song of brother or sister So-
and-So. The song may be found in a hymn book.
However, songs entirely new and the efforts of their
own poetic attempts are often thus circulated. This
gives rise to a new class of Negro spirituals, examples
of which may be seen in the following pages.

Marching Songs. A number of popular spirituals
apparently had their rise in the effort of the church to

satisfy the physical cravings of the Negroes. The church branded the fiddle and the dance as instruments of the devil, and although the Negro was and is passionately fond of dancing, he was forbidden by the church to do so. The church needed some kind of substitute for rhythm and excitement of the dance that would satisfy and still be "in the Lord." Consequently marching services were often instituted. The benches were piled up together and marching room left for the worshipers. They had various orders for this service and many forms of it have been known to exist. Sometimes they marched two by two, a "sister and brother in the Lord," sometimes they marched singly, and at other times they marched in a general "mix-up." At first they followed a leader to a simple melody, keeping step and working into a rhythmic swing. Then as they became more excited they became more expressive, and with the elaboration of the march into a dance their songs became marching songs. Often they thus marched, with intervals for rest, until the hours of the morning. Sometimes they all sang; sometimes the leader sang the leading part and all joined in the chorus with more satisfactory effect. In the march the Negroes swayed back and forth, to and fro, and found the usual satisfaction that comes from absolute lack of restraint. As the songs given in the following pages indicate, the Negroes often imagined themselves to be the children of Israel, while their marching songs represented Moses leading them out from under the bondage of Pharaoh, or they considered themselves as marching around the wall of some besieged city. Victory would be theirs sooner or later. This is not confined to the songs composed by the slavery Negroes, but is common in the later songs. Such scenes are often portrayed by Negro preachers of the present day and very appropriate applications, as they think, are made. The march songs that have been found current today were composed since emancipation. Often the Negroes enacted similar scenes without the formal putting away of the benches in the church, and the same general results were the outcome. Shouting scenes in Negro worship today are very much similar to the old marches except that they are more promiscuous. The "strange, sweet harmonies and melodies" of the old songs are still good shouting songs.

Spontaneous Origins. Individuals have composed spirituals while at work or while wandering from place to place, as a simple outgrowth of the circumstances. The expression, so common in Negro songs, "O my Lord," seems to have been introduced into a number of songs in this way. The single expression repeated, itself forms a favorite melody that is often sung. A group of Negroes sing while working; one sings a new verse of the song. "Wher you git dat?" "I made hit maself, didn't you know I'm a songster?" And he did make it, and thus gratified, tries further; others join him and they have become "songsters." Negroes, in order to verify a boast that they know a certain song to exist, have been known to compose on the moment just such a song, mixing all sorts of songs together with the ideas that arise. Others who have been offered an attractive price for songs have composed them without scruples of conscience, and, when asked to sing then, have done so with perfect ease. They were paid for the songs, thinking that they had "fooled that white man," who valued his song thus composed as much perhaps as an old spiritual that was still current.   What the Negro composed accidentally he learned to sing, and thus introduced a real song in his community, which was soon to be carried to other localities.   The Negro is going to sing whether he has a formal song or not.   The following song appears to have originated with two Negro laborers, apparently in a dialogue.   The lines may be sung to any tune and put to any chorus.

> The church bell a ringin', how sweet I do declar'.
> Why don't you go to meetin' an' pray all day long?
> I'm goin' to church an' pray all day long.
> Of course I'm a sinner but prayin' might do me good,
> An' if I do succeed I sure will tell the news.

Another song that was composed spontaneously in the effort to dignify conversation is the following. It will be seen that for the most part it is composed of phrases common to other songs, and it is only the combination that is new.

> Walk right an' do right an' trust in the Lord—
> Lay down all yo' sinful ways an' trust in the Lord.

> I am goin' to trust in the Lord,
> I am goin' to trust in the Lord,
> I'm goin' to trust in the Lord till I die.
> My God he's wonderful God an' trust in the Lord,
> He will answer yo' prayers don't care wher' you are,
> An' trust in the Lord.

The next example was offered by a Negro man after he had "come through."   He always loved to talk of what he had seen, what he knew would happen and how he could get out of difficulties.   Along with this he had an unusually imaginative mind and told many ingenious stories. Here is the song:

> The devil come down to the worl' one day
> An' I heard him holler, "Hoo-ray, hoo-ray!
> Come out, I'm havin' a holiday."
>
> That was the word I heard him say,
> But I knowed if I danced to his holiday,
> There'd be something doing an' the devil to pay.

The above song is difficult to classify. It would seem to be very much like some rhymes that the Negro had seen published in a newspaper, but for all his purposes it was a good song and it mattered little where he had obtained the ideas. It was indeed his own song. One other example of an effort to compose a new song shows the tendency of the Negro to mix his serious themes with ridiculous expressions.

> There was a man by the name of Cy,
> He never prayed an' he never try.
> So when ole Cy was come to die,
> He hollow out, "In hell I'll cry."
>
> In hell ole Cy did cry,
> In hell ole Cy did cry,
> In hell ole Cy did cry,
> Now don't you die like ole Cy die.

The song is a variation of two or three secular songs and becomes a religious song because of its chorus. It was actually sung in the churches. The "author" continued,

> Ole Cy did lead a mighty bad life,
> He was always after some other man's wife,

which clearly showed the trace of the secular element; this phrase is applied to many of the notorious characters in the Negro secular songs. Still there was an opportunity for the moral and the song represents the peculiar gratification which the Negroes find in having composed something more or less original.

Essential Value. Enough has been said to give a definite idea concerning the actual and possible origin of some of the Negro folk songs. Further examples will be given when the discussion of the Negro's secular song has been reached. The manifestation of Negro music and song is not difficult to understand in the light of the facts already suggested. His plaintive appeals in prayer, his emotional and religious nature, his love of rhythm and melody, his feelings and imagination, his interpretation of life and Scripture, his faith in dreams and visions quickly exaggerated into fabrications, his whole nature—all these reveal within him what we call the musical nature of the race. Motion and song are inseparable. Systematic movement is more conducive to singing than a careless, haphazard motion. Movement and song give rhythm that is not to be found under other circumstances. Regularity and rhythm in movement, emphasis and rhythm in music, these give the Negro songs essential pleasure-giving qualities that appeal strongly to the Negro's entire being. If his music is primitive and if it has much of the sensuous in it, if his songs and verse are full of primitive art having many elemental qualities of great worth, this is all the more reason for the continuous presentation and evaluation of their merit.

The Devil in Song. An analysis of songs that have been preserved will give us at once a better conception of the Negro's folk songs and his religion. The references are reproduced in their exact forms in order that they may serve as an aid in the study of the verse contained in the common songs of the Negroes from the time of slavery to the present day. Only the chief conceptions which have been portrayed in Negro song are given here; further analysis may be made in connection with the songs themselves. The devil is prominent in the religious songs of the Negroes. He is the constant terror and proverbial enemy of the race. He is alive, alert and concrete. He represents the demon trickster incarnate in the form of a man. He is the opposite of God but always less powerful. He is the enemy against whom the battle is always on; it is a personal battle, but he is usually outwitted or disappointed. Here are some pictures of "Old Satan" as found in the songs of the slave and the Negro of today:[1]

> Ef you want to see old Satan run,
> Jes fire off dat gospel gun.

> Old Satan is a liar an' conjurer, too,
> An' if you don't mind he'll conjure you.

Other forms are

> An' if you don't mind he'll cut you in two,
> An' if you don't mind he'll cut you through.

> Ole Satan lak a snake in the grass,
> Always in some Christian's path,

Or

> If you don't mind he'll git you at las'.

---

[1] For verses not found in the present-day Negro spirituals, see *Slave Songs in the United States*, W. F. Allen, New York, 1867; *The Jubilee Singers*, New York, 1873; *Plantation and Cabin Songs*, New York, 1892.

Ole Satan weahs a mighty loose shoe,
If you don't min' gwine a slip it on you.

Ole Satan like dat hunting dog,
He hunt dem Christians home to God.

O shout, shout, de debbil's about,
O shut yo' do' an' keep him out.

All de debbils in hell can't pluck me out,
An' I wonder what Satan's a grumblin' erbout,
He's boun' in hell an' he can't get out
But he shall be loose an' hav his way,
Yonder at de great reserection day.

I went down de hillside to make a one prayer,
An' when I get dere ole Satan was dere,
O what you think he said to me?
Said "Off frum here you better be."

Old Satan tole me to my face,
"I'll git you when-a you leave this place";
O brother dat scere me to my heart,
I was feared to walk-a when it wus dark.

I started home but I did pray,
An' I met ole Satan on de way.
Ole Satan made-a one grab at me,
But he missed my soul an' I went free.

I tell you brother you better not laugh,
Ole Satan'll run you down his path,
If he runs you lak he run me,
You'll be glad to fall upon yo' knee.

We shout so fas' de debbil look,
An' he gits away wid his cluven foot.

Ole Satan is mad an' I am glad,
He missed the soul he thought he had.

What makes ole Satan hate me so?
'Cause he got me once an' let me go.

Ole Satan tole me not to pray;
He want my soul at jedgment day.

I wrestle wid Satan and wrestle wid sin,
Stepped over hell an' come back agin.

Ole Satan tremble when he sees,
The weakest saint upon his knees.

Go 'way, Satan, I doan min' you;
You wonder, too, you can't come through?

O brother, brethren, you better be engaged,
For de debbil he's out on a big rampage.

I plucked one block out O' Satan's wall,
I heard him stumble an' saw him fall.

Ole Satan thought he had me fas';
Broke his chain an' I'm free at las'.

I met ole Satan in my way;
He say, "Young man, you too young to pray."

The devil tries to throw down everything that's good,
He'd fix a way to confuse the righteous if he could,
Thanks be to God-er mighty, he can't be beguiled,
Ole Satan will be done fighting after awhile.

The Negroes have many other phrases which they apply to Satan to picture him in other relations. "Ole Satan is a mighty busy ole man, an' throw rocks in my way." "What makes ole Satan follow me so? Satan ain't got notin' fer to do with me." As a busy man he also has his "shield and sword," not only gives trouble but gets into trouble. Says the Negro: "I

heard de debbil howlin' when I come out'n de wilderness, an' I gib de debbil battle." "Now stan' back,
Satan, an' let me go by . . . why doan de debbil
let-a me be?" "Ole Satan mighty busy, he follow me
night an' day. Ole Satan toss ball at me, he think
ball hit my soul, the ball for hell an' me for heaven."
"Ole Satan gettin' in mighty rage," for "Satan's camp's
afier." "Satan mount de iron gray hoss an' ride halfway
to pilot bar." But "We'll shout ole Satan's kingdom
down, gwine-a pull down Satan's kingdom, gwine-a
win ag'in de debbil." Victory is the Negro's, for he
exclaims: "I saw dem bindin' Satan," and "I saw
ole Satan's kingdom fallin'." But while Satan is a
great schemer and is very busy and "wash his face in
ashes," "put on leather apron," his greatest attribute
is "liar." The Negro cannot give too insistent warning:

> When I got dere Cap'n Satan wus dere.
> Sayin' "Young man, dere's no use to pray,
> For Jesus is daid an' God gone away."
> An' I made 'im out a liar an' went on my way.

With these pictures and warnings the Negro song gives
a final bit of advice. "If you ain't got de grace ob
God in yo' heart, den de debbil will git you sho"; then
the singer rests securely in the knowledge that he is
filled with the grace that holds against the devil.

King Jesus. King Jesus was the name most commonly given to Christ in the spirituals. Besides this
He was the bosom friend of the Negro. He comes in to
intercept Satan and to save the individual from hell.
He is very real and no one is more vividly described
than He. He bears many relations to his people.

Now my Jesus bein' so good an' kind,
My Jesus lowered his mercy down.
An' snatch me from de doors of hell,
An' took me in with him to dwell.

Oh, Jesus tole you once befo',
To go in peace and sin no mo',

I heard o' my Jesus many one say,
Could move po' sinner's sins away.

Den Jesus he come ridin' by,
Gib me wings to ride an' fly.

Jesus Christ the first and las',
No man wuks lak him;
He built a platform in de air,
He meets de saints from eve'ywhere

Virgin Mary had one son,
The cruel Jews had him hung.

Me an' my Jesus goin' live at ease,
Me an' my Jesus goin' do as we please.

If you want' er die like Jesus died,
Fold yo' arms an' clasp yo' eyes.

I tell you brethren an' I tell you twice,
My soul done anchored in Jesus Christ.

Upon de hillside King Jesus spoke,
Out of his mouth come fire an' smoke,

Yer say yo' Jesus set you free;
Why don't you let yo' neighbors be?

Other shorter lines give equally concrete pictures and mention equally definite attributes.

You'll see my Jesus come to wake up de nations underground.
King Jesus died for every man.

An' de son He set me free.
I got my Jesus as well as you.
If you want to see Jesus go in de wilderness.
Gwine serve my Jesus till I die.
I call my Jesus king Emmanuel.
He pluck my feet out'n de miry clay.
He sot dem on de firm rock of ages.
Christ hab bought yo' liberty.
King Jesus settin' in de kingdom.
De win' blow eas' and de win' blow wes' from Jesus.
Oh, yonder comes my Jesus, I know him by his shinin'.
Hear my Jesus when he call you? Hear my Jesus
   callin'?
I'm goin' to hebben where my Jesus dwell.
O, I walk and talk with Jesus.
Jesus loosen de man from under de groun'.
Jesus ain't comin' here to die no mo'.
The Son of Man he dunno where to lay his weary head.

See what wonder Jesus done:
Jesus make 'de dumb to speak.
Jesus make de cripple walk.
Jesus gib de blin' deir sight.
Jesus do mos' anything.

I want to do (or die) like Jesus.
Jesus stan' on de udder side Jordan.
Jesus settin' on de water side.
Jesus is our captain, Jesus got de hellum.
Jesus mount (ride) a milk-white hoss.

You had better follow Jesus.
Daddy Peter set out for Jesus.
Jesus will bring you milk an' honey.
Mas' Jesus is my bosom friend.
Gwine follow King Jesus, I really do believe.
King Jesus he was so strong, my Lord, till he jar down
   de walls ob hell.
Gwine to write to my Jesus.
King Jesus settin' in de heaven.

King Jesus on de mountain top.

O, Jesus is a mighty man.   Ride in, Kind Jesus, who set po' sinner free.

For Jesus come an' lock de do'.

De Jews kill po' Jesus.

Jesus call you—Jesus waitin'.

I wus los' in de wilderness; Jesus hand me de candle down.

Mas' Jesus gib me little broom fer to sweep my heart clean.

Jesus fed me when I was hungry, he clothed me when I was naked, he gave me drink when I was dry.

Jesus rose an' flew away on Sunday morning.

Christ was there four thousand years ago, drinking of the wine.

Jesus he wore the starry crown.   Did you see Jesus when he wore the starry crown?

Jesus he wore long white robe.

King Jesus speaks an' de chariot stops.

King Jesus is the Rock.

Well did you say you love Jesus?

Jesus done bless my soul an' gone to glory.

Won't you ride on Jesus?   O yes.

I look fer Jesus all of my days.

Jesus is a listening all the day long.

The scenes of crucifixion seem to impress the Negroes very forcibly and their songs abound in references to His suffering. Some of these expressions are full of feeling, and are touching in their sentiment.

They nail my Jesus down,
They put him on the crown of thorns (thorny crown).
O see my Jesus hangin' high!
He look so pale an' bleed so free:
O don't you think it was a shame,
He hung three hours in dreadful pain?

God and Jehovah. Next to Jesus and often synonymous with Him is God. He is "My Lord," "My

God," "Lord God-er-mighty," and "King Jehobah," and represents the personal God and the ruler of the world.

Upon de mountain Jehobah spoke,
Out o' his mouth come fire an' smoke.
My God a walkin' down hebbenly road,
Out o' his mouth come two-edged sword.

If yo' find yo' way to God,
The gospel highway mus' be trod.

De Father he look upon de Son an' smile,
De Son he look on me,
De Father redeem my soul from hell,
De Son he set me free.

I'm a chile of God wid my soul set free,
For Christ hab bought my liberty.

I'm going home fer to see my Lord.
My Lord did give me ease.
Ever since my Lord set me free.
I believe it for God he tole me so.
O my Lord's comin' ag'in,
It may be las' time, I don't know.
I goin' to do all I can fer my Lord; I goin' to mourn,
    pray, weep all I can fer my Lord.

The Lord is a listenin' all the day long.
My Lord is a talkin' (preachin') at de jedgment day.
De Lord goin to wake up the dead.
My Lord come down wid de key an' unlock de jail
    house do'.
O My Lord's a rock in a weary lan';
My Lord's a preachin' and teachin, and walkin' in a
    weary lan'.
My Lord calls me by the thunder; by the lightning.
Dat mus' be my Lord in de cloud.

My Lord says there's room enough.
I'm goin' to tell God 'bout my trials.
Thank God-a-mighty, My God's been here.
When I talk I talk wid God.

Gwine to chatter wid de Fadder.
My Fadder call an' I mus' go.
My righteous Lord shall fin' you out.
Look to de Lord wid a tender heart.
O de Lord He plant de garden dere and raise de fruit
   for you to eat.
O de Lord He comfort sinner.
God did go to Moses' house an tell him who He wus.
God an' Moses walked and talked an' God did show him
   who He wus.

God sits in Heaven an' answers prayer.
I gwine tell God how you sarved me.
Look in my God's right hand.

His chariot wheels roll round.
God's goin' call dem chilluns frum de distant lan'.
My Lord's a ridin' all the time.
De Lord has been here an' de love come tricklin' down.
Me an' my God goin' to walk an' talk.
O God don't talk lak a nat'ral man.
My Lord God-ermighty come a steppin' down, come a
   steppin' down on a sea ob glass.

Heaven and Hell.   Heaven for the Negro is an eternal place where he shall occupy the best place.
It is a place of glory and splendor in the material
sense.   Nor does he think that he will fail to miss his
home when he dies.   Hell is a place for thieves and
sinners and liars, but such persons are far removed
from him.   His religion is the panacea for all evils and
all sins, and when he has the "love of God in his heart"
nothing can doom him, for has he not been "washed
in the blood of the Lamb"?   And has not the "blood

done sign his name"? His ideas of heaven are those which his mind naturally conceives of as applying to a home; his conclusions from the Scriptures are not unusual. A few of the references to heaven will give a better conception of the Negro's reality and vividness of interpretation.

> I want to go to heaven when I die,
> To shout salvation as I fly.

> You say yer aiming fer de skies,
> Why don't yer quit yer tellin' lies?

> I hope I git dere by an' by,
> To jine de number in de sky.

> When I git to heaven gwine to ease, ease,
> Me an' my God goin' do as we please,
> Settin' down side o' holy Lamb.

> When I git to heaven goin set right down,
> Gwin-er ask my Lord fer starry crown.
> Now wait till I gits my gospel shoes,
> Gwin-er walk 'bout heaven an' carry de news.

> We'll walk up an' down dem golden streets,
> We'll walk about Zion.

> Gwine sit in de kingdom, I raly do believe, where Sab-
>   baths have no end.
> Look way in de heaven—hope I'll jine de band—Sittin'
>   in de kingdom.
> I done bin to heaven an' I done bin tried.
> Dere's a long white robe in de heaven for me,
> Dere's a golden crown, golden harp, starry crown,
> Silver slippers in heaven for me I know.
> O yes, I'm gwine up to see my Lord; gwine all de way up
>   to see my robe; O de heaven is shinin', shinin'.
> Gwine shout in hebben, gwine hab a big meetin'.

If you want to go to heaven come along wid me.
Take my flight up to de skies in de mornin'.
O de heaven gates are open.
Gwine up to heaven where my Jesus dwells.
My Jesus walkin' de hebbenly road.
De bell is ringin' in odder bright worl'.
If you touch one string de whole hebben ring.
De sun gib light in de hebben all round.
I wish I wus in de kingdom settin' side o' my Lord.
No more hard trial in de kingdom; no more tribulation,
    no more parting, no more quarreling, back-biting in
    de kingdom,
No more sunshine fer to bu'n you; no more rain fer to
    wet you.
Ev'y day will be Sunday in heaven.
Sweet music in heaven jes beginning to roll.
Goin' feast off'n milk an' honey.

The Negro does not dwell upon thoughts of hell as
he does of heaven. Even if he has "stepped over hell
an' come back again," he does not reveal so much of
its character. Some conceptions, however, are definite
enough.

O hell is deep an' hell is wide,
O hell aint got no bottom or side.

I'd rather pray myself away,
Than live in hell an' burn one day.

O when I git to hebben, I'll be able to tell,
How I shunned dat dismal hell.

Ev'y since my Lord done set me free,
Dis ole worl' bin a hell to me.

When I come to find out I's on de road to hell,
I fleed to Jesus.

The Negro's song finds little satisfaction in his
various ideas of hell. "This ole world's a hell to me,"

says the Negro; but "hell is a dark and dismal place," so that the only immediate conclusion which he can reach is that he must "shun de gates of hell" and make for the home beyond the Jordan.

Biblical Folk. A rich variety of references to Scriptural characters is seen in the majority of the Negro spirituals, both of the past and of the present. The Negro portrays the conduct of heroes in the past with imaginative skill. His songs are often running stories of Scripture, in which the effort is made to include as many characters as possible and at the same time draw conclusions which have suitable morals, but these songs may be better studied in the examples that follow. Some of the typical references to the Scriptures will show the average interpretation given them by the Negroes.

> O sisters, can't you help me sing?
> For Moses' sister did help him.

> Where wus Ezekiel when de church fell down?
> Down in de valley wid his head hung down.

> Ezekiel said he spied de train a comin',
> He got on board an' she never stop runnin',

> God made Adam an' Adam wus first,
> God made Adam out o' the dust o' the earth.

> Well, God show Noah de rainbow sign,
> No more water but fire nex' time.

> Moses live 'till he got old,
> Buried in de mountain so I'm told.

> Mary wept and Martha mourned,
> Jesus Christ laid de corner stone.

Mary wore the golden chain,
Every link was in Jesus' name.

Judas was a deceitful man—
Well he betrayed the innercent Lam'.

John wrote a letter an' he wrote it in haste.
If yer want to go to heaven, you better make haste.

John declar' he saw a man,
Wid seven lamps in his right han'.

The Negroes wonder "wher's sister Mary, Martha, Brudder Moses, Brudder Daniel (and the others) gone." So too, "Sister Hannah, Hagar, Brudder Moses" and the rest "took dey seat." And again, "Wondah whar good ole Daniel, doubtin' Thomas, sinkin' Peter" and others. Moses "smote de water," and the Negro says:

I want to go where Moses trod,
For Moses gone to de house o' God.

Peter is commanded again and again to "go ring dem bells"; "Daddy Peter go to Jesus," "Fisherman Peter out at sea," the latter perhaps being the origin of "sinkin' Peter." Elijah is one of the favorites of the Old Testament. "Elijah gwine ride in de chariot in de mornin'"; and Isaiah, who "mounted on de wheel o' time," is a kindred character to Ezekiel and Elijah. Jacob's ladder and his struggle are vivid enough to be sung: "I'm gwine climb up Jacob's ladder"; "Rastlin' Jacob, let me go"; "Jacob tremblin' on a limb." Noah's victory is a common theme. "Dey call Brudder Noah a foolish man," but that makes no difference for "de Lord tole Noah fer to build him ark," and "de

ole ark a-moverin.'' The Negro remarks character-
istically; "God placed Adam in de garden, was 'bout
de cool o' day." Gabriel is proverbial and the attitude
of the singer is always ready "fer to hear Gabriel
blow his horn." "Don't you hear Gabriel's trumpet
in de mornin'?" "Little David play on de harp"
has been a shining example for many another "David"
who loved to blow on his harp. "Father Abraham
sittin' down side o' de holy Lamb," is almost synonymous with Christ. Prominent among the clear impressions made by the Scriptures is that of the delivery of Daniel, the Hebrew children and Jonah.
However, one must read the songs in order to get the
full significance of the references.

The Bible and Angels. Although the Negro bases
everything in his religion upon the Bible, and his
songs and sermons and exhortations abound in quotations from the "Holy word," he has comparatively
little to say of the Bible itself as a book. He thinks
sometimes that it is a "cumpass" and also bases his
convictions on the truth of the Bible. He sings: "How
do you know? For my Bible hit tell me so."

> For in dat Bible you will see,
> Jesus died fer you an' me.
> Matthew, Mark, Luke an' John
> Tell me where my Master's gone.
>
> Go read de fifth of Matthew
> An' read de chapter through,
> It is de guide to Christians,
> An' tell 'em what to do.
>
> Now take yo' Bible an' read it through,
> An' ev'y word you fin' is true.

As the Bible is the compass, so sometimes the Holy Ghost is thought of as the pilot. The Holy Ghost is too vague for the Negro to fathom and is not tangible enough for his imagination. He says: "If this ain't de Holy Ghost I don't know," but goes little further.

Just as the Negro expects to talk and walk with God and Jesus, so he looks forward to seeing the angels in heaven. He wants to see them with their white robes and hear them sing; he even says they mourn. "Bright angels hoverin' on de water by de light" are but a part of the angel band which he hopes to join. "Join de hebben wid de angels" is his watchword, and by it he sees in his childlike fancy all the beauties of ideal creatures.

> I'm gwine to keep a climbin' high.
> Till I meet dem angels in de sky.
>
> Dem pooty angels I shall see—
> Why doan de debbil let-a me be?
>
> O when I get to heaven goin' sit an' tell,
> Three archangels gwine er ring dem bells.
>
> Two white angels come a walkin' down,
> Long white robes an' starry crown.
>
> What's dat yonder dat I see?
> Big, tall angel comin' after me.

The Judgment Day. The Negro makes a remarkable picture of the terrible day of judgment. For him it means everything that could possibly happen at the end of the world. It is the destruction of the sinner and the glory of the righteous. Nor does he hesitate to affirm that the Christian in heaven will shout amen to the sinner's damnation. The sinner will see his mother and friends in heaven while he is doomed to hell. It serves as a warning theme for the song more than it indicates reality of thought. But here is a part of his picture:

My Lord, what a morning when de stars begin to fall,
You'll see de worl' on fire,
You'll see de moon a bleedin' an'
De moon will turn to blood,
Den you'll see de elements a meltin',
You'll see de stars a fallin',
O yes, de stars in de elements a fallin',
An' de moon drips way in blood,
When God goin' call dem chilluns from de distant lan',
Den you see de coffins bustin',
Den you see de bones a creepin',
Den you see po' sinner risin',
Den you hear de tombstones crackin',
An' you see de graves a bustin'.
Hell an' seas gwine give up their daid,
Den you see de forked lightnin',
Den yo hear de rollin' thunder,
Earth shall reel an' totter,
Hell shall be uncapped,
De dragon be loosed—
Don't you hear them sinners cryin?

Such a scene vividly told of at a revival and sung to the associations of the moment is too much for the average Negro; the sinner cries for mercy and turns to a Christian; the latter sings: "Fare you well, po' sinner," and

A mighty sea of glass mingled wid fier,
Good-bye, brother, I'm goin' higher.

Along with the scenes which are associated with the resurrection and judgment go the sadder strains of the "mourners"; "weepin' mournin', cry'n"—these will be much in evidence. A study of the songs that follow will give some idea of the emotional nature of the themes. The Negro sings sympathy. "Weepin' Mary, weep no mo' "—"Mary wept, Martha cried"; why can't he too? "Now ain't dis hard trial and tribulation?" He sings often of hard times and trials. "When you see me," he says, "pity me." "Nobody knows de trubble I seen," but "I boun' to leave dis worl' "; "Fare you well, dere's a better day comin'." His prayers are more pathetic than his songs; his appeals interpret the spirit of song and of worship. But one would scarcely look for a more pathetic wail than that of the Negro who sings

> Sometimes I hangs my head an' cries,
> But Jesus goin' to wipe my weep'n' eyes.

Shouting and Happiness. If the Negro mourns and if his songs are full of sadness and pathos, he also shouts and vigorously defends the right to shout as much as he pleases. His songs have many "hallelu-jahs" in them; many notes of victory may be read in the songs of his choice. He often sings, however, the songs which should be the most joyous in the same plaintive tone of the sadder ones. He forgets the words. In many, however, the shouting takes away any sadness and these livelier songs voice the light and sensuous emotions equally as well as the more serious ones tell of hardships. The Negro maintains that always and everywhere "You'll hear the Christian shout." "De richest man I ever seed, his heart was fill wid Jesus an' Holy Ghost." "I got de glory in my soul," he says and

> I real'y do b'lieve widout a doubt,
> Dat de church hab a mighty right to shout.
>
> I tell you what I lak de bes'
> It is dem shoutin' Mefodes.

If the Negro's mother and sister and father and preacher and the others, as the songs put it, "died a shoutin'," then he is "goin' die shoutin' too."

> Gwine hab happy meetin'
> Gwine shout in hebben,
> Gwine shout an' nebber tire,
> O slap yo' han's, chilluns,
> O pat yo' feets, chilluns;
> I feels de spirit movin',
> O now I'm gittin' happy.

Of true love and devotion to God one finds little definite and concrete expressions as compared with other themes. The Negro is constantly affirming his love of "his Jesus" and offering his eternal allegiance in a general way. But in the average instance the testimony is subordinated to some special word or phrase which receives the greater part of the significance in the song. What does he mean when he asks: "Does yo' love continue true?" or when he insists: "I wants to know, does you love yo' Jesus?" The Negroes are often heard to say that they want to do something "for the Lord." In the same way they sing: "I goin' weep all I can for my Lord, I goin' pray all I can for my Lord, I goin' to do all I can for my Lord." In each case the relation of the Negro and his God is ideal, and he conceives of his own deeds as being not in the practical everyday life, but in the future when there will be nothing unpleasant about them.[1]

Nature in Song. Nature contributes something to the Negro spirituals. Certain parts of nature are symbolic and serve to convey the picture of a vivid imagination as nothing else can do. The wonders of God and the terrors of the judgment must be seen in their relation and effect upon the forces of nature. Certain natural phenomena inspire awe and reverence; they add thus to the Negro's conception of religious fear. Other references to nature convey, as they only could, pleasing features of life, hence of heaven and God. The Negro refers to the "break o' day," the "settin' o' the sun," the "cool o' the evenin'," and each is very expressive. Morning and evening are common; he prays in the evening perhaps; in the morning he is going to heaven. The hillside, the mountain and mountain top, the valley, signify and typify the experiences of the Christian of the past and present; the heavenly breeze comes from the valley. The Negro sees a paradise and a wilderness, a sunshine and a storm. But

> Dere's a tree in paradise,
> Christians call de tree ob life,

and he faithfully sings, "I specs to eat de fruit off'n dat tree." The earth trembles and is jarred; the sky is "shook." The river is "chilly an' cold, wide an'

---

[1] It was doubted if the Negro's ideas of God and heaven and his relation to them were truly expressed in his songs. Several experiments were made with Negro children, wherein questions were answered by them at the time they were given, others being carried to their homes or teachers. Their ideas of hell and heaven, God and the angels are almost identical with those found in the songs.

deep." The "rock" is better than the miry clay. The stars, moon, and world fall, bleed, and burn. The thunder and the lightning are in the stormy cloud; Jesus may be, too. Satan is a snake in the grass and a hunting dog. Young lambs and the sheep "done know de road." The summer, spring, flowers and the field are mentioned. The Negro wishes he had wings like Noah's dove. He is sometimes awed:

> I looked toward dat northern pole,
> I seed black clouds of fire roll.

With his vivid imagination the Negro feels much of the thought expressed in the folk song. Thus sin and the sinner are intimately connected with life and death, religion and repentance. How skillfully the songs express the folk feeling may better be inferred from further analysis of characteristic songs.

CHAPTER III

EXAMPLES OF RELIGIOUS SONGS

An exact classification of the current Negro songs presented in this collection, either as to subject-matter or as to form, would scarcely be possible. There is little unity of thought in their content; their meters conform to no consistent standards. A single favorite stanza, regardless of its meaning, is constantly being sung in a dozen different songs. It is a distinct song and it matters little to which one it belongs; it serves its purpose in any one of them. So in the form of the verse, a single tune is adapted to lines that differ greatly in length; likewise a single line is not infrequently made to fit into any tune that is desired. Again no final version of any song can be given. The lines are rarely sung twice in exactly the same form. There are ordinarily as many versions of a line as there are combinations of the words without spoiling the effect of the rhyme or emphatic word. The stanzas have no order of sequence, but are sung as they occur in the mind of the singer; a song does not have a standard number of stanzas, but the length depends upon the time in which it is wanted to sing that particular song. In the songs that follow the most common versions are given. In giving the dialect no attempt is made at consistency, for the Negro of the present generation has no consistency of speech. He uses "the" and "de", "them" and "dem", "gwine" and "goin'," "and" and "an'," together with many other varied forms, which were noted in Chapter I. Nor does it matter that each of the forms is used in the same line or stanza. In the old songs that are here quoted for comparisons, the exact form of speech in which they have been published is used. In the miscellaneous songs gathered here and there, what may be called the average dialect is used. The songs that form the basis of this work are those that are found among the present-day Negroes of the South; in many cases the corresponding song of earlier days is given in order that a better study of the folk songs may be made and the many points of resemblance noted. In all instances the basis of the chapter is the present-day song, and these should not be confused with those that have already been published. Further particulars will be pointed out in connection with the several songs.

Perhaps no better beginning can be made towards general classification of the religious songs of the Negroes than by introducing some that combine several characteristics, but still have a general theme predominating. Sin is an important factor in the religious life of the Negro and his songs refer to it in many forms. The three general tones which pervade the theme are: A note of victory over sin and the conception of it as being in the past or belonging to some other person; the conception of sin as being present and the singer as being in its grasp; and, thirdly, the "sinner-man" himself and warnings given him.

ALL MY SINS DONE TAKEN AWAY

This very popular song is typical of the first class mentioned above. There is no reason why the stanzas given below should come in the order presented, except that they are heard in this arrangement as much as in any other. The stanzas consist of two rhymed lines with the refrain. These, however, are usually extended to four, the first two and refrain being sung slowly and in a more or less plaintive tone, while the repetition of the same lines with the rhymed line and refrain is rapid and joyous. The common version follows:

> I'm goin' to heaven an' I don't want ter stop,
> Yes, I'm goin' to heaven an' I don't want ter stop,
>   All o' my sins done taken away, taken away;
> I'm goin' to heaven an' I don't want ter stop,
> An' I don't want ter be no stumblin' block,
>   All my sins done taken away, taken away.

Instead of repeating the chorus line at the end of the first two lines that are sung, the Negroes often vary the song by repeating the last half of the line, as in the following stanza:

> Well, "M" for Mary, an' "P" for Paul,
> Well, "M" for Mary, an' "P" for Paul,
>   An' "P" for Paul;
> Well, "M" for Mary, an' "P" for Paul.
> "C" for Chris' who died for us all,
>   All o' my sins done taken away, taken away.

The chorus is again varied from "all my sins" to "all o' my sins," "done taken away," or "bin taken away," while the entire line is sometimes changed in a single stanza. Sometimes it is sung as given above; at other times the line goes: "All my sins done taken away, bin' taken away," or omitting either "done" or "bin" it is sung equally well as "All my sins taken away, taken away," while in the grand chorus at the climax of the song the chorus goes:

> Yes, all o' my sins bin taken away,
> Yes, all my sins done taken away,
> Yes, all o' my sins done taken away,
> Yes, all my sins done taken away.
> Glory, glory to His name,
> All my sins done taken away, taken away.

This last chorus may be repeated whenever the singers do not think of words to fit in with the songs, although this is rarely necessary. The following stanzas are sung in the same manner as those just given.

> If I had er died when I wus young,
> I never would a had dis race to run,
> All o' my sins done taken away, taken away.

> Well you oughter bin dere to see de sight,
> The peoples come runnin' both cullud an' white.

> My feet got wet in de midnight dew,
> An' de mornin' star was a witness, too.

> If you doan b'lieve I bin redeem,
> Jes follow me down to Jordan stream.

> When a sinner see me it make him laugh,
> Thank God-a-mighty, I'm free at las'.

> Mary wept and Martha mourned,
> Mary wept all 'round the throne.

> Mary wept an' Martha mourned,
> All because deir brother done daid an' gone.

> Mary wept an' Martha cried,
> All 'cause dey brother done gone an' died.

I'm goin' to ride on de mornin' train,
All don't see me goin' ter hear me sing.

I'm gwine to heaven on eagle's wing,
All don't see me goin' ter hear me sing.

My mother's sick an' my father's daid,
Got nowhere to lay my weary head.

I went down in de valley to pray,
My soul got happy an' I stayed all day.

A number of other versions are common. Instead of "Mary wept all 'round the throne" is sung "all 'round God's hebbenly throne." Instead of the morning star as a witness the old songs have it "angels witness too." Instead of in the valley, the old songs also had "on de mountain" and also inserted "I didn't go dere to stay." This version is sung in some of the songs still.

DAT SABBATH HATH NO END

This is the name of a favorite somewhat similar to "All My Sins Done Taken Away." It has a number of forms for the chorus.

I went down in de valley,
I didn't go ter stay;
My little soul got happy
An' I like to a stayed all day.

I thought I had religion, I b'lieve,
I thought I had religion, I b'lieve,
I thought I had religion, I b'lieve,
Dat Sabbath hath no end.

I wouldn't be a sinner,
Tell you de reason why—
Feard de good Lord might call me,
An' I wouldn't be ready ter die.

Gwine rock trubble over, I b'lieve,
Rock trubbel over, I b'lieve,
Rock trubbel over, I b'lieve,
Dat Sabbath has no end.

Ole Satan's mighty busy,
Fixin' up his snares;
He'll ketch all dem mourners,
If dey don't keep deir prayers.

Yer better get ready, I b'lieve,
Yer better get ready, I b'lieve,
Yer better get ready, I b'lieve,
Dat Sabbath has no end.

I AM DE LIGHT UV DE WORL'

The singer is a little more definite in his convictions in the next song. He is no longer a sinner and looks forward to the time when he will "cross de ribber."

Halleluyer, good Lord,
I am de light uv de worl';
Halleluyer, good Lord,
I am de light uv de worl'.

Ever since my Lord done sot me free,
Dis ole worl' bin a hell to me;
I am de light uv de worl'.

I looked toward dat northern pole,
I seed black clouds of fier roll;
I am de light uv de worl'.

I gwine 'clare de word,
I am de light uv de worl'.
I'm gwine 'clare de word,
I am de light uv de worl'.

Der ain't but one train on his track,
Goes straight to heaven an' run right back.
I am de light uv de worl'.

Ever since I bin in de worl',
I am de light uv de worl';
Ever since I bin in de worl',
I am de light uv de worl';

When I cross Jordan I'll be free,
Gwine a slip an' slide dem golden streets;
I am de light uv de worl'.

'Way up in de kingdom, Lord,
I am de light uv de worl';
'Way up in de kingdom, Lord,
I am de light uv de worl'.

JESUS DONE BLESS MY SOUL

The Negro is not troubled because he cannot see his Lord; he has heard Him speak and believes that He has gone "on to glory." His personal relation with Jesus is satisfactory and he sings His praises often as he tells of his own experiences. Says he:

One day, one day, while walkin' along,
Jesus done bless my soul;
I heard a voice an' saw no one,
Jesus done bless my soul.

Oh, go an' tell it on de mountain,
Jesus done bless my soul;
Oh, go an' tell it in de valley,
Jesus done bless my soul.

He done bless my soul an' gone on to glory.
Jesus done bless my soul;
Done bin here an' bless my soul an' gone on to glory,
Jesus done bless my soul.

In one of the old plantation songs a similar idea is given of the blessing, but in a different version.

One day when I wus walkin' along, oh, yes, Lord,
De element opened, an' de Love came down, oh, yes,
    Lord.
I never shall forget dat day, oh, yes, Lord,
When Jesus washed my sins away, oh, yes, Lord.

Another chorus inquired: "Oh, brothers where were you? Oh, sisters where were you? Oh, sinners, (Oh, Christians, Oh, mourners, etc.) where were you?" "My good Lord's bin here, bin here, bin here; my good Lord's bin here, an' he blessed my soul an' gone." So the Negro exhorters often conclude their services saying that the Lord has been to the meeting and gone. Said one deacon who was exhorting for a large collection: "De good Lord's done bin with us tonight— I know he has; done bin here an' gone, an' now we want to git down to bizness, I wants some money."

LORD, I JUST GOT OVER

The Negro, fresh and enthusiastic from his religious experience and having "come through," sings with some relief:

I have been tryin' a great long while,
Lord, I jus' got over on yo' side.

Lord, I jus' got over-er,
Lord, I jus' got over,
Lord, I jus' got over-er,
I jus' got over on yo' side.

I prayed an' I prayed till I come over,
Lord, I jus' got over on yo' side.

OH, THE SUNSHINE!

So also he "weeps" and he "mourns" and "cries"
till he "gets over on the Lawd's side." Then he sings:

Oh, the sunshine!   Oh, the sunshine!
Oh, sunshine in my soul this mornin';
Yes, the sunshine, the sunshine,
Yes, sunshine in my soul.

Down in the valley, down on my knees,
Sunshine in my soul;
There I met that heavenly breeze,
Sunshine in my soul.

Ole devil like a snake in the grass,
Sunshine in my soul;
He's always in some sister's path,
Sunshine in my soul.

LORD BLESS THE NAME

Very much mixed and somewhat similar to some of
the songs already given is "Bless the Name."

I've got to go to judgment, I don't know how soon,
Lord bless the name, Lord bless the name;
I've got to go to judgment to hear my sins,
Lord bless the name, Lord bless the name.

My Jesus fed me when I's hungry, gave me drink when
   I's dry,
Lord bless the name, Lord bless the name.
My Jesus clothed me when I was naked,
Lord bless the name, Lord bless the name.

In the same song and with the same tune are sung the

shorter lines that follow. "Lord bless the name,"
is a form of the phrase "Bless the name of the Lord."
It is used as a refrain after each line or it may be
omitted.

> Mary wept and Martha mourned,
> Lord bless the name, Lord bless the name;
> Jesus Chris' laid the corner stone,
> Lord bless the name, Lord bless the name.
>
> Mary wore the golden chain,
> Every link was in Jesus' name.
>
> You may talk about me just as you please,
> I'll talk about you when I git on my knees.
>
> God made man an' man was sure,
> There was no sin an' his heart was pure.
>
> God made Adam an' Adam was first,
> God made Adam out o' the dust o' the earth.

FREE, FREE, MY LORD

It proves an interesting task to follow the development and changes in a song that has survived
from slavery days. In "Free Free, My Lord," one
of the verses was quite a puzzle. On one occasion the
following stanza was heard:

> The moon came down like a piper's stem,
> The sun 'fuse to shine;
> An' ev'y star disappear,
> King Jesus set me free.

Inquiry was made in order to see if the words had
not been misunderstood. The older Negroes gave
this version and insisted that it was correct, but none

of them could explain what it meant.　It was thought that perhaps it was a figure applied to the moon's rays or that the loss of the sun might have meant the peculiar appearance of the moon.　Anyway, they maintained, this was the "way we got de song an' guess it must be right."　The words of the original song were:

> The moon run down in purple stream,
> 　The sun forbear to shine,
> An' ev'y star disappear,
> 　King Jesus shall be mine.

Of this there seemed to be several versions.　Other verses that are found today are:

> As I went down in de valley one day,
> 　I fell upon my knees,
> I begged and cried fer pardon,
> 　The Lord did give me ease.

> Free, free, my lord,
> Free, free, my lord,
> Free, free, my lord,
> To march de heaven's highway.

> My mother look at de son an' smile,
> 　My father look at me;
> My mother turn my soul from hell,
> 　King Jesus set me free.

> Free, free, etc.

The last verse is an unusual variation and interpretation of the old song; just how and when the Negroes inserted the idea of mother would be difficult to ascertain; perhaps it came from "master," or more likely it was introduced by them while they interpreted father and son as names of the ordinary members of a human family. The original form seems to have been,

> De Father, he looked on de Son and smiled,
> De Son, he looked on me;
> De Father, he redeemed my soul from hell;
> An' de.Son, he set me free.

The chorus, too, has been much confused and is sometimes given as "Children light on dat cross, God bless you forever mo'." The song is not a common one among the Negroes and is not known, apparently, among the younger ones.

GLAD I GOT RELIGION

In contrast with this favorite of the older Negroes may be given a favorite of the younger generation, "Glad I Got Religion." The repetition represents pretty well the relative depth of the feeling which the convert experiences. But he loves to sing it for its pleasing sound and for the faith it gives him in his own religious state. The song is a long and continued chorus and may well be taken as a type of the song which reflects the Negro's feeling of immunity from sin.

> I'm so glad, so glad; I'm so glad, so glad;
> Glad I got religion, so glad.
> Glad I got religion, so glad.

> I'm so glad, so glad; I'm so glad, so glad;
> I'm glad all over, so glad,
> I'm glad all over, so glad.

> I'm so glad, so glad; I'm so glad, so glad;
> Glad I bin changed, so glad.
> Glad I bin changed, so glad.

And so he continues singing; he is glad that he is going to heaven, he is glad that he is not a sinner, glad he has been set free, and many other such states. Then when he has finished he begins all over again, if he wishes, and sings: "Sister, ain't you glad?" "Brother, ain't you glad?" and goes through with as many of these as he wishes—preacher, mourner, auntie, and others.

GOD KNOWS IT'S TIME

The "sinner-man" is the theme for many verses of the Negro favorites. Directed at him are warnings and admonitions. He is told what he must do and when; how he must do and why. He is told of the experiences of the Christians and he is told of the doom of the damned. The Negro rejoices over his own safety and boasts of the sinner's destruction; at the same time he constantly refers to the "po' sinner" in a sympathetic way. But the sinner must be warned:

> God know it's time, it's time, it's time,
> That a sinner was makin' up his min'
> It's time, it's time he was makin' up his min' to die.

> A sinner was walkin' off his time, his time,
> An' when my God call him he did not have the time,
> God know it was time, it was time, it was time for him
>   to die.

Again the words of the righteous to the sinner are driven home by repetition and by a dark and dismal picture:

> Oh, hell is deep an' hell is wide,
> Oh, hell is deep an' hell is wide,
> Oh, hell is deep an' hell is wide,
> Oh, hell ain't got no bottom or side.

Well, before I lay in hell all day, hell all day,
Well, before I lay in hell all day, hell all day,
Well, before I lay in hell all day, hell all day,
I goin' to sing an' pray myself away, self away.

O sinner, don't you let this harves' pass, harves' pass,
O sinner, don't you let this harves' pass, harves' pass,
O sinner, don't you let this harves' páss, harves' pass,
Do you die an' go to hell at las', hell at las'.

WORKIN' ON THE BUILDING

The sinner may be a gambler or a dancer or a rogue
or a drunkard. But each name has the same sig-
nification in the religious phraseology of the Negro
song. There are various ways of repenting and of
serving the Lord just as there are many ways of of-
fending and sinning against him. "Workin' on the
Building" appeals to the average Negro.

If I wus a sinner man, I tell you what I'd do,
I'd lay down all my sinful ways an' work on the building
too.

I'm workin' on the building fer my Lord,
Fer my Lord, fer my Lord,
I'm workin' on the building fer my Lord,
. I'm workin' on the building, too.

If I wus a gamblin' man, I tell you what I'd do,
I'd lay down all my gamblin', an' work on the building,
too.

If I was a 'ho'-munger, I tell you what I'd do,
I'd lay down all my munglin' and work on the building,
too.

And so on for the dancer and the drunkard and the
"cussin' man."

IF I WAS A MOURNER

In another song the Negro sings of the sinners and mourners.

> If I wus a mourner jus' like you, um-u,
> I'd go to church an' try to come thru, um-u.
> When I was a mourner, um-u', jus' lak you,
> I prayed an' prayed till I come thru, um-u.
>
> Upon de mountain King Jesus spoke, um-u,
> Out of his mouth come fier an' smoke, um-u.
> Now, mourner, won't you please come on, um-u,
> An' join us in that heavenly lan', um-u.

THE DOWNWARD ROAD IS CROWDED[1]

In "The Downward Road Is Crowded" a mournful picture is given of the sinner who failed to repent. His example is held up for the contemplation of those who are following in his steps.

> Young people who delight in sin,
> I tell you what I lately seen;
> A po' godless sinner die,
> An' he said: "In hell I soon'll lie."
>
> Hark, the downward road is crowded, crowded, crowded;
> Yes, the downward road is crowded with onbelievin' souls.
>
> He call his mother to his bed,
> An' these is the dyin words he said:
> "Mother, mother, a long farewell,
> Your wicked son is damned in hell."
>
> He dance an' play hisself away,
> An' still put off his dyin' day,
> Until at las' ole death was sent,
> An' it 'us too late fer him to repent.

---

[1] Compare "Wicked Polly" in Cox's *Folk Songs of the South,* Harvard University Press, 1925, p. 411.

They also sing of brother and sister and others being called to the bedside. The old plantation song of the same name has a similar chorus but the stanzas were quite different.

> When I wus a sinner,
>   I loved my distance well,
> But when I come to fin' myself,
>   I was hangin' over hell.

> Ole Satan's mighty busy,
>   He follers me night an' day,
> An' everywhere (I'm 'pinted,)
>   Dere's something in my way.

MY LORD'S COMIN' AGAIN

The Lord will come to judge the world and wake up the dead. It is the supreme ambition of the singer to be ready to meet his Lord when He comes. Just what form the Lord will take the Negro does not say; perhaps it will be in a cloud of fire or He will come as in the days of Moses. "My Lord's Comin' Again" gives a general conception.

> Oh, my Lord's comin' again,
> Oh, my Lord's comin' again,
>   (Talk about it:)
> Yes, my Lord's comin' again,
> It may be las' time, I don't know.

> Well he's comin' to judge the worl',
> Well he's comin' to judge the worl',
>   (Talk about it:)
> Yes my Lord's comin' to judge the worl',
> It may be las' time, I don't know.

Well you had better put off lyin' shoes,
Well you better put off lyin' shoes,
   (Talk about it:)
Better put off lyin' shoes,
For it may be las' time, I don't know.

And so he sings "Better put off dancin' shoes," "better put off gamblin' shoes." For the sinner's shoes will not be suitable to "walk on the cross."

GOD'S GOIN' TO WAKE UP THE DEAD

Goin' to wake up the dead,
Goin' to wake up the dead,
God goin' to wake up the dead,
Who's a sleepin' in the grave,
God is goin' to wake up the dead.

You had better min', my brother, how you walk on the
   cross,
God's goin' to wake up the dead;
If yo' right foot slip, then yo' soul be los'
God goin' wake up the dead.

Then "you better min', my sister," my mother, my preacher, is sung. The old song contained words similar to the lines just given:

My brudder, better mind how you walk on de cross,
For yo' foot might slip an' yo' soul git lost,
Better mind dat sun, and see how she run,
An' mind, don't let her catch ye wid yer works undone.

SINNER DIE

"Time is comin' when sinner mus' die," and there is none so pitiable as the lost sinner.

Sinner die, sinner die,
Sinner dies wid his head hung down,
Sinner die, sinner die,
Sinner die in de midnight dew.

Sinner die, sinner die,
Sinner die, with achin' heart,
Sinner die, sinner die,
Sinner die with weary min'.

Stump'ty up an' stump'ty down,
Time is comin' when sinner mus' die,
Hurry home, hurry home;
Time is a comin' sinner mus' die.

Don't you let that sinner change yo' min',
Time is comin' sinner mus' die.
Hurry home, hurry home;
Time is comin' sinner mus' die.

The plantation song of some years ago, sometimes called "Oh Sinner, You Better Get Ready," has the same line refrain, "Time is a comin' dat sinner mus' die." The repetition of "sinner die" is a new addition. In the old song were lines similar to those quoted:

O sinner man, you better pray
For it look-a like judgment every day.

I heard a lumb'ring in de sky,
Dat make-a me t'ink my time was nigh.

I heard of my Jesus a-many one say,
Could move poor sinner's sins away.

Yes, I rather pray myself away,
Dan to lie in hell an' burn-a one day.

I think I heard my mother say—
'Twas a pretty thing to serve the Lord.

Oh, when I git to heaven I'll be able fer to tell,
Oh, how I shun dat dismal hell.

What You Goin' Do?

An interesting type of song is that in which an imaginary conversation is carried on between two parties. If the song is correctly rendered the leader or one part of the chorus sings the first part or takes the words of one of the speakers, while the other chorus takes up the other speaker's words. Both then join in the grand refrain, which in the following song is "Lord, I'm on my way."

Sinner, what you goin' to do
    When de devil git you?
What you goin' do
    When de devil git you?
What you goin' do
    When de devil git you?
    Lord, I'm on my way.

I'm goin' run to the rocks;
    Well, they can't hide you.
Goin' run to the rocks;
    They can't hide you.
Run to the rocks;
    Well, they can't hide you;
    Lord, I'm on my way.

I'm goin' to run to the water;
    An' water goin' to cry "fire."
Goin' to run to the water;
    An' water cry "fire."
Run to the water,
    An' water cry "fire";
    Lord, I'm on my way.

And so the sinner will then "run to the mountain," and "De mountain fly open" or "De mountain cry mercy." The sinner must needs be hopeless at his death and there is neither mercy nor pity for him. It is the idea of the Negro that at the great day "we won't be bothered with them any mo'." A sad picture he makes of the poor and forsaken man who dies "with achin' heart," with "weary min'," and with his "head hung down."

COME, SINNER, COME

Consequently it is not surprising to find appeals of all sorts made to the sinner man; now he is told of his doom, now of possible salvation, now of the joys of being saved, now of immediate satisfaction. Sung like the above song is "Come, Sinner, Come."

> Won't you come, won't you come?
> Come, sinner, come;
> Great day of wrath is comin';
> Come, sinner, come.
>
> Look over yonder what I see;
> Come, sinner, come;
> Two tall angels comin' after me;
> Come, sinner, come.

In the same manner he sings any number of verses, as

> Ole Satan like a snake in de grass,
> Always in some sister's path.
>
> Ole Satan weahs mighty loose ole shoe
> Ef you don't min' gwine slip it on you.

Up on hillside King Jesus spoke,
Out of his mouth come fier an' smoke.

Down in de valley, down on my knees,
Ask de Lord to save me if He please.

The old plantation song was as follows:

O whar you runnin', sinner?
   I do love de Lord;
De Judgment day is comin',
   I do love de Lord;

You'll see de worl' on fire,
   I do love de Lord;
You'll see de element a meltin',
   I do love the Lord.

Besides these stanzas there were sung the various other warnings such as have been given in the idea of judgment and resurrection already noted. In the old slave song the sinner asks:

What shall I do for hiding place?
I run to de sea but de sea run dry.
I run to de gate but de gate shut fast.
No hiding place for sinner dere,
For I am gone an' sent to hell.

I LOOK FOR JESUS ALL MY DAYS

Instead of the regular refrain which is sung by the chorus of voices in response to a line by the leader, the Negroes often respond with "um-u" in a general mingling of chant, humming and "amens." For the most part they do this with closed lips; the volume is surprisingly strong, however, and makes a stirring effect. The meaning of the expression is something

like "Yes" or "Of course, we know it is true," or
"Sure, you talkin', brother." The singer says: "I
look for Jesus all my days," and the chorus answers,
"um-u." He then continues:

>An' when I found him this is what he said, um-u
>"Yo' sin forgiven an' yo' soul set free," um-u.
>
>I pray all night, an' I pray all day, um-u, um-u;
>Then my Lord taken my sins away, um-u, um-u.
>
>Nex' day, nex' day while walkin' along, um-u, um-u,
>I heard a voice and saw no one, um-u, um-u;
>It said, "Sinner man, you better come home," um-u,
>um-u.
>
>One day I was walkin' long dat lonesome road, um-u,
>um-u,
>King Jesus spoke unto me an' lifted off dat load, um-u.

BROTHER, YOU'D BETTER BE A-PRAYIN

"Brother, You'd Better Be a Prayin'," while mostly
repetition, makes a long song when sung to its limit.
"Sister," "sinner," "backslider," "mourner," "children," each serves to make a complete stanza of eight
lines:

>Brother, you'd better be a prayin',
>Brother, you'd better be a prayin',
>My brother, you'd better be a prayin'.
>An' I'll be carried above,
>An' I'll be carried above,
>An' I'll be carried above.
>I'll see King Jesus in his reign,
>An' I'll be carried above.

WHEEL IN MIDDLE OF WHEEL

The chorus song, "Wheel in Middle of Wheel," is most likely a variation of the old song, "Wheel in a Wheel." Sometimes the wheel was conceived of as being a "Little wheel-a-turnin' in my heart," in which case it signified some sort of feeling. The phrase means nothing more than a chorus in the present-day song.

> O sinner man, how can it be?
>> Wheel in de middle of wheel;
> If you don't serve God you can't serve me,
>> Wheel in de middle of wheel.

> In the wheel, in the wheel,
>> Wheel in de middle of wheel,
> In the wheel, in the wheel,
>> Wheel in the middle of wheel.

> Well, don't you know it's prayin' time?
>> Wheel in middle of wheel;
> Lay down yo' way and go to God,
>> Wheel in middle of wheel.

> Well, don't you know it's mournin' time?
>> Wheel in middle of wheel;
> He'll hear yo' prayers an' sanctify,
>> Wheel in middle of wheel.

JESUS IS LISTENIN'

Jesus and God are represented as "listenin' all the day long," and the sinner is directed to pray. The plantation song called to him: "Where you goin' sinner? Oh, come back, don't go dat way." And one of the singers affirmed that "about the break o' day" his sins were forgiven and "his soul set free."

The song "Jesus Is Listenin' " seems at some time to have been considerably corrupted. The Negroes have sung it: "I've been a-listenin' all the day long (all night long) to hear some sinner pray." However, the correct version now seems to be:

Jesus is a listenin' all the day long,
He keep listenin' all day long,
He keep listenin' all the day long,
For to hear some sinner pray.

If I was a sinner I would please him,
I would pray an' pray all day;
So when I got to heaven,
He could say he heard me pray.

BEAR YO' BURDEN

But in "Bear Yo' Burden, Sinner," another version is given of the same idea. This song is a popular one, while the figures used give a definite conviction.

The Lord is a listenin' all the day long,
    Bear yo' burden, sinner.
If you will only pray, he will bear you on,
Bear yo' burden in the heat o' the day.

    Bear yo' burden, sinner,
    Bear yo' burden, sinner,
    Bear yo' burden in the heat o' the day.

I'm goin' home fer to see my Lord,
    Bear yo' burden, sinner;
An' don't you wish you could go 'long,
    Bear yo' burden, let in the heat.

The way to bear yo' burden is to get down on yo' knees,
    Bear yo' burden, sinner, let in the heat;
Ask God to forgive you if you please,
    Bear yo' burden in the heat of the day.

This last stanza is an improvisation made by a young Negro of some twenty-five years, although he claimed that it belonged to the song that was regularly sung, maintaining that they only forgot to sing it in the church on that special occasion.

TRUE RELIGION

"True Religion" gives one view of the requisites of him who will be saved. The song is based in form on a current secular song, and belongs to the class of colloquies.

> Well you must have that true religion,
> You must have that true religion an' yo' soul converted,
> You must have that true religion
> Or you can't cross dere.

> Where are you goin' sinner,
> Where are you goin', I say?
> I goin' down to de river of Jordan,
> An' you can't cross dere.

He continues, "Where are you goin', gambler, backslider, drunkard, liar, hypocrite?" and answers each with, "An' you can't cross dere," while the entire chorus, "You must have that true religion," is often repeated after each. The sinner is asked still other questions, one of which is given in the next song.

HE IS WAITING

> Why does you tarry, sinner,
> Why does you wait so long?
> For my Lord is a waitin',
> Why don't you come to His call?

He is waitin', Lord,
He is waitin', Lord,
He is awaitin' fer the good Lord
To come, my Lord.

But when my Lord get here,
You won't have time to pray at all,
For he is goin' to judge you,
An' hell you be bound.

TALK ABOUT ME

The Negro preacher often rebukes his flock for talking about one another in uncomplimentary terms. Sometimes the "sisters" who do not like the preacher retort variously, "I heard you talkin' 'bout So-and-So, and you know I did," or "We gwine talk 'bout you," or "Yes, you knows it." Slander and gossip are fast runners and the average Negro assumes that somebody is talking about him or something which he has done. Out of this has grown the song "Talk About Me" and others.

Yes, I know you goin' talk 'bout me,
Yes, I know you goin' talk 'bout me,
For you talk 'bout my father when he's on his knees
    a prayin'
An' you know you goin' talk 'bout me.

For you talk about my mother when she's on her bed
    a-dyin';
An' you know you goin' talk 'bout me.

He actually sings, father, brother, mother, sister, mourner, preacher, to both "on his knees a prayin'" and "on bed a dyin'." A very popular stanza which is regularly sung in a number of songs goes:

You may talk about me just as you please,
I'm goin' to talk about you when I git on my knees.

GET IN THE UNION

The old slave and plantation song asked: "Who'll jine de Union?" saying, "Say, ef you belong to de union ban', den here's my heart an' here's my hand." There have been societies known as "The Union" or "Union Band" both in the church and outside. The name "Union" itself is a favorite one among the Negro societies and organizations. It was thought in the old days that a union band would march to heaven and that these only would be enabled to reach the destination. It is almost certain that a number of references in their songs referred to the Union army in and after the war. However, the exact origin of the song as it is now sung has not been found, but appears to be a general corruption of several songs.

> Get in the Union, Jesus is a listenin';
> Get in the Union, Jesus die.
> Well, won't you get in the Union?
> Jesus is a listenin', Jesus die.
>
> Where was Ezekiel when the church fell down?
> Down in de valley wid his head hung down.
>
> Hypocrite, hypocrite, God do despise,
> Tongue so keen till he will tell lies.
>
> Upon the mountain Jehober spoke,
> Out of His mouth come fier an' smoke.

With this chorus are sung also as already given, "Satan like a snake in the grass," "Ole Satan weah mighty loose ole shoe," etc. The "hallelujah" so common among the old songs is less frequently heard now; it will be found to some degree in the shouting songs and songs of heaven.

BLOW, GABLE, BLOW

Not least among the warnings to the sinner were to be reckoned the times when "Gable" should blow his horn. "Gable" has been proverbial among the Negroes; Gabriel and the trumpet are, however, significant in the same way among the whites in the vulgar reference. Many ideas of "Gable's" trumpet have appeared in the Negro songs. Sometimes it is "blow louder, Gable!" "How loud mus' I blow?" The song "Blow, Gable, Blow" has changed considerably from the old plantation songs of the same name.

> Blow, Gable, at the judgment,
> Blow, Gable, at the judgment bar,
> For my God is a talkin' at the judgment,
> For my God is a talkin' at the judgment bar.
>
> Now won't you blow, Gable, at the judgment?
> For my God is a preachin' at the judgment bar.
>
> Now won't you blow, Gable, at the judgment bar?
> Well, I'm goin' to meet my preacher at the judgment bar.

In the same manner, making a four-line stanza of each one, are sung, "Goin' to meet brother," (mother, sister, etc.) and also, "My God is a walkin' (tryin', etc.) at the judgment bar." So, too, it is "prayin' time (mournin' time, singin' time, shoutin' time, tryin' time, etc.) at the judgment bar." This song may be given as the last one of the class peculiar to warnings and admonitions to sinners. It closes with still other verses that give vivid pictures of the judgment bar.

> Well, sinners, keep a prayin' at the judgment bar.
> Well, it's too late to pray at the judgment bar.
> Why didn't you take heed at the judgment?
> Some come crippled at judgment.
> O, I look for my mother, (brother, sister) at de judgment.

OH, WHAT A HARD TIME!

The sinner as well as the seeker has a "hard time" during his experience. The duties of everyday life, too, often seem hard. Now on his knees, now shouting, now sorrowful and now glad, the Negro comes from "hanging over hell" to die and "set by de Fadder's side." The average negro appears to pity himself, and his song intensifies the feeling. The songs that follow may be classed as those that give the state of uncertainty and doubt, together with pity mingled now and then with the note of triumph. In "Oh, What a Hard Time!" sisters, brothers, children, preachers, seekers—all have the same difficulties.

> Oh, what a hard time! Oh, what a hard time!
> Oh, what a hard time—all God's children have a hard time.
> Oh, what a hard time! Oh, what a hard time!
> Oh, what a hard time! My Lord had a hard time, too.

In another division will be given the song "My Trouble Is Hard," the idea of which seems to be derived from the old plantation songs, though the new song is entirely different from the old ones. The plantation Negroes used to sing "Nobody knows the trouble I've seen," in which they were "sometimes up, sometimes down, sometimes almost to de groun'." Others sang it "Nobody knows the trouble I see," (or "I've had,") and asked: "Brother, sister, preacher, will you pray for me?"

PO' SINNER MAN

In the same pathetic tone the "sinner man" gives another phase of the feeling.

> My mother 'n' yo' mother both daid an' gone,
> My mother 'n' yo' mother both daid an' gone,
> My mother 'n' yo' mother both daid an' gone,
>   Po' sinner man he so hard to believe.
>
> My folks an' yo' folks both daid an' gone,
>   Po' sinner man he so hard to believe.
>
> My brother 'n' yo' brother both daid an' gone,
>   Po' sinner man he so hard to believe.

As usual "my sister," etc., completes the song, with favorite lines, "Down in de valley," "Up on mountain Jehober spoke," etc., being inserted as often as they are needed.

HANGIN' OVER HELL

The next one gives more intensity to the feeling of the sinner. He says

> When I wus hangin' over hell, over hell,
> When I wus hangin' over hell, over hell,
> Well, I had no one to pity poor me, poor me.
>
> Well, my mother sick an' my father daid, father daid,
> Well, my mother sick an' my father daid, father daid,
> Well, I ain't got no one to pity poor me, poor me.

Well, I ain't got no one to pray for me, to pray for me.

I ain't got no one to feel for me, feel for me.

Likewise he has no one to "cry" for him, to "mourn " or to "care" for him.

KEEP INCHIN' ALONG

The struggle is well represented by the song "Keep Inchin' Along," which was also common in the old plantation melodies; the chorus is the same, while the words are entirely different from the other song.

> Keep er-inchin' erlong, keep er-inchin' erlong,
> Jesus 'll come by an' by
> Keep er-inchin', keep er-inchin' erlong,
> Jesus 'll come by an' by.
>
> De road is rocky here below,
> But Jesus 'll come by an' by.
> But Jesus leads me as I go,
> Jesus 'll come by an' by.
>
> Sometimes I hang my head an' cries,
> But Jesus 'll come by an' by.
> An' He goin' wipe mer weepin' eyes,
> Jesus 'll come by an' by.
>
> Oh, run 'long, mourner, an' git yo' crown,
> By yo' Father's side set down.
>
> I'm glad that I'm bo'n ter die,
> Frum trouble here my soul goin' fly.

CROSS ME OVER

In the same hopeful strain the Negro sings "Boun' ter cross Jord'n in dat mornin'," which has a large

number of stanzas, none of which conforms closely to
the general theme.

> Yonder come er sister all dressed in black,
> She look lak er hipercrit jes' got back.
> I'm boun' ter cross Jord'n in dat mornin'.
>
> Cross me over,
> Great Jehover,
> My Lord, I'm boun' ter cross Jord'n in dat mornin'.
>
> See dat Christian on his knees,
> He's gwin' ter cross dem jasper seas.
> I'm boun' ter cross Jord'n in dat mornin'.
>
> Swing low, chariots, in er line,
> Carry me ter glory in due time.
> I'm boun' ter cross Jord'n in dat mornin'.
>
> Ain't but the one thing grieve my min',
> Sister goin' to heaven an' leave me behin'.
> I'm boun' ter cross Jord'n in dat mornin'.

FOR MY LORD

It is a favorite theme of the Negroes to sing much
of their "Lord" and "God." Much has been said of
the names and attributes which Deity holds in the
Negro songs. As his friend the Negro believes that
God is always true; consequently he sings his loyalty
to him. The old plantation song "Tell Jesus" had
as its chorus:

> Tell Jesus done done all I can,
> Tell Jesus done done all I can,
> Tell Jesus done done all I can;
> I can't do no more.

Very much like it is the song "For My Lord" that is much in demand among the present-day Negroes.

> I goin' to do all I can fer my Lord,
> I goin' to do all I can fer my Lord,
> I goin' to do all I can fer my Lord,
> I goin' to do all I can fer my Lord,
> I do all I can till I can't do no more;
> I goin' to do all I can fer my Lord.

Likewise he sings: "I goin' weep all I can till I can't weep no more," "I goin' pray all I can till I can't pray no more." The phrase, "till I can't do no mo'," is characteristic of the Negro's prayers. He usually closes his church prayers "Now Lord, when we's done prayin' an' can't pray no mo'; when we' done meetin' an' can't meet no mo'," etc. The closing scene, the final act of life, seems to appeal to the Negro with wonderful dramatic power.

GWINE LAY DOWN MY LIFE FOR MY LORD

This song is similar in theme to "For My Lord," but excels it in variety of expression.

> De Lord giv' me mer trumpet an' tole me ter blow,
> He giv' me mer cummission an' tole me ter go.
>
> Fer my Lord, fer my Lord, fer my Lord,
> Gwine lay down my life fer my Lord.
>
> You can hinder me here but you can't hinder me dere,
> For de Lord in Heaven gwine hear my prayer.
>
> De enemy's great but my Cap'n is strong,
> Um fightin' fer de city an' de time ain't long.
>
> When I git dar I'll be able fer to tell,
> How I whipped ole Satan at de door ob hell.

Mer head got wet wid de midnight dew,
Dat mornin' star was shinin' too.

DO, LORD, REMEMBER ME

It is but natural that the Negro would call upon the Lord to remember him. The old plantation song "Do, Lord, Remember Me," was apparently based upon the idea of being remembered at Christmas time; indeed the Negroes always asked to be remembered at such a time by the "white folks." The song now current is very likely an entirely different one.

> Do, my Lord, remember me,
> Do, my Lord, remember me,
> Do, my Lord, remember me,
>   Do, Lord, remember me.
>
> Up on de housetop an' can't come down,
>   Do, Lord, remember me.
> Up on de house and can't come down,
>   Do, Lord, remember me.
>
> When I am hungry do feed me, Lord,
>   Do, Lord, remember me.
> When I am thirsty do give me drink,
>   Do, Lord, remember me.

KING JESUS IS THE ROCK

The Negroes sometimes call the following song the "riddle song," because the leader asks, "Who is the Rock?" while the answer comes back, "King Jesus is the Rock."

> Lead me to the Rock, lead me to the Rock,
> Lead me to the Rock, that is higher an' higher.
> Oh, lead me to the Rock,
> Yes, lead me to the Rock that is higher an' higher.

King Jesus is the Rock, yes, King Jesus is the Rock,
King Jesus is the Rock that is higher an' higher.
Oh, King Jesus is the Rock,
Yes, King Jesus is the Rock that is higher an' higher.

Standing on the Rock, yes, standing on the Rock,
Standing on the Rock that is higher an' higher.
Oh, standing on the Rock,
Yes, standing on the Rock that is higher an' higher.

DERE'S NO ONE LAK JESUS

As Jesus is the Rock, so the Negroes have sung, 'Dere's no one lak Jesus." The chorus-line was common in the old songs; the verses of the song of to-day are different.

I think I heard a rumblin' in de sky,
Dar's no one lak Jesus;
It mus' be mer Lord passin' by,
Dar's no one lak Jesus.

Stan' still, walk study, keep de faith,
Dar's no one lak Jesus.

Sister Mary went up on de mount'n top,
Dar's no one lak Jesus.
She sung a li'l song an' she never did stop,
Dar's no one lak Jesus.

She argued wid de Fadder an' chatter'd wid de Son,
Dar's no one lak Jesus.
She talk'd erbout the ole worl' she cum frum,
Dar's no one lak Jesus.

GIVE ME JESUS

The song "Give Me Jesus" was said to have been the product of "over-free spirit and super-religious-ness" just after the Civil War. The Negro claims that the white man took him at his word when he sang "Give me Jesus, You can have all this worl'," and has left him nothing in this world but Jesus. At least this is one view of the song, which is represented as a bargain which the white man wants the Negro to keep. The song is a typical and well-known one, said to have been first sung by a blind Negro preacher.

In de mornin' when I rise,
In de mornin' when I rise,
In de mornin' when I rise,
　　Give me Jesus.

Give me Jesus,
Give me Jesus,
You may hab' all dis worl'.

Ef it's midnight when I rise,
Ef it's midnight when I rise,
Ef it's midnight when I rise,
　　Give me Jesus.

Jes' 'fore day when I cried,
　　Give me Jesus.

When I wade death's cold stream,
　　Give me Jesus.

LOVE THE LORD

The Negro says that if one loves Jesus he "can't keep it," and that he is duty bound to let the world know it. It is a common custom to ask "members" at the class-meeting and revival whether or not they "love the Lord." It is the duty of the class leader to see to the religious welfare of the members. The song, "Love The Lord," represents this phase of worship.

> Well, did you say that you love Jesus?
> Did you say that you love the Lord?
>
> > Yes, I say that I love Jesus;
> > Yes, I say I love the Lord.
>
> All I wants to know is, does you love Jesus?
> All I wants to know is, does you love the Lord?
>
> > Yes, I say that I love Jesus.
> > Yes, I say I love the Lord.
>
> If you love Jesus, you can't keep it,
> All I wants to know is, does you love the Lord?
>
> > Yes, my mother, I love Jesus,
> > Yes, my mother, I love the Lord.

The chorus then varies from "Yes, I say" to "Yes, my mother," "Yes, my sister," "Yes, my brother."

I GOT A HOME

In striking contrast to his earthly life, the Negro sings of his heavenly home. If in slavery days he had no home, it was natural that he should look to heaven for his home. This conception, intensified by the Negro's emotional nature and self-pity, is still prominent. Not only is his home to be a happy one, but it is to be exclusive; only the fortunate, of whom he is the chiefest, may go there. This class of songs—of heaven and home—is perhaps as large as any. The Negro sings:

I got a home where liars can't go,
　　Don't you see?
Jus' between the heaven an' earth,
Where my Saviour bled an' died,
I got a home where liars can't go,
　　Dont' you see?

I got a home where sinners can't go,
　　Don't you see?
Jus' between the earth an' sky,
Where my Saviour bleed an' die,
　　Don't you see?

When the earth begin to shake,
　　Don't you see?
You better get a ticket or you'll be late,
　　Don't you see?

The singers repeat, using the words "drunkards," "hypocrites," and other sinners. Sometimes instead of saying, "I got a home where the drunkards can't come," the singer will say, "where the drunkards can't find me."

DON'T YOU SEE?

Another version of the same song is found in different localities:

I got a home in the Rock,
　　Don't you see?
Just between the heaven an' earth,
Well, yes, I got a home in the Rock,
　　Don't you see?

Judas was a deceitful man,
　　Dont' you see?
Well, he betrayed the innercent Lam',
Well, he lost a home in the Rock,
　　Don't you see?

Well, the sun refuse to shine,
    Don't you see?
The sun refuse to shine,
An' the sun refuse to shine,
    Don't you see?

God don't talk like a natural man,
    Don't you see?
God don't talk like a natural man,
He talk so sinners can understan',
    Don't you see?

Well I don't want to stumble,
    Don't you see?
Well I don't want to fall,
I read that writin' on de wall,
    Don't you see?

YOU GOT A ROBE

The chorus of this and the following song is made unusually effective when the "heaven" is hummed softly with lips closed. It is a chorus that appeals much to both old and young Negroes.

You got a robe, I got a robe,
All God's chillun got a robe.
Goin' to try on my robe an' if it fits me,
Goin' to wear it all around God's heaven.

Heaven—heaven, ev'ybody goin' to heaven,
An' I'm goin' dere, too.

Gamblers here an' gamblers dere,
I'm so glad dat God declare,
Dere aint no gamblers in heaven.

This version and wording is rather that of the children, who are fond of singing it. They continue "Heaven so high you can't go over it," "Heaven so low you can't go under it," "Heaven so deep you can't go through it," and "Heaven so wide you can't go round it." The most common form of the song is "Heaven," a variation of the above. Sinners, gamblers, dancers, liars, drunkards are everywhere, but not in heaven.

HEAVEN

Well, there are sinners here and sinners there,
An' there are sinners eve'ywhere;
But I thank God that God declare,
That there ain't no sinners in heaven.

    Heaven, Heaven,
    Everybody talkin' 'bout heaven ain't goin' there.
    Heaven, Heaven,
    Goin' to shine all 'round God's heaven.

Well, there are drunkards here an' drunkards there,
An' there are drunkards everywhere;
But I'm so glad that God declare,
There ain't no drunkards in heaven.

    Heaven, Heaven,
    Preachers all preachin' 'bout heaven ain't goin'
      there.
    Heaven, Heaven,
    Goin' to shine all 'round God's heaven.

IF I KEEP PRAYIN' ON

As has been indicated, many of the Negro songs consist of single lines repeated in couplets or by fours in order to give length to the singing. The most simple sentences that could be devised may serve as a good song. The Negro happens to think of an ordinary truth; he then sings it to his tune and chorus

I'm goin' to be a Christian if I keep a-prayin' on,
I goin' to be a Christian if I keep a-prayin' on,
I goin' to be a Christian, I'm goin' to be a Christian,
I goin' to be a Christian if I keep a-prayin' on.

An' when I git religion, I goin' to keep a-prayin on.

I goin' to see my Jesus if I keep a-prayin on.

I goin' to see my mother if I keep a-prayin on.

The singer is going to see his father, brother, master, preacher and others. He sings each line four times, altering it as he desires and putting in any chorus that appeals to his fancy.

GREAT JUDGMENT DAY

The next song shows a typical variation of a line, and the Negro sometimes sings the second version with more determination than the first.

Lord, I want to go to heaven fer to stan' my trials,
Lord, I want to go to heaven fer to stan' my trials,
Yes, I want to go to heaven fer to stan' my trials,
        Great judgment day.

Well, I'm goin' to heaven fer to stan' my trials,
An' I'm goin' to heaven fer to stan' my trials,
Yes, I'm goin' to heaven fer to stan' my trials,
        Great judgment day.

I'M ON MY JOURNEY HOME

The slaves used to sing, "Hail, hail, hail, I'm gwine jine saints above, I'm on my journey home." In many of their songs the "promise lan'" was held out as the goal of future happiness. So it is today.

Sister, when you pray you mus' pray to de Lord,
For I hab some hopes ob glory;
I feel like, I feel like I'm on my journey home,
I feel like, I feel like, I'm on my journey home.

I'll away, I'll away to de promise lan'.
My Father calls me, I mus' go,
To meet Him in de promise lan'.

I have a father in the promise lan',
Go meet him in de promise lan';
I feel like, I feel like I'm on my journey home,
I feel like, I feel like I'm on my journey home.

The singer also has a mother, a sister, an auntie and others in the "promise lan'." Likewise he says, instead of "sister, when you pray," brother, member, mourner, sinner, preacher and others.

IN THE MORNING

As a rule morning signified to the Negro the time for going to heaven and for the resurrection. The morning star shone as a witness to his conversion, and the midnight dew typified the early morning time of his religion. "In the Morning" is sung as of old.

I have been tempted, O yes,
An' I have been tried, O yes;
I have been to the river an' been baptize,
An' I want to go to heaven in the morning.

Won't you ride on, Jesus?
Ride on, Jesus, ride on, Crowning King;
For I want to go to heaven in the morning.

If you see my mother, O yes,
Please tell her for me, O yes,
That the angels in heaven done change my name,
An' I want to go to heaven in the morning.

I ain't goin' to study war no more

The song once so popular, "Yes, I'll Be Dere When Gen'ral Roll Call," is still heard occasionally. Many songs of this kind have been corrupted and changed, consolidated and revised into new songs. Such a song is "Study War No Mo'," which combines the old camp meeting song "Down by the River Side," and a new element of peace, the origin of which is not known.

Well, there's goin' to be a big camp meetin',
Well, there's goin' to be a big camp meetin',
Well, there's goin' to be a big camp meetin',
    Down by the river side.

Well, I ain't goin' to study war no mo',
Well, I ain't goin' to study war no mo',
Well, I ain't goin' to study war no mo'.

Well, such a shoutin' an' prayin',
    Down by the river side.

Well, I goin' to meet my sister,
    Down by the river side.

Well, the brothers got to shoutin',
    Down by the river side.

My soul's goin' to heaven

Said the old singers: "Some o' dese mornin's, hope I'll see my mother, hope I'll jine de ban', hope I'll walk about Zion, talk wid de angels, talk my trouble over." Now the negro sings:

Goin' to weep, goin' to mourn,
Goin' to git up early in de morn,
Fo' my soul's goin' to heaven jes' sho's you born;
Brother Gabriel goin' to blow his horn.

Goin' to sing, goin' to pray,
Goin' to pack all my things away,
For my soul's goin' to heaven jes' sho's you born;
Brother Gabriel goin' ter blow his horn.

DRY BONES GOIN' RISE

"Pray come an' go wid me," sings the Christian, for "I'm on my journey home to the New Jerusalem." If refused he says, "Now don't let me beg you to follow me, for I'm on my journey home," and finally he sings, "Well brother, come an' go wid me." If the sinner needs other exhortation he may listen to the mixed song, "Dry Bones Goin' to Rise Ergin," in which there is first warning, then hope of glory.

Some go ter meetin' to sing an' shout,
    Dry bones goin' ter rise ergin;
'Fore six months dey's all turned out,
    Dry bones goin' ter rise ergin.

Oh. little chillun, oh, little chillun,
Oh, little chillun, dry bones goin' rise ergin.

Talk erbout me but 'tain't my fault,
    Dry bones goin' ter rise ergin;
But me an' God-er-mighty goin' walk an' talk,
    Dry bones goin' ter rise ergin.

Ef you want ter go to heaven when you die,
    Dry bones goin' rise ergin;
Jes' stop yo' tongue from tellin' lies,
    Dry bones goin' ter rise ergin.

In the old plantation song Ezekiel was represented down in a valley "full of bones as dry as dust" and

He gib de bone a mighty shake,
Fin' de ole sinners too dry to quake.

JOIN DE HEAVEN WID DE ANGELS

In "Join De Heaven Wid De Angels" the rich voice of one or two leaders and the swelling chorus produce an effect scarcely surpassed.

> Oh, join on, join my Lord,
>   Join de heaven wid de angels;
> Oh, join on, join my Lord,
>   Join de heaven wid de angels.
>
> What kin' er shoes is dem you wear?
>   Join de heaven wid de angels;
> Dat you kin walk upon de air?
>   Join de heaven wid de angels.
>
> Oh, God don't talk like a natural man,
>   Join de heaven wid de angels;
> He talk to de sinner, he understan',
>   Join de heaven wid de angels.
>
> I'm Baptis' bred an' I'm Baptis' born,
>   Join de heaven wid de angels;
> An' when I die dey's a Baptis' gone,
>   Join de heaven wid de angels.
>
> Jes so de tree fall jes so it lie,
>   Join de heaven wid de angels;
> Jes so de sinner lib', jes so he die,
>   Join de heaven wid de angels.

The song has been found in several forms, among which one has it that John is to be "in de heaven with the angels." In fact, the probable origin of "join on" seems to have been "John saw de heaven wid de angels." In one of the old songs the singer answers:

> Dem shoes I wears is gospel shoes,
>   View de lan', view de lan';
> An' you can wear dem if you choose,
>   View de lan', view de lan'.

THE ANGEL BAND

"The Angel Band," while a very simple song in which the chorus constitutes the greater part, is one of the most beautiful that the Negroes sing. The power of the song seems to lie in the tender interest which centers about the vivid portrayal of the little angels in the heavenly band. The chorus is repeated after each stanza, while each stanza is the repetition of a single line. From one to ten, from ten to twenty, and so on to one hundred is ordinarily sung, thus making a lengthy song. The children love to sing the chorus; two forms are ordinarily found, varying the monotony enough to please the Negro.

> Dere's one little, two little, three little angels,
> Dere's four little, five little, six little angels,
> Dere's seven little, eight little, nine little angels,
> Dere's ten little angels in de band.

> Dere's leben, dere's twelve, dere's thirteen little angels,
> Dere's fourteen, dere's fifteen, dere's sixteen little angels,
> Dere's seventeen, dere's eighteen, dere's nineteen little
>   angels,
> Dere's twenty little angels in de ban.

The "little" in the chorus is preferred to the "dere's" as a rule, apparently serving to describe the angels. The stanzas of the song are as unlimited and as simple as the chorus. "Sunday morning" is the most common factor in the verses; sometimes it is omitted.

Jesus rose on Sunday mornin',
Jesus rose on Sunday mornin',
Jesus rose on Sunday mornin',
On Sunday mornin' so soon.

He rose an' flew away on Sunday mornin'.

My mother died on Sunday mornin'.

Oh wasn't that sad on Sunday mornin'?

Dere's goin' to be a mournin' on Sunday mornin'.

Mourners got to shoutin' on Sunday mornin.

I'm goin' away to leave you on Sunday mornin'.

Well, my sister's goin' to heaven on Sunday mornin'.

While this form of the song may be continued indefinitely, other verses may also be inserted. Instead of the "on Sunday mornin' " is often substituted "Fer to see my Lord."

Well, my sister's goin' to heaven fer to see my Lord,
    To see my Lord, to see my Lord;
Well, my sister's goin' to heaven fer to see my Lord,
    What's de onbelievin' soul?

And so it continues with preacher, brother, mother, auntie, and any others that the singer wishes to enumerate. As a shouting song or as a "collection" song, it is not surpassed.

'WAY IN DE MIDDLE OF DE AIR

The Negro's fancies of the "Heaven's bright home" are not exceeded by the world's fairy tales. There are silver and golden slippers; there are crowns of stars

and jewels and belts of gold. There are robes of
spotless white and wings all be-jeweled with heavenly
gems. Beyond the jasper seas he will outshine the
sun; the golden streets and the fruit of the tree of
life are far superior to any golden apples or silver
pears of a Mother Goose. In fact the Negro's fairy
stories center on heaven; the children's definitions of
heaven consist entirely of pictures of splendor and
glory. To this place the Negro imagines he will go,
and who knows but that he may fly there?

> Some o' dese mornin's bright an' fair,
>   'Way in de middle of de air;
> Goin' hitch on my wings an' try de air.
>   'Way in de middle of de air.
>
> Come over, den, John saw de holy number,
>   'Way in de middle of de air;
> John saw de holy number
>   'Way in de middle of de air.
>
> If yer wanter dream dem heavenly dreams.
>   'Way in de middle of de air;
> Lay yo' head on Jord'n's stream,
>   'Way in de middle of de air.
>
> I got a book, goin' read it thru',
>   'Way in de middle of de air;
> I got my Jesus well as you,
>   'Way in de middle of de air.

I GOIN' TRY THE AIR

With a golden "band all round his waist, an' de
palms ob victory in-a his hands," the Negro sings in
reality, "Pray come an' go wid me," for so vivid is
his picture that he has been known to start up a post

or pillar in the church, saying, "Good bye, brothers,
I'm gone." His songs make much of flying; different
from that just given, is—

> One mornin' soon,
> One mornin' soon, my Lord,
> One mornin' soon,
> I goin' try the air,
> I goin' try the air;
> Pray come an' go wid me.
>
> Well, I got on my travelin' shoes,
> Well, I got on my travelin' shoes,
> Well, I got on my travelin' shoes;
> Pray come an' go wid me.

He sings, too: "I goin' to put on my long white
robe," "We'll try on de slippah shoe and wear de
golden belt."

i goin' put on my golden shoes

Again he sings of his doings on the great resurrection
day:

> In the morning—um-u,
> In the morning—um-u,
> In the morning—um-u,
> I goin' put on my golden shoes.
>
> In the midnight—um-u,
> In the midnight—um-u,
> In the midnight—um-u,
> I goin' put on my long white robe.
>
> Talk about it—um-u,
> Talk about it—um-u,
> Talk about it—um-u,
> I goin' wear that starry crown.

JESUS WORE THE CROWN

The angels and Jesus wear starry crowns and long white robes; there will be no separating line between us and God in the next world. "Oh, how I long to go dere, too," sang the old Negroes. Now they picture again the appearance of Jesus.

> Jesus, he wore the starry crown,
> Jesus, he wore the starry crown,
> Jesus, he wore the starry crown, starry crown.
>
> How does you know he wore the crown?
> How does you know he wore the crown?
> How does you know he wore the crown, wore the crown?
>
> For the Bible it tell me so,
> For the Bible it tell me so,
> For the Bible it tell me so, tell me so.
>
> Jesus, he wore the long white robe,—etc.

I DON'T CARE FOR RICHES

More than the world or riches or dress the singer claims he values the treasures of heaven. In this assertion he is doubtless sincere, both because he is thinking only of his religious state while he sings, and because he has little opportunity for obtaining these earthly riches. Says he:

> I don't care for riches,
> Neither dress so fine;
> Jes' giv' me my long white robe,
> An' I want my starry crown.
>
> For my Lord done bin here,
> Done bless my soul an' gone away.

Po' man goin' to heaven,
Rich man goin' to hell;
For po' man got his starry crown,
Rich man got his wealth.

DEATH IS IN DIS LAND

"This ole worl' bin a hell to me" indicates the contrast between the everyday life of the world and that which the Negro will enjoy after death. In his eagerness and impatience to rest in the "promise lan'," the Negro does not always think kindly of the world and he does not care even though "death is in dis lan'."

Ever since my Lord has set me free,
    Death is in dis lan';
This ole worl' bin a hell to me,
    Death is in dis lan'.

I'm so glad death is in dis lan'.
I'm so glad death is in dis lan'.

O run 'long, mourner, 'n' git yo' crown,
    Death is in dis land;
By yo' father's side set down,
    Death is in dis lan'.

Some er dese mornin's bright and fair,
    Death is in dis lan';
Goin' er hitch on my wings and try de air,
    Death is in dis lan'.

GOIN' TO OUTSHINE THE SUN

If the Negro expects to go to heaven and there mingle with God, the angels and his loved ones, he also expects to sing in all the glory and splendor imaginable. The Negroes used to sing: "Den my little soul gwine shine." So they sang of a mother, father, brother in heaven who "outshines de sun"; and when "we" get to heaven "we will outshine de sun." In very much the same way Negroes sing today in one of their favorites, "Goin' to Outshine de Sun."

Well, my mother's goin' to heaven,
She's goin' to outshine the sun, O Lord.
Well, my mother's goin' to heaven,
She goin' to outshine the sun,
Yes, my mother's goin' to heaven to outshine the sun,
An' it's 'way beyon' the moon.

You got a home in the promise lan',
Goin' to outshine the sun, O Lord,
An' it's 'way beyon' the moon.

The crown that my Jesus give me,
Goin' to outshine the sun, my Lord,
An' it's 'way beyond the moon.

Goin' to put on my crown in glory,
An' outshine the sun, O Lord,
'Way beyond the moon.

CHAPTER IV

EXAMPLES OF RELIGIOUS SONGS (*Concluded*)

The next group of songs presented will appear very much like those already given, except that they show more uniformity, a little more length, and in the last of this chapter, more of the mixed type of song. This group will deal with such themes as the gospel train, the grandeur of heaven and the judgment, the impressive personalities of the Bible, typical variations of song, and specimen poetic efforts to make new songs.

WHEN DE TRAIN COME ALONG

In these illustrations it will be seen that the Negro uses many figures and symbols. He sees vividly the chariot of fire. It took Elijah, perhaps it will take him. Christ and the angels ascended; perhaps he will. And there is the gospel train; the same train that took the others! What fascination the train has for the Negro may be seen further from the "train song," illustrations of which are given in Chapter VI.

Well, I may be sick an' cannot rise,
But I meet you at de station when de train come along.

When de train come along,
When de train come along,
I'll meet you at de station when de train come along.

Well, I may be blind an' cannot see,
But I meet you at de station when de train come along.

Well, I may be lame and cannot walk,
But I'll meet you at de station when de train come along.

While no mention is made of the exact kind of train, it is generally understood to mean the gospel train. This song also has a popular variant which is used in a secular way. In either case it expresses in a very forceful way the importance of meeting the train.

SAME TRAIN

In proportion as a picture resembles real life or magnifies that which has been imaged, to that degree does it bring home its truth to the Negro's mind. The Negro continues to sing of the train on which he is to ride into the Kingdom. Says he:

> I am talkin' 'bout the same train,
> Same train that carried my father,
>   Same train.
>
> Same train that carried my mother,
>   Same train,
> Same train will be back tomorrow,
>   Same train.
>
> Same train will be here tomorrow,
>   Same train,
> Well you better be ready,
>   It's the same train.

The "same train" also carried his brother, sister, preacher and others.

YOU BETTER GIT YO' TICKET

But the train which will come back tomorrow will not wait always. One must not only be at the station but must also have a ticket. There is plenty of room, according to the Negro's conception, but there is not plenty of time. It would be a wistful Negro that looked upon the train pulling out for heaven and leaving him behind. He sings:

> Well, you better git yo' ticket,
> Well, you better git yo' ticket,
> Well, you better git yo' ticket,
>   By and by.
>
> There's a great day er comin',
> There's a great day er comin',
> There's a great day er comin',
>   By and by.
>
> For the train it's er comin',
> For the train it's er comin',
> For the train it's er comin',
>   By and by.
>
> I am sure God is ready,
> I am sure God is ready,
> I am sure God is ready,
>   By and by.

Instead of the chorus just given he often sings: "I sure God am ready," and "I sho God is ready." With this in view he is willing and glad for the train to come along. If he is ready, all the better for him to be on his journey.

THE GOSPEL TRAIN

He continues in another song to sing of the gospel train:

> If God was to call me I would not care—um-u,
> For he done move away my fears—um-u.
> I'm goin' to heaven, an' I'm goin' fo' long—um-u,
> All don't see me will hear my song—um-u.

When de gospel train come 'long—um-u,
That's the train goin' carry me home—um-u.
Wake up, sinner, you will be too late—um-u,
Gospel train done pass yo' gate—um-u.

In the old plantation songs the exhortation was
given to "Git on board, little children, dere's room
for many a-mo'," and—

De gospel train's a comin',
I hear it jus' at hand,
I hear de car wheels rumblin',
An' rollin' thru de land.

I hear de train a comin',
She's comin' around de curve,
She's loosened all her steam an' brakes,
An strainin' eb'ry nerve.

De fare is cheap an' all can go,
De rich an' pore are dere,
No second class aboard dis train,
No difference in de fare.

Other verses of "The Gospel Train" as it was sung
by the Jubilee Singers are:

There's Moses and Noah and Abraham,
And all the prophets, too;
Our friends in Christ are all on board,
Oh, what a heavenly crew.

We soon shall reach the station,
Oh, how we then shall sing;
With all the heavenly army,
We'll make the welkin ring.

She's nearing now the station,
    O sinner, don't be vain,
But come an' get your ticket,
    And be ready for the train.

No signal for the other train,
    To follow on the line;
O sinner, you're forever lost,
    If once you're left behind.

While the song as reported by the Jubilee Singers does not possess the usual characteristics of form and dialect, it nevertheless appeals to the Negroes and it is sometimes sung.

I CANNOT STAY HERE BY MYSELF

One of the fears of the Negro is that others may go to heaven and he be left behind. This, as has been indicated, constitutes the sum total of misery. So he has a number of songs in which he expresses this feeling and prays that he may not be left behind in the race of life for the eternal goal. One of the most touching of these songs represents the Negro as an orphan who is unwilling to stay alone in the world:

My muther an' my father both are dead, both are dead,
My muther an' my father both are dead,
My muther an' my father both are dead,
Good Lord, I cannot stay here by merself.

I'm er pore little orphan chile in de worl', chile in de
    worl',
I'm er pore little orphan chile in de worl',
I'm a pore little orphan chile in de worl',
Good Lord, I cannot stay here by merself.

De train done whistled an' de cars done gone, cars done
    gone;
De train done whistled an' de cars er gone,
De train done whistled an' de cars er gone,
Ezekiel, I cannot stay here by merself.

My brothers an' my sisters are all gone, all gone,
My brothers an' my sisters 're all gone, all gone,
My brothers an' sisters all are gone,
Mer Jesus, I cannot stay here by merself.

Git me ticket fer de train, fer de train,
Git me ticket fer de train,
I got mer ticket fer de train,
Thank God, I ain't gwine stay here by merself.

Very much like the song just given the Negroes used
to sing: "Dar's room in dar, room in dar, room in de
heaven; Lord, I can't stay behin'." Again they sang
the "good news, de chariot's comin', I doan want her
to leave a-me behind." In a prayer the Negro sang:
"Jesus, don't leave me behind." In his songs today
the Negro says:

THIS OLE WORLD'S A HELL TO ME

Dear brother, don't you leave,
Dear brother, don't you leave,
Dear brother, don't you leave,
This ole world's a hell to me.

This ole world's a hell to me,
This ole world's a hell to me.

Yes I 'bleeged to leave this world,
Yes, I 'bleeged to leave this world,
Sister, I's 'bleeged to leave this world,
For it's a hell to me.

YOU CAN'T STAY AWAY

While the old Negroes used to sing "Oh, brother, sisters, mourners, don't stay away, For my Lord says there's room enough," the modern Negro sings "You can't stay away."

> Sister, you can't stay away,
> Sister, you can't stay away,
> Sister, you can't stay away.
>
> My Lord is callin' an' you can't stay away,
> My Lord is a callin' an' you can't stay away,
> Yes, my Lord is a callin' an' you can't stay away,
>   An' you can't stay away.
>
> King Jesus is a ridin' an' you can't stay away,
> King Jesus is a ridin' an' you can't stay away,
> King Jesus is a ridin' an' you can't stay away,
>   O preacher, you can't stay away.

OLE SHIP OF ZION

There have been a great many versions of the song "Ole Ship of Zion," none of which differs materially. There were four of five versions common during slavery. The coast Negroes had many songs that originated in ideas suggested by the boats. Today the river Negroes have songs of their own, but they are not of a religious nature. The "Ole Ship of Zion," however, is sung, but only as a less elaborate remnant of the former song.

> This ole ship is a reelin' an' a rockin'
> This ole ship is a reelin' an' a rockin', rockin', rockin',
>   Makin' fer de promise lan'.

While the Negro sings, he sees the ship "reelin' an' rockin'," and repeats these phrases in a rhythmic manner

so that he imitates the imagined motion of the ship.
The other stanzas of the song are practically the same
as those of the earlier days.

> O my Lord, shall I be the one?
> O my Lord, shall I be the one?
> O my Lord, shall I be the one?
>   Makin' for the promise lan'?
>
> Yes, 'tis that good ole ship of Zion, of Zion,
> Yes, 'tis that good ole ship of Zion, of Zion,
> Yes, 'tis that good ole ship of Zion,
>   Makin' for the promise lan'.
>
> O the ship is heavy loaded, loaded, loaded,
>   Makin' for the promise lan'.
> It's loaded with many er thousand, thousand, thousand,
>   Makin' fer the promise lan'.

THIS OLE WORL'S A ROLLIN'

"This Ole Worl' Is A-Rollin'" is most likely a figure
of the ship and modeled on the same song. However,
it conveys a different idea, one of judgment and the
end of the world.

> Well, the ole worl' is a rollin', rollin', rollin',
> Yes, the ole worl' is rollin', rollin' away.
>
> Well, ain't you goin' to get ready?
> Yes, ain't you goin' to get ready, for it's rollin' away?
>
> Well, get on board, little children, children, children,
> Well, get on board, for this ole worl's rollin' away.

He sings for the sinner, mourner, and all his friends
and relatives to get on board the world as it rolls away.
It reminds one somewhat of the song once current
among the Negroes: "O de ole ferry boat stan'
a-waitin' at de landin', Chilluns, we's all gwine home."

I KNOW MY TIME AIN'T LONG

The same idea of motion and the end of the world as is indicated in the moving of the train, ship, and the world itself is also reflected in the next song.

> Oh, the lightnin' flashin' an' the thunder rollin', rollin', rollin',
> Oh, the lightnin' flashin' an' the thunder rollin', rollin', rollin',
> Oh, the lightnin' flashin' an' thunder rollin',
> Lawd, I know my time ain't long; Lawd, I know my time ain't long.
>
> The hearse wheel rollin' an' graveyard openin', openin', openin',
> The hearse wheel rollin' an' graveyard openin', openin', openin',
> The hearse wheel rollin' an' the graveyard openin',
> Lawd, I know my time ain't long, my time ain't long.

EVERY DAY

Very much like the foregoing song is "Every Day." It is so similiar to other songs that one concludes that it is only a putting together of what the singer already knew. The Bahama Negroes have a song, "If Hev'ry Day Was Judgment Day," that has almost exactly the same meaning as this one. "Every Day," however, is powerful and seems to be gaining in popularity.

> Well, the hearse wheel rollin',
>   Every day, every day,
> Carryin' yo' brother to the graveyard,
>   Every day, every day; move, Zion, move.

> Well, ain't it a pity, pity?
>   Every day, every day.
> Well, ain't it a pity, ain't it a pity?
>   Every day, every day; move, Zion, move.
>
> Well, they're carryin' a sinner, sinner,
>   Every day, every day.
> Yes, they're carryin' a sinner,
>   Every day, every day; move, Zion, move.
>
> Move, Zion, move, for you got to go to judgment,
>   Every day, every day.
> Move, Zion, move, for you got to go to judgment,
>   Every day, every day; move, Zion, move.

MY MOTHER GOT A LETTER

The getting of mail, and especially of letters, usually means much to the Negroes. Perhaps it is simply because they receive little mail. To have a letter from a distinguished person is superlative honor and the recipient usually makes the fact known generally. Just how the Negro conceived of receiving letters from God, or why he imagined the angels and apostles as writing letters does not appear clear. One gets a letter, another reads it; one writes a letter and all know its contents. Such a reference is found in a number of songs that serve as a warning or admonition.

> Well, my mother got a letter, oh, yes;
> Well, she could not read it, oh, yes.
> What you reckon that letter said?
> That she didn't have long to stay here.
>
> Won't you come, won't you come?
> Won't you come an' get ready to die?
> Won't you come, for my Lord is callin' you?

How do you know that my Lord is callin'? oh, yes,
If you look at this letter, oh, yes,
You see it come from the Hebrews, oh, yes.
Won't you come, for my Lord is callin' you?

IT JUST SUITS ME

Perhaps the idea of the letter came from the epistles of the New Testament. John and Peter wrote letters; Mary and Martha read them. The letters of the Hebrews and Ephesians are spoken of. The idea in "It Just Suits Me" seems to have sprung up from satisfaction in reading the Scripture or in hearing the preacher.

John wrote a letter and he wrote it in haste,
    An' it jus' suit me.
John wrote a letter and he wrote it in haste,
    An' it jus' suit me.

John wrote a letter and he wrote it in haste,
If yer want to go to heaven yer better make haste,
    An' it jus' suit me.

I'll tell you a little thing that was in John's letter,
The Holy Ghost came to make us better,
    An' it jus' suit me.

If this isn't the Holy Ghost I don't know,
I never felt such a love befo',
    But it jus' suit me.

O my brother, you oughter been at de pool,
To see me put on my gospel shoes,
    An' it jus' suit me.

Ezekiel said he spied the train a comin',
We got on board an' she never stopped runnin',
    An' it jus' suit me.

This kind er religion is better than gold,
It's better felt than ever told,
      An' it jus' suit me.

I tell you a little thing you can't do,
You can't serve God and the devil, too,
      But it jus' suit me.

When trouble is done an' conflicts have passed,
I rise to reign in peace at last,
      An' it jus' suit me.

THE BLOOD DONE SIGN MY NAME

It is gratifying to the Negro that his sins have been "washed in the blood of the Lamb." The Negro singers have exhibited a characteristic specimen of their word combinations, concrete pictures, and theological principles in their song, "De Blood Done Sign My Name."

O de blood, O de blood,
O de blood done sign my name;
O Jesus said so, Jesus said so,
O de blood done sign my name.

I believe it, for God he tole me,
That the blood done sign my name,
I believe it, for God he tole me,
That the blood done sign my name,
Yes, the blood done sign my name.

How do you know so?   God he said so,
That the blood done sign my name.

Well, it's written in de Kingdom,
That the blood done sign my name.

Well, in the Lamb's book it is written,
That the blood done sign my name.

Well, the wheels a turnin', wheels a turnin',
Blood done sign my name.

I'm boun' for glory, boun' for glory,
The blood done sign my name.

On de mountain, on de mountain,
The blood done sign my name.

In the valley, in the valley,
Blood done sign my name.

DE UDDER WORL' IS NOT LAK DIS

But the Christian does not have an easy time after his conversion. Satan is always at hand and ready to lead him away if there is a chance. The Negro's idea of the devil has been noted. In his march songs the Negro imagines that he is marching against his foe; this foe is sometimes Satan himself.

I er's walkin' 'long de udder day,
    De udder worl' is not lak dis.
I met ole Satan on de way,
    De udder worl' is not lak dis.
He said, "Young man, you're too young to pray."
    De udder worl' is not lak dis.

Tell all dis worl',
Tell all dis worl',
Tell all dis worl',
    De udder worl' is not lak dis.

As I went down in de valley to pray,
    De udder worl' is not lak dis,
I met a little looker on de way,
    De udder worl' is not lak dis.
He said: "Look out fer de jedgment day."
    De udder worl' is not lak dis.

GOIN' DOWN TO JORDAN

Another marching song that is a favorite is "Goin' Down to Jordan." It represents, like the one just given, the attributes of Satan and his relation to the Christian. The scene as pictured, the army marching on down to Jordan, the imaginary foe, and the rhythi of the song make it irresistible for the Negro.

> Halleluyer to the Lam'!
>   Goin' on down to Jordan,
> Lord God's on that givin' han',
>   Goin' on down to Jordan.
>
>   Goin' down to Jordan,
>   Goin' down to Jordan,
>   I got my breas' plate, sword an' shield.
>   Goin' down to Jordan,
>   Boldly marchin' thru' the field,
>   Goin' on down to Jordan.
>
> I plucked one block out'n Satan's wall,
>   Goin' on down to Jordan,
> I heard him stumble an' saw him fall,
>   Goin' on down to Jordan.
>
> Ole Satan's a liar an' a conjurer, too,
>   Goin' on down to Jordan.
> If you don't mind he'll conjure you,
>   Goin' on down to Jordan.
>
> Ole Satan mad an' I am glad,
> He missed a soul he thought he had.
>
> Ole Satan thought he had me fast,
> Broke his chain an' I'm free at last.
>
> I've landed my feet on Jordan's sho',
> Now I'm free forever mo',
>   Goin' on down to Jordan.

THEY NAIL HIM TO THE CROSS

The old songs asked: "Wus you dere when dey crucified my Lord? When dey put the crown of thorns on?" In some of the songs the Negroes sang, "I wus dere when," etc., while still others only affirm the facts. The songs of the present generation of Negroes are less vivid and less full of feeling for the suffering of the Master. Some of the verses are similar to those of the plantation songs.

> He carried his cross, he carried his cross,
> Up Zion hill, up Zion hill,
> He carried his cross, he carried his cross,
> Up Zion hill, up Zion hill.
> He carried his cross up Zion hill, Zion hill, Zion hill.
>
> They put him on the thorny crown,
> Then they nail my Jesus down.
> They nail him down, nail him down, nail him down.
>
> They lif' the cross high in the air,
> To show the worl' how they nail him there,
> How they nail him there, nail him there, nail him there.

A peculiar corruption of this song represents the prodigal son as being in the place of Christ; now it is the prodigal, now it is the Lord. It indicates the manner of the development of many of these songs, and shows something of the insignificance of the words in the mind of the singer. He sings with his holy laugh:

> Yes, the prodigal son come home, ha, ha!
> Yes, the prodigal son come home, ha, ha!
> The prodigal son come home by hisself.

An' they nail him to the cross, ha, ha!
An' they nail him to the cross, ha, ha!
An' they nail him to the cross on that day.

An' the blood come runnin' down, ha, ha!
The blood come runnin' down, ha, ha!
An' the blood come runnin' down, on that day.

An' they kill the fat'nin' calf, ha, ha!
An' they kill the fat'nin' calf, ha, ha!
They kill the fat'nin' calf on that day.

An' they carried my Lord away, ha, ha!
An' they carried my Lord away, ha, ha!
They carried my Lord away, by hisself.

PAUL AND SILAS

Paul and Silas, Peter and John are models for proper contemplation. One of the old songs represented Peter and Paul as bound in jail. "Togedda dey sung, togedda dey prayed; De Lawd he heard how dey sung an' prayed. Den humble yo'selves, de bell done rung." "Paul an' Silas bound in jail, The Christians pray both night and day," represented another song, one version of which has survived and is current today. Most of the song consists of repetitions.

Paul and Silas bound in jail,
Paul and Silas bound in jail,
Paul and Silas bound in jail,
Paul and Silas bound in jail.

Paul did pray one mournful prayer.

Don't you wish you could pray like Paul?

He prayed an' the good Lord set him free.

Another version prays for the angels to come down and unlock the door of the jail. It has a striking parallel among the secular songs and might have been composed with the idea of the Negro in jail as being rescued.

> Come down, angel, with the key,
> Come down, angel, with the key,
> My Lord, angel, come down with the key.
>
> Unlock the door for me-e-e,
> Unlock the door for me-e-e,
> My Lord, unlock the door for me.
>
> Paul and Silas is in jail,
> Paul and Silas is in jail,
> My Lord, Paul and Silas is in jail.
>
> Unlock the jail-house door,
> Unlock the jail-house door-oor,
> My Lord, unlock the jail-house door.

FOHTY DAYS AN' NIGHTS

Among those of the Bible who have been the special subjects of song, Noah has a prominent place. References to him have been made already. He is always the hero of the flood. In most of the songs wherein a special character has an important part, it is in the chorus or refrain. So in "Fohty Days an' Nights," a general mixture of songs and ideas, Noah and the flood make the chorus.

> Dey calls Bro' Noah a foolish man,
>   Fohty days an' nights,
> He built de ark upon de lan',
>   Fohty days an' nights.

An', ho, ho, didn't it rain?
    O yes, you know it did.
Ho, ho, didn't it rain?
    O yes, you know it did.

Ole Satan wears a iron shoe,
    It's fohty days an' nights;
Ef you don't mind gwine slip it on you,
    Fohty days an' nights.

Some go to meetin' to put on pretense,
    Fohty days an' nights;
Until de day ob grace is spent,
    Fohty days an' nights.

Some go to meetin' to sing an' shout,
    Fohty days an' nights;
Fo' six months dey'll be turned out,
    Fohty days an' nights.

I tell you brother an' I tell you twice,
    It's fohty days an' nights;
My soul done anchored in Jesus Christ,
    Fohty days an' nights.

If you git dar befo' I do,
    Fohty days an' nights;
Look out fer me, I'se comin' too,
    Fohty days an' nights.

You baptize Peter an' you baptize Paul,
    It's fohty days an' nights;
But de Lord-God-er-mighty gwine baptize all,
    It's fohty days an' nights.

didn't it rain?

"De Ole Ark A-Moverin" was the title of a plantation song which gave the story of Noah and the flood.

> Jes' wait a little while, I'm gwine tell you 'bout de ole
> ark.
> De Lord told Noah for to build him an ole ark.
> Den Noah and his sons went to work upon dry lan';
> Dey built dat ark jes' accordin' to comman'.
> Noah an' his sons went to work upon de timber;
> De proud begin to laugh, the silly to point de finger.
> When de ark was finished jes' accordin' to plan,
> Massa Noah took his family both animal an' man.
> When de rain begin to fall and de ark begin to rise,
> De wicked hung round wid der groans and der cries.
> Fohty day and fohty nights de rain it kep' a fallin',
> De wicked clumb de trees an' for help dey kep' callin'.
> Dat awful rain she stopped at las', de water dey subsided,
> An' dat ole ark wid all aboard on Ararat she rided.

This is the picture which the plantation and slave Negro has made for his satisfaction. The present-day song that apparently originated in the above song is less elaborate, having only portions of the old song and not being much in demand. It is called "Didn't It Rain?"

> God told Noah 'bout de rainbow sign,
>   Lawd, didn't it rain?
> No more water but fier nex' time,
>   Oh, didn't it rain?   Halleluyer!
>
> Oh, didn't it rain?   Oh, didn't it rain?
> Halleluyer, didn't it rain?
> Some fohty days an' nights.

Well it rain fohty days an' nights widout stoppin',
   Lawd, didn't it rain?
The sinner got mad 'cause the rain kept a droppin',
   Oh, didn't it rain? Halleluyer!

MY TROUBLE IS HARD

Among the most interesting of all the Negro spirituals are those which have been composed in recent
years. These are significant in their bearing upon the
temperament and religion of the present-day Negro.
These songs are efforts at poetry, while at the same
time they unite Biblical story with song. The following song, which gets its name from the chorus, is
entitled "My Trouble Is Hard," and was composed
by "Sister Bowers." It was printed on a single sheet
for distribution; each person who contributed to the
collection was entitled to a copy or a copy could be
had for a nickel. She sung her new song to crowds
wherever she went, and then was given a pro rata of
the collections. With the chorus repeated after each
stanza, as the Negroes always do, it becomes a song
of unusual length:

I know a man that was here before Christ,
His name was Adam and Eve was his wife.
I'll tell you how this man lived a rugged life,
Just by taking this woman's advice.

    My trouble is hard, oh, yes!
    My trouble is hard, oh, yes!
    My trouble is hard, oh, yes!
    Yes, indeed, my trouble is hard.

Whilst you are sitting on your seat,
Let me tell you something that is sweet.
When all God's people in glory meet,
They will slip and slide the golden street.

Stop, young man, I've something to say;
You know you're sinful and why don't you pray?
You're sinning against a sin-venged God,
Who has power to slay us all.

O Lord, ain't it a pity—ain't it a shame—
To see how my Lord and Saviour was slain?
I hate to call the murderer's name,
I know they are dead but left the stain.

Read the Scriptures and be content,
You are bound to know what Jesus meant.
John was here before his advent;
Stood in the wilderness and cried "Repent."

Christ called his apostles two by two,
He particularly told them what to do:
"Preach my gospel as I command you,
And I'll be with you all the way through."

Just let me tell you what David done,
Old man Jesse's youngest son:
He slayed Goliath that mighty one,
Ole Saul pursued him but he had to run.

Ole Saul pursued poor David's life—
It's a mighty good thing he had a wife;
They went to his house and did surround,
And she took a rope and let him down.

God called Jonah in a powerful way;
He told old Jonah just what to say;
"Tell them people if they don't pray,
I'll destroy the city of Nineveh."

Just let me tell you how this world is fixed:
Satan has got it so full of tricks,
You can go from place to place,
Everybody's runnin' down the colored race.

WITNESS FOR MY LORD

Almost equally interesting is "That's Another Witness for My Lord." It will be noticed in these songs that references and phrases taken from the old songs are often used, but in different combinations. They thus lose their former worth. It will be interesting, also, to compare the Negro's religious conceptions of the Bible and God as expressed in these songs with those expressed in the older productions.

Read in Genesis, you understand,
Methuselah was the oldest man,
Lived nine hundred and sixty-nine,
Died and went to heaven in due time.

Methuselah is a witness for my Lord,
Methuselah is a witness for my Lord.

You read about Samson from his birth,
Strongest man that lived on the earth.
'Way back yonder in ancient times,
He slayed three thousand of the Philistines.

Samson he went wanderin' about,
For his strength hadn't been found out.
His wife dropped down upon her knees,
Said: "Samson, tell me where your strength lies, please."

Deli'a' talked so good and fair,
He told her his strength lie in his hair;
"Shave my head just as clean as your hands,
And my strength'll be like a nachual man's."

Wasn't that a witness for my Lord?
Wasn't that a witness for my Lord?

Isaiah mounted on de wheel o' time,
Spoke to God-er-mighty way down the line:
Said, "O Lord, to me reveal,
How can this vile race be healed?"

God said, "Tell the sons of men,
Unto them'll be born a king.
Them that believe upon his Way,
They shall rest in the latter day."

Isaiah was a witness for my Lord,
Isaiah was a witness for my Lord.

There was a man amongst the Pharisees
Named Nicodemus and he didn't believe,
He went to the Master in the night,
And told him to take him out er human sight.

"You are the Christ, I'm sure it's true,
For none do de miracles dat you do.
But how can a man, now old in sin,
Turn back still and be born again?"

Christ said, "Man, if you want to be wise,
You'd better repent and be baptized;
Believe on me, the Son of Man,
Then you will be born'd again."

Wasn't that a witness for my Lord?
Wasn't that a witness for my Lord?

AFTER 'WHILE

"After 'While" gives a slightly different form of verse but with somewhat the same characteristics in other respects as those just given. There is little regularity in the metrical arrangement, but it makes a good song.

The worl' is full of forms and changes,
It's just now so confuse,
You will find some danger
In everything you use.
But this is consolation to every blood-washed child:
God's goin' to change our station, after 'while.

After 'while, after 'while,
God's goin' to change our station, after 'while.

The devil tries to throw down
Everything that's good;
He'd fix a way to confine
The righteous if he could.
Thanks be to God almighty, who cannot be beguiled,
Ole Satan will be done fightin' after 'while.

Some men and women would help the world along,
By constantly complaining of everything that's done.
They want to be called Christians and all their badness
    hide;
God's goin' to open the secret after 'while.

Preachers in their sermons stand up and tell the truth,
They'll go about and murmur with slander and abuse;
They want the whole arrangement to suit their selfish
    style,
God's goin' to rain down fire after 'while.

WHAR SHALL I BE?

In a general mixture of old songs and new songs, of old traits and new traits, the Negro sings a beautiful song which he has called, "Whar' Shall I Be?" The usual imagery is seen.

Moses lived till he got old,
    Whar shall I be?
Buried in de mountain, so I'm told,
    Whar shall I be?

Whar shall I be when de fust trumpet sounds?
Whar shall I be when it sounds so loud?
When it sound so loud that it wake up the dead,
Whar shall I be when it sounds?

Well, God showed Noar de rainbow sign,
    Whar shall I be?
No more water but fire nex' time,
    Whar shall I be?

Matthew, Mark, Luke and John,
    Whar shall I be?
Tole me whar my Saviour gone,
    Whar shall I be?

John declar'd he saw a man,
    Whar shall I be?
Wid seben lamps in his right han',
    Whar shall I be?

GO, AND I GO WID YOU

The exact meaning of the following song could not be ascertained. It is apparently derived from some idea of the Scriptural invocation and blessing upon the disciples. It is said to have a special message to the preacher, and is sometimes represented as being the words of God, at other times the encouragement of a friend and the reply.

Go, and I will go with you;
Open your mouth and I'll speak for you.
If I go and tell them what you say they won't believe me.

Shout, and I shout with you;
Throw out your arms and I catch you.
If they see you going with me, they won't believe on you.

So it's go and I go with you;
Open your mouth and I speak for you.
Shout and I shout with you;
Throw out your arms and I catch you.
If I go and tell them what you say they won't believe me.

DRINKIN' OF THE WINE

Another song of the modern type seems to appeal to the Negroes very strongly. Again he is seeing a vivid picture of the Christ in the long years ago. But just where he gets the exact ideas by which to make the combinations, it is difficult to say. Perhaps he gets the central thought from the miracle of Cana.

If my mother ask you for me, tell her I gone to Gallerlee,
I ought to a been there four thousand years ago,
    To drink of the wine.

Drinkin' of the wine, drinkin' of the wine,
Drinkin' of the wine, drinkin' of the wine.
Christ was there four thousand years ago,
Drinkin' of the wine.

You may mourn, sinner, mourn, the Lord help you to
    mourn;
Christ was there four thousand years ago,
    Drinkin' of the wine.

THE BLIND MAN STOOD BY THE WAY AND CRIED

In "The Blind Man" the picture is also one of confusing the Scriptural scenes with those of the present and of placing himself in the stead of the central character of the story.

Well, the blind man stood by the way and cried,
Well, the blind man stood by the way and cried,
Yes, the blind man stood by the way and cried.

He cried, "O Lord, don't you hear po' me?"
Hark, the blind man stood by the way and cried,
He cried, "O Lord, don't you hear po' me?"

Brother, don't you hear the blind cries, blind cries?
Brother, don't you hear the blind cries, blind cries?
O brother, don't you hear the blind cries?

Jesus he give de blind man sight, blind man sight,
Jesus he give de blind man sight, blind man sight,
Yes, Jesus he give de blind man sight.

WALKIN' IN THE LIGHT

A peculiar modification of "Walking in the Light"
is the song of the same name among the Negroes,
which seems to have its origin in the Scriptural in-
junction, "Ye are the light of the world."

Let yo' light shine all over the world;
Walkin' in the light, beautiful light.

Mos' wonderful light, shine by night;
Let yo' light shine all over the world.

I am the light, most pitiful light;
Let yo' light shine all over the world.

Follow the light, mos' beautiful light;
Let yo' light shine all over the world.

Sinner, what you gwine do when the lamp stops burnin'?
Let yo' light shine all over the world.

THE PILGRIM'S SONG

The "Pilgrim's Song" which has been considered so
beautiful is still a favorite; the words of the stanzas
differ little. It may be called a standard hymn of the

Negroes. There is a story that Bishop Allen, the founder of the A. M. E. Church, composed the song on his dying bed. He was very well educated and a man of considerable ability and feeling. While the sadly hopeful words of the song are of a higher type than the average spiritual, and while its metrical form is far above the usual, the song still combines many of the ideas and phrases of the favorite spirituals of the slaves. "The Pilgrim's Song" as it is found is:

I am a poor wayfaring stranger,
    While journeying through this world of woe;
But there is no sickness, toil, no danger,
    In that bright world to which I go.

I'm going there to see my classmates,
    They said they'd meet me when I come;
I'm just a going over Jordan,
    I'm just going over home.

I know dark clouds 'll gather 'round me,
    I know my road is rough and steep;
Yet there bright fields are lying just before me,
    Where God's redeemed their vigils keep.

I'm going there to see my mother,
    She said she'd meet me when I come;
I'm just going over Jordan,
    I'm just a going over home.

I'll soon be free from every trial,
    My body will sleep in the old churchyard.
I'll quit the cross of self-denial,
    And enter in my great reward.

I'm going there to see my mother,
    She said she'd meet me when I come;
I'm just a going over Jordan,
    I'm just a going over home.

STEAL AWAY

Very much in the same class of song is "Steal Away." The present version is very similar to the old versions. "Steal Away" is found in some of the church song books today. The most common verses now sung are:

> O the green trees a-bowin',
> An' po' sinner stan' tremblin',
> Well, the trumpet soun' in my soul,
> An' I ain't got long to stay here.

> O steal away, steal away,
> O steal away to my Jesus.
> Steal away, steal away,
> For I ain't got long to stay here.

> My Lord is a callin',
> Po' sinner he can't answer.
> Well, the trumpet sound in my soul,
> An' I ain't got long to stay here.

HEAL ME, JESUS

One of the most beautiful and at the same time simple and pathetic songs of the Negroes is "Heal Me, Jesus." Here the Negro is at his best in prayer; without pretension, without reserve, claiming nothing, he simply pleads:

> O Lord, I'm sick an' I want to be healed,
> O Lord, I'm sick an' I want to be healed,
> O Lord, I'm sick an' I want to be healed,
> O Lord, I'm sick an' I want to be healed.

> Heal me, Jesus, heal me, Jesus,
>   Along the heavenly way,
> Heal me, Jesus, heal me, Jesus,
>   Along the heavenly way.

O Lord, I'm blind an' I want to see,
O Lord, I'm blind an' I want to see,
O Lord, I'm blind an' I want to see,
Heal me, Jesus, along the heavenly way.

O Lord, I'm crippled an' I want to walk,
O Lord, I'm crippled an' I want to walk,
O Lord, I'm crippled an' I want to walk,
Heal me, Jesus, along the heavenly way.

O Lord, I'm deaf an' want to hear, etc.

I HEARD THE ANGELS SINGIN'

The Negroes are great believers in dress and uniform. Color, too, appeals to them as significant, and the more strikingly distinct the color the stronger impression it makes upon their imaginations. This idea of color has become interwoven in many of their songs. The rhyme helps to give the picture its vividness. The following song, with its variants, is still sung with considerable zest.

Who is that yonder all dressed in red?
    I heard the angels singin';
It look like the children Moses led,
    I heard the angels singin'.

Down on my knees,
Down on my knees,
I heard the angels singin'.

Well, who that yonder all dressed in black?
    I heard the angels singin';
It looks like it's de mourners jus' got back,
    I heard the angels singin'.

Yes, who's that yonder all dressed in blue?
It look like the children just come through.

Besides "mourners jus' got back," the Negroes sometimes sing "a sister (a sinner, a hypocrite, etc.) jus'
got back." In one of the old songs the above verses
were sung to the chorus,

> O what you say, John?
> O what you say, John?
> O what you say, John?
> De resurrection drawin' nigh,

with this last line as a refrain after each line of the
song, corresponding to "I heard the angels singing."
In another of the old songs the chorus was:

> Go, Mary, an' ring de bell,
> Come, John, and call de roll;
> I thank God.

THE BIG FISH

The Negro visualizes with a good deal of satisfaction. He imagines that he can see the things about
which he sings. So he has told wonderful stories
about the whale and the gourd vine, about the "cutter
worm" as well as Jonah. The old song, modified and
adapted with characteristic phraseology and expression, still appeals to him. The "big fish" or "sherk"
represents the terror of the sea to the Negro. One
old man explained this fact by saying that is was
because the Negroes were terrified as they were brought
over from Africa, that they "saw de whales and fishes
in de sea," and that "de race hain't nebber got over it
yet." Another ascribed the fear and imagination
much to the Biblical story of the whale and Jonah.
Perhaps neither determines to any marked degree
this feeling. However, the song, "Big Fish Swallow

Jonah," which has been so popular in its paraphrases and in the glee clubs, is still current in this form:

> Lord, the big fish, big fish, big fish, swallow ole Jonah whole;
> The big fish, the big fish, the big fish swallow ole Jonah;
> The big fish, big fish, big fish, swallow ole Jonah whole.
>
> Ole Jonah cried, "Lord, save my soul";
> Ole Jonah, ole Jonah, ole Jonah cried, "Save my, save-m-y-y,"
> Ole Jonah cried, "Lord, save my soul."

In the same manner are sung other lines:

> Lord, the gourd vine, gourd vine, gourd vine growed over Jonah.
>
> Well, the cutter worm, cutter worm, cutter worm, cut that vine down.

In addition to Jonah—and the last two stanzas are not common in the old songs—"Peter on the sea," "Gabriel, blow yo' trumpet" and "Daniel in the lion's den" are sung. Those who have heard the latest form of this song would hardly imagine that it was a very appropriate church song.

THE OLE TIME RELIGION

It has been stated that the Negro makes a song his own by the simple act of singing it. If he is unrestrained and at the same time thoroughly wrought up, he adds enough to his song or changes it sufficiently to make it almost unique. In a common old song like "The Old-time Religion," sung by whites and Negroes alike, there are as many versions as the Negro can make combinations.   He refuses to sing these old-time songs as they are written.   He begins with the chorus:

> 'Tis that ole-time religion,
> 'Tis that ole-time religion,
> 'Tis that ole-time religion,
> It's good enough for me.

But he nearly always varies the chorus with: "Gi' me that ole-time religion," or "Was that ole-time religion," and several others.   The verses defy enumeration, but they usually begin:

> It was good enough for mother,
> It was good enough for mother,
> It was good enough for mother,
> An' it's good enough for me.

Even this kind of verse, however, is varied by the use of "my mother," "my ole mother," etc.   Similarly:

> It was good enough for father.

> It was good enough for sister.

> It was good enough for brother.

> It was good for Paul and Silas.

> It was good for John and Peter.

These verses are often sung in the revivals of the Southern whites in the rural districts.   But the Negro is soon off the beaten path proclaiming that the old time religion is "good when you are dying (living, mourning, praying, talking, etc)."   He continues:

> It is good when in trouble.

> It is good when de worl's on fier.

It is good when de lightnin' flashes.

It is good when de thunder rolls.

It is good when de stars are fallin'.

It is good when de moon is meltin'.

It is good when de graveyards a-openin'.

In short, any line from another song which fits the rhythm is given a place in "The Ole-time Religion," and every new singing is likely to suggest additional verses to the Negro.

BY AND BY I'M GOIN' TO SEE THEM

This song is another good example of the Negro's tendency to make any song his own. It is his version of the old "By and By We'll Go and See Them." The chorus is:

> By and by I'm goin' to see them,
> By and by I'm goin' to see them,
> Well, it's by and by I'm going to see them,
> On de udder shore.

It is varied by the substitution of "him" or "her" for "them." The verses are practically unlimited. They consist of a line repeated three or six times, as the singers prefer, with the refrain "On de udder shore" added to the end of each stanza.

> I got a brother over yonder,
> I got a brother over yonder,
> I got a brother over yonder,
> On de udder shore.

Father, mother, sister, preacher, Paul, Silas, Moses, and others are also "on de udder shore." Sometimes a different element is introduced:

> Well, mournin' time will soon be over,
> Well, mournin' time will soon be over,
> Well, it's mournin' time will soon be over,
> On de udder shore.

> Prayin' time will soon be over, etc.

> Shoutin' time will soon be over, etc.

If the occasion calls for warning to the sinner, others are sung:

> Sinnin' time will soon be over, etc.

> Gamblin' time will soon be over, etc.

The old plantation song was: "Wonder wher's dem Hebrew children (doubtin' Thomas, sinkin' Peter, etc.)? By and by we'll go and meet him." This form is apparently not sung today.

Even the newer songs, many of them the best efforts of the white evangelists, go through this process of transformation when they are appropriated by the Negro. The younger generation is trying to substitute new songs and standard church hymns for the old spirituals, with but little success except in the larger and more formalized urban congregations. Occasionally an educated minister or layman writes a song in formal style, has it printed on a single sheet, and distributes it during church services. The following song, given in the exact form in which it was distributed, will serve to illustrate:

BLESSED HOPE

By Rev. W. E. Bailey

Blessed hope that in Jesus is given,
　　All our sorrow to cheer and sustain,
That soon in the mansions of heaven
　　We shall meet with our loved ones again.

Blessed hope, blessed hope,
　　We shall meet with our loved ones again,
Blessed hope, blessed hope,
　　We shall meet with our loved ones again.

Blessed hope in the word God has spoken,
　　All our peace by that word we obtain,
And as sure as God's word was never broken,
　　We shall meet with our loved ones again.

Blessed hope, how it shines in our sorrows,
　　Like the star over Bethlehem's plain,
We will see our Lord ere the morrow,
　　We shall meet with our loved ones again.

Blessed hope, the bright star of the morning,
　　That shall herald his coming to reign,
He will come and reward all the faithful,
　　We shall meet with our loved ones again.

(Sung by Rev. J. T. Johnson)

Such a song is not a spiritual, yet it has some of the characteristics of the spiritual. Many songs of this kind are introduced and sung to various tunes, but they often undergo variation before they have been sung many times. The older Negroes still cling to the spirituals, and they are often heard to remark that the new songs "don't put a feelin' in you like the ole ones." It may be, then, that for some time to come the church singing of the Negroes in the South will be dominated by the characteristics that have made the spirituals so popular. Song is, indeed, the cornerstone of the Negro's religious life. Perhaps that is why he claims with so much feeling that "religion's so sweet":

> I jus' got home f'um Jordan,
> I jus' got home f'um Jordan,
> I jus' got home f'um Jordan,
>   'Ligion's so-o-o sweet.
>
> My work is done an' I mus' go,
> My work is done an' I mus' go,
> My work is done an' I mus' go,
>   'Ligion's so-o-o sweet.

CHAPTER V

THE SOCIAL SONGS OF THE NEGRO

Increasing Popularity of the Social Songs. In the last twenty years there has been a marked increase in the popularity of the Negro's social songs.[1] Whereas during slavery and for a long time thereafter religious themes predominated in the songs of the Negro, there has now grown up a group of secular songs magnificent in its proportions and rich in variation. These songs vary from the filthiest thoughts of the "rounder" to the loftiest sentiments of the lover, and every Negro child in the South falls heir to some part of this apparently unlimited body of song. Perhaps the diminishing importance of the older religious themes means that the Negro has finally outgrown that former disposition to sing himself *away from* a world of sorrow and trouble and is coming more and more to sing himself and his troubles *through* that world.

Not Pure Folk Songs. The songs in this collection are Negro songs in that they have had their origin and growth among the Negroes, or have been adapted so completely that they have become the common property of the Negroes. As Dr. John Meir has said, they are "folk-poetry which, from whatever source and for whatever reason, has passed into the possession of the folk, the common people, so completely that each

[1] In one sense all songs are social, but the term is used herein to denote the ordinary songs of the Negro's everyday life as distinguished from his purely religious songs.

singer or reciter feels the piece to be his own."[1] Each
singer alters the song according to his own thoughts
and feelings. Clearly many of the songs are adapted
forms of well-known ballads; others, which in all prob-
ability had their origin among the Negroes, resemble
very strongly the folk songs of other people; while still
others combine in a striking way original features
with the borrowed. In any case, the song, when it
has become the common distinctive property of the
Negroes, must be classed with Negro folk songs.

Origins of the Social Songs. Fortunately many of the
songs current among the Negroes today are of such a
nature that their general origins may be traced with
considerable accuracy. All of the songs popularly
called "Nigger songs" are by no means genuine Negro
songs. In fact, the great mass of present-day Negro
songs may be divided into three classes, the third
constituting the folk songs: First, the modern "Nigger
songs," popular "hits" and "blues"; second, such
songs greatly modified and adapted partially by the
Negroes; third, songs originating with the Negroes
or adapted so completely as to become common Negro
songs. The second class easily arises from the popular
songs varied through constant singing or through
misunderstanding of the original versions. These
songs appear to be typical of the process of song-
making and indicate the facility of the Negroes in
producing their own songs from material of any sort.
The third class is made up of the approximate folk
songs. While the variations of the songs of the first
and second classes would afford material for an in-

---

[1] Quoted by Professor H. M. Belden, *Journal of American Folklore*, Vol.
XXIV, p. 3.

teresting study, they are in reality not folk songs. Accordingly, only those that have become adapted are given in this collection.

Origins in White Ballads. Naturally, in his song-making the Negro does not adapt only those songs having Negro themes. He appropriates distinctively white songs and ballads and devises new versions which are distinctively Negro. For instance, the Negro song "Kelley's Love," the chorus of which is,

> You broke de heart o' many a girl,
> But you never will break dis heart o' mine,

is clearly an adaption of parts of the mountain song,

> She broke the heart of many poor fellows,
> But she won't break this heart of mine.

The once popular Western ballad, "Casey Jones," which begins,

> Come, all you rounders, if you want to hear
> The story about a brave engineer;
> Casey Jones was the rounder's name,
> On a heavy eight-wheeler he won his fame,

has its counterpart in the Negro song of the same name which begins,

> Casey Jones was an engineer,
> Told his fireman not to fear;
> All he wanted was boiler hot,
> Run into Canton 'bout four o'clock.

Similarly, such Negro songs as "Jesse James," "Eddy Jones," "Joe Turner," "Brady," "Lilly," "Stagolee," and others are largely made up of the Negro's efforts to make certain white ballads into narratives of Negro life. Resemblances may also be shown between the ballads and song-games of white children and the Negro songs entitled "Won't You Marry Me?", "Miss Lizzie, Won't You Marry Me?", and "The Angel Band."

Origins in Everyday Life. The majority of the Negro's social songs, however, are the product of experience—of life itself. Even in those songs which are most unmistakably borrowed, there would be little of the interesting left if the Negro's own interpretation of his everyday life were removed. Here and there rhythmic words or phrases occurring in conversation or in thought are sung. This gives rise to what the Negroes call one-verse songs. By this they mean a single line, repeated again and again, constituting the entire song. Usually the line is repeated with regularity, so that it makes a stanza of two, four, or six lines, sometimes three or five. The last repetition is usually preceded by some word of exclamation, as "oh," "my," "well," "so," "yes," and others.

The majority of Negro songs now current are one-verse songs, and almost all have arisen and developed along the one-verse method. In this way the origin of a song is simple and natural. Any word may lead to a phrase which itself becomes a one-verse song, and naturally calls for a rhyme and additional verses. A Negro is driving a delivery wagon; the weather is cold, and wind and drizzling rain add to the gloominess of the day. He pulls his coat around him and says, "The wind sho do blow." Not having any special song which he wishes to sing at the moment, he sings these words for a while. Perhaps he adds others:

"Goin' where chilly win' don't blow," or "Ain't goin' to rain no mo'." Still other thoughts may suggest lines which he sings in a sort of monotone, such as "I bin workin' so long—hungry as I can be"; "Where in de worl' you bin?" "I'm goin' 'way some day"; "Had a mighty good time las' night"; or as many others as there are common scenes in his life. Presently he makes a two-line rhyme. Next he might recall two other lines or a single chorus line from some other song which seems appropriate, and the combination easily becomes a three- or a four-line song. If the theme is not unusual, verses from other songs suggest themselves. The addition of one or more of these verses gives length and dignity to the new song and pleases the singer, although the words themselves may be practically meaningless.

Little incidents of everyday life thus constitute an inexhaustible source of song. Once a song is sung before a group and is received with favor, the possibility of numberless additions and variations is created.

"A girl wus luvin' a nigger," explained one singer, "an' she thought he did not go to see any other girl; she found out he did, an' she made a hole in the wall of her house so she could watch an' see did her lover go to see any other nigger. Her luvin' man found this out an' it made him laugh; an' he wus sorry, too." The lover makes a song:

> Dony got a hole in de wall,
> Dony got a hole in de wall,
> Dony got a hole in de wall,
> Oh, my Dony got a hole in de wall.

Baby weahs a number fo' shoe,
Baby weahs a number fo' shoe,
Baby weahs a number fo' shoe,
Oh, my baby weahs a number fo' shoe.

Thus is given the origin of a bit of song. How the first verse suggested the other is not known, but they were sung just as they have been given. Many of the songs which the Negro sings are the outcome of his attempts to build songs around incidents or stories of incidents which appeal to his emotions or imagination. Sometimes the story is exciting or fictitious, so that the imagination of the song-maker has a chance to run riot. More often, however, it falls well within the pale of everyday trivialities. In theory at least, then, the Negro song is based on incident; in practice it develops through the common events of Negro life.

Origins in Improvisations. Many songs owe their origins to the Negro's keenness at improvisation. Undoubtedly many Negroes have a consciousness of power or ability to create new songs when they wish to. Sometimes a boast that he knows a new song or that he knows more songs than some one else compels the singer to produce one in order to make good his assertion. From his unlimited store of songs, sayings, stories, and experiences he takes a theme and begins his song. If he does not immediately think of rhyming lines that would be appropriate, he continues to sing the original line until the song takes further shape in his mind. But, regardless of what the theme is, the needed lines are invariably forthcoming and are fitted into the tune. Nor would one suspect that the song was a new one were it not for its unfinished or incoherent lines and its lack of characteristic folk song qualities. The song which follows is a very good example of such a process of creation.

MULE SONG

I went up Zion Hill this mornin' on a wagon,
I went on a wagon up Zion's Hill this mornin';
The durn ole mule stop right still,
This mornin', this mornin', so soon.

I got out an' went 'round to his head this mornin',
I got out an' went 'round to his head this mornin';
The durn ole mule was standin' there dead,
This mornin', this mornin', so soon.

Yes, I hollow at the mule, an' the mule would not gee,
    this mornin',
Yes, I hollow at the mule, an' the mule would not gee;
An' I hit him on the head with the single-tree,
This mornin', this mornin', so soon.

Thus is produced a song from imagination and experience aided by bits of other songs. At first glance, this might appear to be an advanced composition which was the result of protracted mental effort, but it is more or less a spontaneous creation or assembling of song material. The chorus line, "This mornin', this mornin', so soon" (sometimes "This mornin', this evenin', so soon"), is a very common one in Negro social songs, while the last stanza is very likely taken from a child's rhyme long current among the Negroes. The other two stanzas, however, are clearly made to order in the effort to make song and rhyme.

Further examples of rather rough spontaneous compositions containing made-to-order elements are as follows:

WHOA MULE!

"Say, look here, Jane!
Don't you want to take a ride?"
"Well, I doan care if I do."
So he hitch up his mule an' started out.

Well, it's whoa, mule, git up an' down,
Till I say whoa-er, mule.

Well it's git up an' down
Jus' fas' as you can,
Fer I goin' to buy you
All of de oats an' bran.

An' it's whoa-er mule, git up an' down,
Till I say whoa-er, mule.
"Ain't he a mule, Miss Jane?"—"Um—huh."

POOR JOHN

Yes, he caught poor John with his hawk-tail coat,
    An' he stab him to the fat;
He run the race an' he run so fas'
    Till he bust his beaver hat.

Poor John fell down them winding steps,
    Till he could not fall no further;
    An' the girls all holler murder;
Go tell all policemen on this beat to see
    Can't they catch that coon.

What coon am you talkin' about?
    The coon that stab po' John;
I'm goin', I'm goin', to the shuckin' o' de corn,
    I'm goin' jus' sho's you born.

Other Origins. Occasionally a poem is written with the avowed intention of making a song. Given a poem possessing the proper rhythmic qualities, it is almost inevitable that the Negro will put it to music. One thrifty teacher wrote verses on the sinking of the *Maine* to be sung to the tune of "John Brown's Body," while another called "Hog Killin' Time" to be sung to the tune of "The Old Oaken Bucket." A would-be poet closed his description of a day's plowing in the hot month of June with,

> Dem skeeters dey callin' me cousin,
>   Dem gnats dey calls me frien',
> Dem stingin' flies a buzzin',
>   Dis nigger done gone in;

and doubtless his verses have since been sung more often than they have been recited. While such verses do not ordinarily become standard folk songs, they illustrate the ease with which any sort of song may arise and become current.

How much of the Negro's song is borrowed and how much is original cannot, of course, be discovered, but it is certain that the majority of his social songs owe their origin to his ability to create song from the ordinary experiences of his everyday life or to make entirely new adaptions.

The Role of the "Music Physicianer." Worthy of consideration as makers and disseminators of Negro songs are the "music physicianers," "musicianers," and "songsters." These terms may be synonymous, or they may denote persons of different habits. In general, "songster" is used to denote any Negro who regularly sings or makes songs; "musicianer" applies often to the individual who claims to be expert with the banjo or fiddle; while "music physicianer" is used to denote more nearly a person who is accustomed to travel from place to place and who possesses a combination of these qualities; or each or all of the terms may be applied loosely to any person who sings or plays an instrument. A group of small boys or young men, when gathered together and wrought up to a high degree of abandon, appear to be able to sing an unlimited number of common songs. Perhaps the "music physicianer" knows the "mo'est songs." With a prized "box" (fiddle or guitar), perhaps his only property, such a Negro may wander from town to town, from section to section, loafing in general, working only when compelled to do so, gathering new songs and singing the old ones.

Most of the songs current among the Negroes are, of course, sung without musical accompaniment. In general, however, the majority of the songs of the evening are accompanied by the "box" or fiddle when large or small groups are gathered together for gayety; when a lonely Negro sits on his doorstep or by the fireside, playing and singing; when couples stay late at night with their love songs and jollity; when groups gather after church to sing the lighter melodies; when the "musicianers," "music physicianers," and "song-sters" gather to render music for special occasions, such as church and private "socials," dances, and other social gatherings. Most of these gatherings, and especially the dance, require continuous music for a longer period of time than the average song will last. It thus happens that the Negro could sing the majority of his songs to a single tune if the necessity called for it.

The expert "musicianer" often adds zest to the occasion by making his instrument "talk" and "sing." This he does by skillfully running the back of a knife along the strings of the instrument. A piece of bone, polished and smooth, sometimes serves the same purpose, but the knife is more commonly used. Hence the term "knife song," which is by origin instrumental only, but which is now regularly associated with several songs (see Chapter VII). The "musicianer" places his knife by the side of the instrument while he picks the strings and sings. He can easily take it up and use it at the proper time without interrupting the music. The so-called "train song," examples of which are given in a later chapter, derives its name from the musical imitation of the running train. The train is made to whistle by a prolonged and consecutive striking of several strings, while the bell is rung by the striking of a single string. As the listeners imagine themselves observing the train, or riding on it, the fervor of the occasion is increased. They follow the train "when she blows fer the station," as it "pulls out frum the station," passes crossings, goes up hill and down hill, whistles for smaller stations, stops for water and coal, and takes the siding "when she meets the fas' express." If the piece is instrumental only, the man at the guitar announces the various stages of the run. To his remarks are added the exclamations of the onlookers, such as "Lawd, God, she's a-runnin' now!", "Sho God railroadin'!", and others. The Negroes thus create their train. They see it and hear it as distinctly as if it were a reality. Indeed, when the "train song" is executed by an expert "musicianer," one can easily imagine that he hears the clicking of the train wheels as they pass the joints in the rails.

Are the Negro's Songs an Index to His Life? Originating as they do from the daily life and expe-

rience of the common Negro, these songs may be said
to have considerable value as reflectors of Negro life.
They portray the relation of the singer to his environment; they give some insight into character; they
reflect much of home life and morals, social habits and
ideals; they indicate possible social tendencies and
qualities; and they are themselves testimonials of the
creative ability and esthetic sense of the Negro.   Lest
the absence of the higher ideals of home and woman-
hood, of love and virtue, of industry and thrift, give
rise to a pessimistic attitude, it must be constantly
borne in mind that this collection of songs is representative only of what may be called the Negro lower class.

Home and Home Life.   Home for the singer of these
songs is little more than a place to stay.   The ideal
home is simply a place where he has opportunity to do
as he pleases.   "Everywhere I hang my hat is Home,
Sweet Home, to me," seems to be the prevailing attitude reflected in the Negro's songs.   But it is not
surprising that he feels no more attachment for home,
if the following descriptions are true to life;

> Clothes all dirty, ain't got no broom;
> Ole dirty clothes all hangin' in de room.
>
> Honey babe, honey babe, bring me de broom.
> De lices an' de chinches 'bout to take my room.
>
> Make me a pallet on de flo',
> Make it in de kitchen behin' de do!

It is only when the Negro is far from home that his
songs are filled with references to home.   The wanderer
sings in plaintive tones, "I'm po' boy long way from
home," or

> Out in dis wide worl' alone,
> Ain't got a place to call my home.

But he really loathes the idea of being attached to one home or one place permanently.   All he wants is

> Hat on my head, shoes on my feet,
> An' a few ole clothes to wear;
> A place to eat an' a place to sleep—
> What a-more need I care?

Man and Woman.   Conceptions of woman, love, and sex relations may be interpreted from the Negro's songs.   Woman holds first place among the themes sung by the Negro, but there is almost a total lack of any suggestion of higher conceptions of love, married life, and the relations of the sexes.   The excerpts that follow are typical:

> If I git drunk who's goin' ter carry me home?
> Brown-skin woman, she chocolate to de bone.

> I got a little black woman, honey, name is Mary Lou;
> Treats me better, honey, heap better'n you.

> She's long an' tall an' chocolate to de bone;
> She make you married man an' leave yo' home.

> I got a woman an' sweetheart, too;
> Woman don't love me, sweetheart do.

> Long as I make my nine a week,
> 'Round yo' bedside I goin' to creep.

> Diamon' Joe, you better come an' git me.
> Don't you see my man done quit me?

> Where were you las' night when I was sick in bed?
> Down town wid some other gal, wusn't here to hole my
>   head.

Don't you let my honey catch you here;
He kill you dead, sho's you born.

I got husband, sweetheart, too;
Husband don't love, sweetheart do.

The terms woman, love, sweetheart, baby, honey, and others may all be synonymous in their application. When the singer tells of his "woman" it is more often *a* woman than any particular one. In addition to the characterizations given above, woman is often thought of as being of questionable quality, if the following bits of song mean anything:

Woman is a good thing an' bad thing too;
They quit in the wrong an' start out bran' new.

Don't never git one woman on yo' min',
Keep you in trouble all de time,
Don't never let yo' woman have her way;
Keep you in trouble all yo' day.
Don't never have one woman for yo' frien';
When you out, 'nuther man in.

I thought I'd tell you what nigger woman'll do:
She have 'nuther man, an' play sick on you.

All I hope in dis bright worl',
If I love anybody, don't let it be a girl.

The Wanderer. The migratory habits of the Negro are so well known that they need no explanation. The Negro wanderer has a technique all his own. He has been to Memphis, Atlanta, Birmingham, New Orleans, and "all de big places." He has seldom worked a stroke since he left home, yet he has always had plenty to eat and a place to stay and has sometimes actually had money to spend. Thus he would have one believe, and much of his narrative is true. His songs are the most pathetic and plaintive of all, for he depends upon them to arouse pity and to gain the favors which he desires. He makes much of his hard times, his loneliness, his lack of friends and sympathy; yet he would not change these conditions if he could. He makes conditions of his own liking, and these things constitute his "good time." Sings the Negro wanderer in pitiful tones:

> I wish some scusion train would run,
> Carry me back where I come frum.

> Now my mommer's daid, an' my sweet ole popper, too;
> Got no one fer to carry my troubles to.

> An' if I wus to die so far away frum home,
> The folks fer miles aroun' would mourn.

> I'm goin' tell my mommer when I git home,
> How people treated me far 'way frum home.

> O don't turn good man frum yo' do',
> May be frien', babe, you don't know.

> No need, O babe, to throw me down,
> Po' boy jus' come to town.

> I didn't bring nuthin' in dis bright worl';
> Nuthin' I'll carry away.

> Went down to de railroad, couldn' find a frien'.

> Oh, look down dat lonesome road and cry.

The Hobo and Work. For the most part, the singer loves idleness and shuns work. In the songs of this collection the hobo or vagrant is represented more than is the industrious Negro. The assumption that the life of the hobo is an enviable one appears frequently. The hobo's philosophy in regard to work is: Don't do it except as a last resort. He boasts of his ability to live from the work of the community or some hard-working woman and of his skill at begging "handouts."

> I got it writ on de tail o' my shirt:
> I'm a natu'el-bohn eastman, don't have to work.
>
> If I could get them good hand-outs,
> I'd quit work an' bum all de time.
>
> All I want is my strong hand-out;
> It will make me strong and stout.
>
> Ain't no use me workin' so,
> 'Cause I ain't a-goin' to work no mo'.
>
> When you kill a chicken, save me the whing;
> When you think I'm workin', I ain't doin' a thing.
>
> When you kill a chicken, save me the feet;
> When you think I'm workin', I'm walkin' de street.

On the other hand, the songs indicate that the Negro considers money his *summum bonum*. He is constantly talking of money. Small change is his boon companion, and larger amounts represent the ideal of utopian conditions. He speaks of "a bran' new dollar bill," a "luvin' dime," a "fohty-dollar suit of clothes." He sings dolefully of the three hundred dollars he had when he left Kansas City—"all gone now." He spends his wages a dozen times in his mind before pay-day comes, and he maintains:

Now when you git a dollar, you got a frien',
Will stick to you through thick an' thin.

The Negro Bad Man. The idle Negro develops from the vagrant, bum, or hobo, to the "bully boy" or "bad man." He sings of crimes, of whiskey and beer, of morphine and cocaine, of pistols and murders. He extols the criminal and follows him with admiration. He revels in the exploits of Stagolee, who ran his enemy down and "laid him on de flo'" with his forty-four gun; or of Railroad Bill, who was so bad that he shot all the buttons off the high sheriff's coat; or of Eddy Jones, who died on the "coolin' board" with his "special" in his hand singing "Nearer, My God, to Thee." Thus sings the Negro bad man:

I got de blues, but too damn mean to cry.

I was bohn in a mighty bad lan',
For my name is Bad-lan' Stone;
I want you all fer to understan'
I'm a bad man wid my licker on.

Wake up in de mornin' by city clock bell,
Niggers up town givin' cocaine hell.

I tell you once and I tell you twice,
Next time I tell you, goin' take yo' life.

Went up town wid my hat in my han';
"Good mornin', jedge, done kill my man.
Didn't quite kill him, but I fixed him so
He won't bodder wid me no mo'."

Arrests, court scenes, convictions, jail sentences—all these are taken for granted by the bad man. Policemen, jailers, and judges are no friends of his; they are hard-hearted men. He has doubtless been to court a dozen times, but he always insists that the officer

> Carried me 'round to the court house do',
> Place where I ain't never been befo';

and his impression of the court room is always

> Jedge an' jury all in de stan',
> Great big law books in deir han'.

Just how much importance the bad man assumes in real life it is difficult to say, but the high place which he occupies in the songs of the Negro seems to justify the assumption that he enjoys a prestige out of proportion to his worth as a personality. Recklessness and braggadocio characterize the songs of the Negro bad man, and their careful study would doubtless throw light upon a factor which is of no little importance in the causation of Negro criminality.

Sadness in Social Songs. While there is much recklessness and care-free gayety in the Negro's social songs, there is, nevertheless, a definite vein of sadness running through the majority of them. There are some, of course, who contend that the Negro's sadness is not real, does not reflect an equivalent feeling. But such a thesis is without foundation. In relation to his own life experiences, the pathos expressed in the Negro's songs is sincere and genuine. The reasons for this sadness, however, are not apparent. Do the effects of slavery still linger in the songs of today? Is it that the Negro feels himself oppressed and downtrodden by the whites? Or does the sadness in his songs arise naturally, apart from racial considerations, from the life he lives? Perhaps none of these factors offers an adequate explanation. But, bound down as he is by the eternal force of circumstances, condemned to live a life which is destined to bring him a very small share of the enjoyments and decencies that characterize the civilization of which he has become a part, it is no wonder that he either forgets himself in gayety or purges his feelings with his sad and plaintive outbursts.

Filth and Vulgarity. Enough has been said to indicate in a general way the philosophy and attitudes of the class of Negroes represented by the songs in this collection. Further study of the songs may be made in succeeding chapters. It is to be regretted that a great mass of material cannot be published because of its vulgar and indecent content. These songs tell of every phase of immorality and vice and filth; they represent the superlative of the repulsive. Ordinarily the imagination can picture conditions worse than they are, but in the Negro songs the pictures go far beyond the conception of the real. The prevailing theme is that of sexual relations, and there is no restraint in expression. In comparison with the indecency that has come to light in the vulgar songs of other peoples, those of the Negro stand out undoubtedly in a class of their own. They are sung in groups of boys and girls, men and women. Children of ten or twelve know scores of them, varying in all degrees of suggestiveness. Often these songs are the favorites; and many of the songs in this volume have been shortened by the omission of stanzas unfit for publication.

Classification Difficult. Classification of songs and fragments of songs like those in this collection is very difficult. Classification by localities from which they were collected would hardly be satisfactory. Division according to subject-matter is, of course, more logical, but even this is not wholly satisfactory. Many songs have no unifying thread of thought, so that any one of three or four titles would only partially describe any particular song. Certain songs might be classed as dance songs, but practically every Negro song is, or could be, used as a dance accompaniment. There are very few pure dance songs. Again, some might be classed as love songs, but such a group would contain productions that would fall as easily into other classes such as work songs, wanderer's songs, bad man songs, and many others. It is common for the Negro to mingle every kind of song into one, so that what he naively calls "coon songs," "devil songs," "knife songs," "corn songs," "work songs," and "ragtimes" may all alike become love songs or dancing "breakdowns." It has been thought best, therefore, to present the songs in general groups. In the following chapter will be found the shorter songs, while the next chapter contains the longer ones, expecially those which are narrative in style. At the same time the songs have been grouped roughly according to subject-matter.

CHAPTER VI

EXAMPLES OF SOCIAL SONGS

In this chapter will be presented the songs which might be classed in a general way as songs of the Negro wanderer and songs dealing with woman. An effort is made to avoid repetition as much as possible, and at the same time to report the songs in such a way as to do justice to the characteristic qualities of the song. Hence stanzas that have been given in one song will not always be given in full in others in which they are found. The dialect is that of the average singing; for the Negro, in his social and secular songs, even more than in his religious songs, uses no consistent speech. The language is neither that of the whites nor that of the blacks, but a freely mingled and varied usage of dialect and common speech. Colloquialisms are frequent. The omission of pronouns and connectives marks many Negro verses, while the insertion of interjections and senseless phrases goes to the other extreme. Such peculiarities may be best noted when the songs are studied. It should be remembered that the song not only begins and ends with the regular chorus, but each stanza is followed by the same chorus, thus doubling the length of the song.

Perhaps no person is sung more among the Negroes than the homeless and friendless wanderer, with his disappointments in love and adventure. In no phases of Negro life do self-feeling and self-pity manifest themselves more than in the plaintive appeals of the wanderer. With his characteristic manner, he appeals to both whites and blacks for sympathy and assistance. He especially appeals to his women friends, and thus moves them to pity him. His pleas for their sympathy are usually effective; and the Negro thus gets shelter, food and attention. The wandering "songster" takes great pride in singing with skill his favorite songs; then he can boast of his achievements as "a bad man" with his "box." As he wanders from community to community he finds lodging and solace. The Negroes at each place take up the songs and sing them to their companions, this constituting the most effective method of courtship. In these songs the roving, rambling thoughts of the Negro are well brought out by the quick shifting of scenes; so his rambling and unsteady habits are depicted with unerring though unconscious skill.

po' boy long way from home

In the following song, which is sometimes sung with the knife instrumental described in Chapter V, each stanza consists of a single line repeated several times.

I'm po' boy long way from home,
Oh, I'm po' boy long way from home.

I wish a 'scushion train would run,
Carry me back where I cum frum.

My mother daid an' my father gone astray,
You never miss you mother till she done gone away.

No need, O babe, try to throw me down,
A po' little boy jus' come to town.

I wish that ole engeneer wus dead,
Brought me 'way from my home.

Central, gi' me long-distance phone,
Talk to my babe all night long.

If I die in State of Alabam',
Send my papa great long telegram.

Come here, babe, an' sit on yo' papa's knee.

You brought me here an' let 'em throw me down.

I ain't got a frien' in dis town.

I'm out in de wide worl' alone.

If you mistreat me, you sho will see it again.

Come 'way to Georgia, babe, to git in a home.

Sometimes the following "one-verse" songs are added:

Shake hands an' tell yo' babe good-bye.

Bad luck in de family, sho God, fell on me.

Have you got lucky, babe, an' then got broke?

I'm goin' 'way, comin' back some day.

Good ole boy, jus' ain't treated right.

I'm Tennessee raise, Georgia bohn.

I'm Georgia bohn, Alabama raise.

ON A HOG

Very much like the above song is "On a Hog,"
which means the condition of a "broke hobo" or tramp.
By "broke" he means the usual state of being without
money, or place to sleep, or food to eat. The song

like the above one, consists of lines repeated, without a chorus. There is little sense or connection in the words and verses. It represents the characteristic blending of all kinds of words to make some sort of song. At the same time its verses are classics in Negro song.

> Come 'way to Georgia to git on a hog,
> Come 'way to Georgia to git on a hog,
> Come 'way to Georgia to git on a hog.
> Lord, come 'way to Georgia to git on a hog.

> If you will go, babe, please don't go now,
> But heave-a-hora, heave-a-hora, babe, heave!

> I didn't come here to be nobody's dog.

> I jest come here to stay a little while.

> Well, I ain't goin' in Georgia long.

And with characteristic rhyme-making, a Negro, after he had finished the few verses that he knew, began adding others. Said he,

> I didn't come here to be nobody's dog,
> Jes come here to git off'n dat hog.

FRISCO RAG-TIME

Even more disjointed and senseless is the song known among the Negroes as "Frisco Rag-time," "K. C.," or any other railroad name that happens to be desired. The song may be sung by a man or a woman or by both. It is expected that the viewpoint of man be indicated in the use of woman as the object and woman's viewpoint be indicated in the reference to man. Such is sometimes the case; but usually the Negro sings the song through, shifting from time to time from man to woman without so much as noticing the incongruity of meaning. In the verses which follow, the scenes are portrayed with clear vision by the Negro singer.

> Got up in the mornin', couldn't keep from cryin'.
> Got up in the mornin', couldn't keep from cryin'.
> Got up in the mornin', couldn't keep from cryin;
> Thinkin' 'bout that brown-skin man o' mine.
>
> Yonder comes that lovin' man o' mine,
> Comin' to pay his baby's fine.
>
> Well, I begged the jedge to low' my baby's fine,
> Said de jedge done fine her, clerk done wrote it down.
>
> Couldn't pay dat fine, so taken her to de jail.
>
> So she laid in jail, back to de wall,
> Dis brown-skin man cause of it all.
>
> No need, babe, tryin' to throw me down,
> Cause I'm po' boy jus' come to town.
>
> But if you don't want me, please don't dog me 'round,
> Give me this money, sho will leave this town.
>
> Ain't no use tryin' to send me 'roun',
> I got plenty money to pay my fine.

It will be observed that the last-named verses are practically the same as those given in other songs and have no connection with the theme with which the song was begun; yet they formed an integral part of the song. In the same way single lines repeated four times are sung at length, although one would need to search diligently for the connection of meaning.

> If you don't find me here, come to Larkey's dance.

If you don't find me there, come to ole Birmingham.

Ain't goin' to be in jungles long.

Yonder comes that easy-goin' man o' mine.

Ain't Jedge Briles a hard ole man?

"Jedge Briles" is only a local name which was applied to Judge Broyles of Atlanta. His reputation is widely known among the Negroes of Georgia. Instead of this name are often inserted the names of local characters, which serves to add concreteness to the song. Instead of Birmingham, the Negro may sing Atlanta, Chattanooga, or any other city that ranks as a favorite.

LOOKED DOWN DE ROAD

The following song might well be a continuation of those just given. It is sung, however, to a different tune, and should be ranked as a separate song. Its form is not unlike that already cited—repetition of a single line twice, or, in rare instances, a rhymed couplet.

Looked down de road jes' far as I could see,
Well, the band did play "Nearer, My God, to Thee."

I got the blues, but too damn mean to cry.
I got the blues, but too damn mean to cry.

Now when you git a dollar, you got a frien'
Will stick to you through thick an' thin.

I didn't come here fer to steal nobody's find,
I didn't jes come here to serve my time.

I ask jailer, "Captain, how can I sleep?
All 'round my bedside polices creep."

The jailer said, "Let me tell you what's best:
Go 'way back in yo' dark cell an' take yo' rest."

If my kind man quit me, my main man throw me down,
I goin' run to de river, jump overboard 'n' drown.

The local policeman is always spoken of as creeping around the bedside. It makes an interesting comparison to note the contrast between the police and the angels of the old wish-rhyme. Various versions of the above stanzas are given, some of which are far from elegant. Profanity is inserted in the songs in proportion as the singer is accustomed to use it, or as the occasion demands or permits its use.

IF I DIE IN ARKANSAS

Ridiculous and amusing in its pathos, "If I Die in Arkansas" is typical and representative. It is quite impressive when sung with feeling. The Negro gets a kind of satisfaction in believing that he is utterly forlorn, yet begs to be delivered from such a condition.

If I die in Arkansaw,
Oh, if I die in Arkansaw,
If I die in Arkansaw,
Des ship my body to my mother-in-law.

If my mother refuse me, ship it to my pa,
If my mother refuse me, ship it to my pa.

If my papa refuse me, ship it to my girl,
If my papa refuse me, ship it to my girl.

If my girl refuse me, shove me into de sea,
Where de fishes an' de whales make a fuss over me.

And then after this remarkable rhyme and sentiment,

the singer merges into plaintive appeal, and sings
further:

> Poor ole boy, long ways from home,
> Out in dis wide worl' alone.

Somewhat similar in spirit is a song given by Talley[1]
under the title "When My Wife Dies," one stanza of
which is as follows:

> Railly, w'en I'se been dead, you needn' bury me at tall.
> You mought pickle my bones down in alkihall;
> Den fold my han's "so", right across my breas';
> An' go an' tell de folks I'se done gone to res'.

GOT NO WHERE TO LAY MY WEARY HEAD

This song, also called "Po' Boy 'Way From Home,"
repeats much the same sentiment. Besides many
verses of other songs, the singer adds:

> I want to see do my baby know right from wrong,
> I want to see do my baby know right from wrong,
> I want to see do my baby know right from wrong,
>   O babe!

> Well, I got no where to lay my weary head,
>   O babe!

> Well, a rock was my pillar las' night
>   O girl!

Thus repetition makes a long story of a short one.

BABY, YOU SHO LOOKIN' WARM

In the next song, "Baby, You Sho Lookin' Warm,"
three lines in a stanza are alike, while the fourth

---

[1] Thomas W. Talley, *Negro Folk Rhymes*, Macmillan, 1922. For further
description see Bibliographical Notes.

varies only by an exclamation.   This, too, is an appeal
to the "baby" or sweetheart for pity and admission
into the house.

> Baby, you sho lookin' warm,
> Baby, you sho lookin' warm,
> Baby, you sho lookin' warm.
> O my babe, you sho' lookin' warm.
>
> Baby, I'm feelin' so tired,
> O my babe, I'm feelin' so tired.
>
> Got nowhar to lay my weary head,
> O my babe, got nowhar to lay my weary head.
>
> Sometimes I'm fallin' to my face,
> O my babe, sometimes I'm fallin' to my face.
>
> I'm goin' whar de water drinks like wine.
>
> Gwine whar' I never been befo'.
>
> Baby, I love the clothes you wear.
>
> Whar in de worl' my baby gone?
>
> Gone away, never come back no more.

TAKE YO' TIME

"Take Your Time" represents the Negro in a more
tranquil and independent state of mind.   It portrays
varied circumstances from the home to the court.   It
is a popular favorite.

> Baby, baby, didn't you say
> You'd work for me both night and day?
> Take yo' time, take yo' time.

Baby, baby, don't you know
I can git a girl anywhere I go?
Take yo' time, take yo' time.

Baby, baby, can't you see,
How my girl git away from me?
Take yo' time, take yo' time.

Went down country to see my frien',
In come yaller dog burnin' the win'.
Take yo' time, take yo' time.

'Tain't but the one thing grieve my mind:
Goin' 'way, babe, an' leave you behin'.
Take yo' time, take yo' time.

Carried me 'roun' to de courthouse do',
Place wher' I never had been befo',
Take yo' time, take yo' time.

Jedge an' jury all in de stan',
Great big law-books in deir han'.
Take yo' time, take yo' time.

Went up town 'bout four o'clock,
Rapt on door, an' door was locked.
Take yo' time, take yo' time.

'TAIN'T NOBODY'S BIZNESS BUT MY OWN

Jingling rhymes are sought at the sacrifice of meaning and the sense of song. If the sentiment of the subject of the song appeals to the singer, he may take it and make his own rhymes, departing from the original version. The frequent omission of words and the mixing of dialect and modern slang usually result. "Tain't Nobody's Bizness but My Own" represents the more reckless temperament of the wanderer.

Baby, you ought-a tole me,
Six months before you roll me;
I'd had some other place to go.
'Tain't nobody's bizness but my own.

Sometimes my baby gets boozy,
An' foolish 'bout her head,
An' I can't rule her,
'Tain't nobody's bizness but my own.

I want to see my Hanner,
Turn tricks in my manner,
'Tain't nobody's bizness but my own.

Don't care if I don't make a dollar,
Jes so I wear my shirt an' collar.
'Tain't nobody's bizness but my own.

I'm going 'way

The swaggering tramp decides to leave the town, as indeed he is often doing; but he expects to come back again. He looks forward to the adventures of the trip with pleasure, not with fear, although he knows he must ride the rods, go without food, and sleep where he may. He sings:

I'm goin' 'way, comin' back some day,
I'm goin' 'way, comin' back some day.
I'm just from the country, come to town—
A zoo-loo-shaker from my head on down.
If I git drunk who's goin' ter carry me home?
Brown-skin woman, she's chocolate to de bone.

O babe!

The following song really has little meaning, but it is probably the "rounder's" attempt to boast of his adventurous life.

Late every evenin' 'bout half pas' three,
I hire smart coon to read the news to me.
O babe! O my babe! O my babe!

O babe! O babe! O my babe! take a one on me,
An' my partnah', too, that's the way sports do.
O babe! O my babe! O my babe!

Well, you talk 'bout one thing, you talk 'bout another.
But if you talk 'bout me, gwine talk 'bout yo' mother.
O babe! O my babe! O my babe!

SWEET TENNESSEE

To be sure, the wanderer will not work. He will have his own way, where the "water drinks like wine," and where the "wimmins" are "stuck" on him. He bids farewell, in an appeal of great force.

Come an' go to sweet Tennessee,
Where de money grows on trees,
Where de rounders do as they please, babe!
Come an' go to sweet Tennessee.

Come an' go to sweet Tennessee,
Where the wimmins all live at ease,
Where the rounders do as they please, babe!
Come an' go to sweet Tennessee.

Come an' go to sweet Tennessee,
Where the wimmins do as they please,
Where the money grows on trees, babe!
Come an' go to sweet Tennessee.

I AIN'T BOTHER YET

As woman occupies a prominent place in the songs of the wanderer, so woman and sweetheart occupy the most prominent part in the general social songs. The

Negro's conception of woman as seen in his songs has been observed. Few exalted opinions of woman, little permanent love for sweetheart, or strong and pure love emotions will be found in the songs. Sensual love, physical characteristics, and jealousy are predominant. The singer is not different from the wanderer who figures as the hero in the class of songs just given. Woman here is not unlike woman there. The Negro sings:

> I got a woman an' sweetheart too,
> If woman don't love me, sweetheart do.
> Yet, I ain't bother yet, I ain't bother yet.

> Honey babe, I can't see
> How my money got away from me.
> Yet, I ain't bother yet, ain't bother yet.

Or the woman sings in retort to the husband who does not support her properly, or has failed to please her in some manner:

> I got a husband, a sweetheart, too,
> Husband don't love me, but sweetheart do.

I'M ON MY LAST GO-ROUND

The Negro lover sometimes gets more or less despondent. The theme of rejected love is strong, but the sorrow short. While this feeling lasts, however, the lover, in his jealousy, shows desperation. Sometimes he is determined.

> It's no use you sendin' no word,
> It's no use you sendin' or writin' no letter,
> I'm comin' home pay-day.

I'm on my last go-round,
I'm on my last go-round,
I'm on my last go-round.
God knows Albirdie won't write to me.

There's mo' pretty girls 'an one,
Swing, an' clang an' don't git lost,
There's mo' pretty girls 'an one.

LEARN ME TO LET ALL WOMEN ALONE

The Negro is constantly singing of woman and trouble. In a large per cent of his quarrels and fights the cause of the trouble is the "woman in the case." It is she who gets his money and makes him do all manner of trifling things to please her fancy. He claims that she turns from him as soon as she gets all he has. It is not surprising to hear the song "Learn Me to Let All Women Alone" as the expression of a disgruntled laborer.

One was a boy, an' one was a girl.
If I ever specs to see 'em again,
I'll see 'em in de other worl':
Learn me to let all women alone.

All I hope in this bright worl',
If I love anybody, don't let it be a girl:
Learn me to let all women alone.

Firs' girl I love, she gi' me her right han'.
She's quit me in de wrong fer anudder man:
Learn me to let all women alone.

Woman is a good thing, an' a bad thing too,
They quit in the wrong an' start out bran-new:
Learn me to let all women alone.

I got up early nex' mornin', to meet 'fo' day train,
Goin' up the railroad to find me a man:
Learn me to let all women alone.

In Talley's collection occurs a song in which a
"roustabout" narrates in some detail the story of how
he rid himself of a wife who abused him. The sentiment of the closing stanza is similar to "Learn Me
to Let All Women Alone":

WHEN I WAS A "ROUSTABOUT"
(Talley, p. 145)

On a Sund'y mornin', as I laid on my bed,
I didn' have no nigger wife to bother my head.
Now whiskey an' brandy jug's my bigges' bes' friend,
An' my long week's wuk is about at its end.

O MY BABE, WON'T YOU COME HOME?

The Negro sings, "I don't know what I'll do! Oh,
I don't know what I'll do!" "Oh, I'll take time to
bundle up my clothes! Oh, I'll take time to bundle
up my clothes! Oh, I'll take time to bundle up my
clothes," and he is off; but he is soon involved again,
and sings his promiscuous allegiance.

I love my babe and wouldn't put her out of doors,
I'd love to see her kill a kid wid fohty-dollar suit o'
clothes,
O my babe, won't you come home?

Some people give you nickel, some give you dime;
I ain't goin' give you frazzlin' thing, you ain't no girl
o' mine.
O my babe, won't you come home?

Remember, babe, remember givin' me yo' han';
When you come to marry, I may be yo' man.
O my babe, won't yo' come home?

Went to sea, sea look so wide,
Thought about my babe, hung my head an' cried.
O my babe, won't you come home?

MAKE ME A PALAT ON DE FLO'

Perhaps the lover is again turned out of doors, and pines around the house. "That's all right, treat me mean, treat me wrong, babe. Fare you well forever mo', how would you like to have a luvin' girl turn you out o' doors?" he sings, and pretends to leave. But true to the Negro proverb, "Nigger ain't gone ever' time he say good-bye," he returns again to sing:

Make me a palat on de flo',
Make it in de kitchen behin' de do'.
Oh, don't turn good man from yo' do',
May be a frien', babe, you don't know.

Oh, look down dat lonesome lane,
Make me a palat on de flo!
Oh, de reason I love Sarah Jane,
Made me a palat on de flo'."

CAN'T BE YO' TURTLE ANY MO'

Somewhat similar is the song "Can't Be Yo' Turtle Any Mo'," localized to apply to Atlanta, Memphis, or other specific places.

Goin' to Atlanta, goin' to ride de rod,
Goin' to leave my babe in de hands o' God.
Sorry, sorry, can't be your turtle any mo'.

Goin' up town, goin' hurry right back,
Honey got sumpin' I certainly lak.
Sorry, sorry, can't be yo' warbler any mo'!

NO MORE GOOD TIMES

The Negro adds much zest and fun to his song when
he introduces local characters. In the next song it is
sometimes "Police Johnson, woman, knockin' at de
do'," or in other localities it is the name of the most
dreaded officer. He sings these and laughs heartily,
boasting now and then of fortunate excapes. "No
More Good Times" portrays a common scene.

No more good times, woman, like we used to have,
Police knockin', woman, at my back do'!

Meet me at the depot, bring my dirty clothes,
Meet me at the depot, woman, when the train comes
down.

For I goin' 'way to leave you, ain't comin' back no mo';
You treated me so dirty, ain't comin' back no mo'.

I got a little black woman, honey, an' her name's Mary
Lou,
She treat me better, baby, heap better than you.

DIAMON' JOE

Very much like the above in general tone, but sung
by a woman, "Diamon' Joe" typifies a custom all too
common in the Negro community. It is a love song.

Diamon' Joe, you better come an' git me:
Don't you see my man done quit?
Diamon' Joe, com'n' git me.

Diamon' Joe he had a wife, they parted every night.
When the weather it got cool,
Ole Joe he come back to that black gal.

But time come to pass,
When old Joe quit his last;
An' he never went to see her any mo'.

BABY, WHAT HAVE I DONE?

"Baby, What Have I Done?" introduces other scenes of Negro love life. The same wail of "knockin' at de do' " is heard again and again—a hint at infidelity, which is so often sung in the next few songs.

Late las' night an' night befo',
Heard such a knockin' at my do',
Jumped up in stockin' feet, skipped across the flo':
Baby, don't never knock at my do' no mo'.

O me, O my! baby, what have I done?
O me, O my! baby, what have I done?
O me, O my! baby, what have I done?
O me, O my! baby, what have I done?

Where were you las' Saturday night,
When I lay sick in my bed?
You down town wid some other ole girl,
Wasn't here to hold my head.

Ain't it hard to love an' not be loved?

Other verses of one long line are divided into two short lines or repeated each four times to make the stanza.

It's ninety-six miles from Birmingham,
I tramped it day by day.

It's fifteen cents' wuth o' morphine,
A dollar's all I crave.

I didn't bring nuthin' in this bright worl',
Nuthin' I'll carry away.

I laid my head in bar-room do',
Ain't goin' to get drunk no mo'.

Han' me down my grip-sack
An' all my ole dirty clothes.

If my baby ask for me,
Tell her I boun' to go.

THINGS AIN'T SAME, BABE, SINCE I WENT 'WAY

Both men and women appear changeable in their affections. A husband and wife quarrel the first of the week, separate, vow never to speak again; but the latter part of the week may find them back again. This does not happen once, but many times. A Negro man will often give his entire week's or month's wages in order to pacify his wife who has threatened to go live with some other man. She spends the money and begins to quarrel again. In the same way the wife may often beg to be received back after she has left him. She is often received, sometimes with a beating, sometimes not at all. A typical appeal of these characters is sung:

Things ain't same, babe, since I went 'way;
Now I return, please let me stay.
I'm sorry I lef' you in this worl' alone;
I'm on my way, babe, I'm comin' home.

BABY, LET ME BRING MY CLOTHES BACK HOME

Another appeal is a little more forceful. It is the present moment that counts. So the Negro often makes promises of fidelity, if only he will be given another chance.

> The burly coon, you know,
> He packed his clothes to go,
> Well, he come back las' night,
> His wife said, "Honey, I'm tired o' coon,
> I goin' to pass for white."

> But the coon got mad—
> He's 'bliged to play bad,
> Because his color was black.
> "O my lovin' baby! don't you make me go;
> I git a job, if you let me, sho.

> "I'll wuk both night an' day,
> An' let you draw my pay.
> Baby, let me bring my clothes back home.
> When you kill chicken, save me the bone;
> When you bag beer, give me the foam.

> "I'll work both night an' day,
> An' let you draw the pay.
> Baby, let me bring my clothes back home."
> When she make them strange remarks,
> He look surprise—goin' roll them white eyes;
> "Goin' cry, baby, don't make me go!"

LONG AN' TALL AN' CHOCOLATE TO THE BONE

The Negro often makes trouble for the meddler in his home. Here arise many of his capital crimes. Jealousy runs riot among both men and women. In the following song a hint is given of the boasting spirit of the Negro.

Well, I'm goin' to buy me a little railroad of my own;
Ain't goin' to let nobody ride but the chocolate to the
    bone.

Well, I goin' to buy me a hotel of my own;
Ain't goin' to let nobody eat but the chocolate to the
    bone.

She's long an' tall an' chocolate to the bone.

Well, I goin' to start a little graveyard of my own,
If you don't, ole nigger, let my woman alone.

She's long an' tall an' chocolate to the bone.
She make you married man, then leave yo' home.

Well, if that's yo' man, you'd better buy a lock an' key,
    O babe!
An' stop yo' man from runnin' after me-e-e.

Well, I goin' back to sweet Memphis, Tennessee, O babe!
Where de good-lookin' wimmins take on over me.

Now, a good-lookin' man can git a home anywhare he go,
The reason why is, the wimmins tell me so.

She change a dollar an' give me a lovin' dime,
I'll see her when her trouble like mine.

STARTED TO LEAVE

The sense of humor is very marked in many of the
verses sung by the Negroes. The commonplace,
matter-of-fact statement in the following illustrates.
Says the Negro,

I'm goin' 'way,
Goin' sleep under the trees till weather gits warmer.
Well, me an' my baby can't agree,
Oh, that's the reason I'm goin' to leave.

But, as in other cases, the Negro does not stay long. Perhaps it is too cold under the trees for him; perhaps the song has it all wrong, anyway.

> Well, I started to leave, an' got 'way down the track;
> Got to thinkin' 'bout my woman, come runnin' back,
>   O babe!

> She have got a bad man, an' he's as bad as hell, I know,
> For ev'body, sho God, tell me so.

> I thought I'd tell you what yo' nigger woman'll do:
> She have another man an' play sick on you.

I COULDN'T GIT IN

The spirit of infidelity, already touched upon in the songs given, may be shown further in "I Couldn't Git In."

> Lawd, I went to my woman's do',
> Jus' lak I bin goin' befo';
> " I got my all-night trick, baby,
> An' you can't git in.

> "Come back 'bout half pas' fo',
> If I'm done, I'll open de do'.
> Got my all-night trick, baby,
> An' you can't git in."

> I keep rappin' on my woman's do',
> Lak I never had been dere befo';
> She got a midnight creeper dere,
> An' I couldn't git in.

> Buddy, you oughter to do lak me:
> Git a good woman, let the cheap ones be,
> Fur dey always got a midnight creeper,
> An' you can't come in.

Buddy, stop an' let me tell you
What yo' woman'll do:
She have 'nuther man in, play sick on you.
She got all-night creeper, buddy,
An' you can't git in.

You go home; well, she layin' in bed,
With red rag tied all 'round her head.
She done had 'fo'-day creeper in here,
Dat's de reason you couldn't git in.

WHAT'S STIRRIN', BABE?

The singer uses the common slang "fallin' den" for his bed. As he has sung of his love and jealousies, so he sings of varied affection and infidelity, but with abandon.

Went up town 'bout four o'clock;
  What's stirrin', babe; stirrin', babe?
When I got dere, door was locked;
  What's stirrin', babe, what's stirrin', babe?

Went to de window an' den peeped in:
  What's stirrin', babe; stirrin', babe?
Somebody in my fallin' den—
  What's stirrin', babe; stirrin', babe?"

The woman tells the "creeper" that he had best be watchful while he is about her house. At the same time, besides his general rowdyism, he is perhaps eating all the provisions in the house. She sings:

Don't you let my honey catch you here—
He'll kill you dead jus' sho's you born.

HOP RIGHT

It will thus be seen that the songs of the most characteristic type are far from elegant. They go beyond the interesting point to the trite and repulsive themes. Nor can a great many of the common songs be given at all. But these are songs current among the common Negroes, and as such are powerful comment upon the special characteristic of the group. A few of the shorter themes thus sung will illustrate further.

> Hop right! goin' to see my baby Lou.
> Goin' to walk an' talk wid my honey,
> Goin' to hug an' kiss my honey,
>   Hop right, my baby!

> I wouldn't have a yellow gal
> Tell you de reason why:
> Her neck so long, 'fraid she never die.

> I wouldn't have a black gal,
> Tell you de reason why:
> Her hair so kinky, she break every comb I buy.

Talley has several songs containing themes like those in the second and third stanzas of "Hop Right." The following examples are taken from his "I Would Not Marry a Black Girl" (p. 56) and "I Wouldn't Marry a Yellow or a White Negro Girl" (p. 63) respectively:

> I wouldn' marry a black gal,
> I'll tell you de reason why:
> When she goes to comb dat head
> De naps 'll 'gin to fly.

> I wouldn' marry dat yaller nigger gal,
> An' I'll tell you de reason why:
> Her neck's drawed out so stringy an' long,
> I'se afraid she 'ould never die.

IF YOU WANT TO GO A COURTIN'

While there is not much sense to the next song, it gives some insight into the life of the common Negroes.

> If you want to go a courtin', I show you where to go,
> Right down yonder in de house below.
>
> Clothes all dirty an' ain't got no broom:
> Ole dirty clothes all hangin' in de room.
>
> Ask'd me to table, thought I'd take a seat.
> First thing I saw was big chunk o' meat.
>
> Big as my head, hard as a maul—
> Ash-cake, corn-bread, bran' an' all.

IF YOU WANT TO MARRY

Similar to some of the songs used in children's games in the Colonial days is "Marry Me." The song has come to be thought a Negro song, but is apparently a form of the old rhyme, "If you will marry, marry, marry, If you will marry me." The Negro sings:

> If you want to marry, come an' marry me-e-e:
> Silk an' satin you shall wear, but trouble you shall
>   see-e-e.
>
> If you want to marry, marry the sailor's daughter;
> Put her in a coffee-pot and sen' her cross the water.
>
> I marry black gal; she was black, you know,
> For when I went to see her, she look like a crow-ow,
>   She look like a crow-ow-ow.

HONEY, TAKE A ONE ON ME

A variation of the once popular song, "Honey, Take a One on Me," has a great number of verses that are undoubtedly Negro verses. Most of these, however, are not suitable for publication. An idea may be given of the song.

> Comin' down State Street, comin' down Main,
> Lookin' for de woman dat use cocaine.
> Honey, take a one on me!
>
> Goin' down Peter Street, comin' down Main,
> Lookin' for de woman ain't got no man.
> Honey, take a one on me!

HONEY, TAKE A WHIFF ON ME

Another version of "Honey, Take a One on Me" also shows something of the attitude toward woman.

> A yellow girl I do despise,
> But a jut-black girl I can't denies,
>   O honey! take a whiff on me.
>
> A jut black nigger, jus' black as tar,
> Tryin' to git to heaven on eligater car.
>   O honey! take a whiff on me.
>
> Hattie don't love me, Esther does,
> Because I wear my Sunday clothes,
>   Honey, take a whiff on me.

I LOVE THAT MAN, O GOD, I DO

More serious and of much better sentiment is the lover's song, ordinarily sung as the lament of a woman.

I love that man, O God, I do,
I love him till the day he die;
If I thought that he didn't love me,
I'd eat morphine an' die.

If I had listened to what mamma said,
I wouldn't a been here today;
But bein' so young, I throwed
That young body o' mine away.

Look down po' lonesome road,
Hacks all dead in line.
Some give nickel, some give dime,
To bury dis po' body o' mine.

KELLY'S LOVE

In "Kelly's Love" the note of disappointed affection is sounded:

Love, Kelly's love,
Love, Kelly's love,
Love, Kelly's love.
You broke de heart o' many a girl,
You never break dis heart o' mine.

When I wo' my aprons low,
When I wo' my aprons low,
When I wo' my aprons low,
Couldn't keep you from my do'.

Now I weahs my aprons high,
Sca'cely ever see you passin' by.

Now I weahs my aprons to my chin,
You pass my do' but can't come in.

See what Kelly's love have done.
See what Kelly's love have done.

If I had listened to what my mamma said,
I would a been at home in mamma's bed.

FAREWELL

Nearer the simple longing of a sincere affection is the chorus, "Farewell."

My love for you is all I knew,
My love for you is all I knew,
My love for you is all I knew.
Hope I will see you again.

Farewell, my darling, farewell!
Farewell, my darling, farewell!
Farewell, my darling, farewell!
Hope I will see you again.

SWEET FORGET-ME-NOT

The singer grows imaginative when he thinks of things absent. He longs to see his sweetheart. He thinks of all the good times he has had, and sometimes he sings plaintively that they are gone.

O girl, O girl! what have I done?
Sweet forget-me-not.

I've got a girl dat's on de way,
Sweet forget-me-not.

Times ain't like dey use ter be,
Sweet forget-me-not.

Times have been, won't be no more,
Sweet forget-me-not.

CHAPTER VII

EXAMPLES OF SOCIAL SONGS (*Concluded*)

The songs in this chapter are in many respects like those in the preceding chapter. They are, however, usually longer, and they sometimes approximate ballad and epic in combinations fearfully and wonderfully made. Difficulties of classification are at once apparent. One class of songs stands out clearly, however, namely, the songs having to do with the Negro "Bad Man" or bully. These are presented first. Other groups include train songs, dance songs, and various miscellaneous types.

STAGOLEE

The notorious character is sung as a hero of the tribe. His deeds are marvelous, his personality is interesting. He is admired by young and old in song and story and undoubtedly has an important influence upon the group.

> Stagolee, Stagolee, what's dat in you' grip?
> Nothin' but my Sunday clothes, I'm goin' to take a trip.
> Oh, dat man, bad man, Stagolee done come.
>
> Stagolee, Stagolee, where you been so long?
> I been out on de battle fiel' shootin' an' havin' fun.
> Oh, dat man, bad man, Stagolee done come.
>
> Stagolee was a bully man, an' ev'ybody knowed,
> When dey seed Stagolee comin' to give Stagolee de road.
> Oh, dat man, bad man, Stagolee done come.

The refrain "Oh, dat man, bad man, Stagolee done come," is sung at the end of each stanza and adds much to the charm of the song, giving characteristic thought to the words and rhythmical swing to the music.   The singer continues his narrative:

Stagolee started out, he give his wife his han';
"Good bye, darlin', I'm goin' to kill a man."

Stagolee killed a man an' laid him on de flo',
What's dat he kill him wid?   Dat same ole fohty-fo'.

Stagolee killed a man an' laid him on his side,
What's dat he kill him wid?   Dat same ole fohty-five.

Out of house an' down de street Stagolee did run,
In his hand he held a great big smok'n' gun.

Stagolee, Stagolee, I'll tell you what I'll do:
If you'll git me out'n dis trouble I'll do as much for you.

Ain't it a pity, ain't it a shame?
Stagolee was shot, but he don't want no name.

Stagolee, Stagolee, look what you done done:
Killed de best ole citerzen; now you'll have to be hung.

Stagolee cried to de jury, "Please don't take my life.
I have only three little children an' one little lovin' wife."
Oh, dat man, bad man, Stagolee done come.

STAGOLEE DONE KILL DAT BULLY

The foregoing version is more usually sung in Mississippi, Louisiana and Tennessee, though it is known in Alabama and Georgia, besides being sung by the Negro vagrants all over the country.   Another version, more common in Georgia, celebrates Stagolee as a somewhat different character, and the song is sung to different music.

> I got up one mornin' jes' 'bout four o'clock;
> Stagolee an' big bully done have one finish' fight.
> What 'bout?   All 'bout dat rawhide Stetson hat.
>
> Stagolee shot bully; bully fell down on de flo',
> Bully cry out: "Dat fohty-fo' it hurts me so."
> Stagolee done kill dat bully now.
>
> Sent for de wagon, wagon didn't come,
> Loaded down wid pistols an' all dat gatlin' gun.
> Stagolee done kill dat bully now.
>
> Some give a nickel, some give a dime;
> I didn't give a red copper cent, 'cause he's no friend o'
>   mine.
> Stagolee done kill dat bully now.
>
> Fohty dollar coffin, eighty dollar hack,
> Carried po' man to cemetery but failed to bring him
>   back,
> Ev'ybody been dodgin' Stagolee.

From the home to the cemetery he has gone the road of many a Negro "rounder."   Sometimes the man killed is at a picnic or public gathering, sometimes elsewhere.   The scenes of the burial, with its customs, are but a part of the life, hence they are portrayed with equal diligence.

RAILROAD BILL

But Stagolee has his equal, if not his superior. "Railroad Bill" has had a wonderful career in song and story. He is the Negro's hero of the track. One must take all the versions of the song in order to appreciate fully the ideal of such a character.

Some one went home an' tole my wife
All about—well, my pas' life.
    It was that bad Railroad Bill.

Railroad Bill, Railroad Bill,
He never work an' he never will.
    Well, it's that bad Railroad Bill.

Railroad Bill so mean an' so bad,
Till he tuk ev'thing that farmer had.
    It's that bad Railroad Bill.

I'm goin' home an' tell my wife,
Railroad Bill try to take my life.
    It's that bad Railroad Bill.

Railroad Bill so desp'rate an' so bad,
He take ev'ything po' womens had.
    An' it's that bad Railroad Bill.

IT'S THAT BAD RAILROAD BILL

With all these crimes to his credit, it is high time that some one was going after Railroad Bill. The singer starts on his journey as quickly as he can, but has to make many trips.

I went down on Number One,
Railroad Bill had jus' begun,
    It's lookin' fer Railroad Bill.

I come up on Number Two,
Railroad Bill had jus' got through.
    It's that bad Railroad Bill.

I caught Number Three and went back down the road,
Railroad Bill was marchin' to an' fro.
    It's that bad Railroad Bill.

An' jus' as I caught that Number Fo',
Somebody shot at me with a fohty-fo'.
   It's that bad Railroad Bill.

I went back on Number Five,
Goin' to bring him back, dead or alive.
   Lookin' fer Railroad Bill.

When I come up on Number Six,
All the peoples had done got sick.
   Lookin' fer Railroad Bill.

When I went down on Number Seven,
All the peoples wish'd they's in heaven.
   A-lookin' fer Railroad Bill.

I come back on Number Eight,
The folks say I was a minit too late.
   It's lookin' fer Railroad Bill.

When I come back on Number Nine,
Folks say, "You're just in time
   To catch that Railroad Bill."

When I got my men, they amounted to ten;
An that's when I run po' Railroad Bill in.
   An' that was last of po' Railroad Bill.

IT'S LOOKIN' FER RAILROAD BILL

But Railroad Bill soon appears again, and now he is worse than before. The next version differs only slightly from the foregoing one. One must remember that the chorus line follows each couplet, and the contrast in meaning makes a most interesting song.

Railroad Bill mighty bad man,
Shoot dem lights out o' de brakeman's han'.
   It's lookin' fer Railroad Bill.

Railroad Bill mighty bad man,
Shoot the lamps all off the stan'.
    An' it's lookin' fer Railroad Bill.

First on table, next on wall;
Ole corn whiskey cause of it all.
    It's lookin' fer Railroad Bill.

Ole McMillan had a special train;
When he got there was shower of rain.
    Wus lookin' fer Railroad Bill.

Ev'ybody tole him he better turn back;
Railroad Bill wus goin' down track.
    An' it's lookin' fer Railroad Bill.

Well, the policemen all dressed in blue,
Comin' down sidewalk two by two,
    Wus lookin' fer Railroad Bill.

Railroad Bill had no wife,
Always lookin' fer somebody's life.
    An' it's lookin' fer Railroad Bill.

Railroad Bill was the worst ole coon:
Killed McMillan by de light o' de moon.
    It's lookin' fer Railroad Bill.

One Culpepper went up on Number five,
Goin' bring him back, dead or alive.
    Wus lookin' fer Railroad Bill.

The Negroes sing different forms of these verses, as they are suggested at the moment:

McMillan had a special train,
When he got there, it was spring.

Two policemen all dressed in blue
Come down street in two an' two.

Railroad Bill led a mighty bad life,
Always after some other man's wife.

Railroad Bill went out Wes',
Thought he had dem cowboys bes'.

Railroad Bill mighty bad man,
Kill McGruder by de light o' de moon.

RIGHT ON, DESPERADO BILL

It is not surprising that a song so popular as "Railroad Bill" should find its way into others of similar type. Another version of the same song adds recklessness to the achievements of the desperado and combines gambling, criminal tendencies, and his general immorality, in one. The following version is somewhat mixed, but is known as a "Railroad Bill" song. There are two forms of the chorus, and they are given first.

Lose, lose—I don't keer;
If I win, let me win lak a man.
If I lose all my money, I'll be gamblin' for my honey;
Ev'y man ought to know when he lose.

Lose, lose, I don't keer;
If I win, let me win lak a man.
Lost fohty-one dollars tryin' to win a dime;
Ev'y man plays in tough luck some time.

Railroad Bill was mighty sport,
Shot all buttons off high sheriff's coat,
Den hollered, "Right on, Desperado Bill!"

Honey babe, honey babe, where you been so long?
I ain't been happy since you been gone.
Dat's all right, dat's all right, honey babe.

Honey, babe, Honey babe, bring me de broom,
De lices an' chinches 'bout to take my room.
Oh, my baby, baby, honey, chile!

Honey babe, honey babe, what in de worl' is dat,
Got on tan shoes an' black silk hat?
Honey babe, give it all to me.

Talk 'bout yo' five an' ten dollar bill,
Ain't no Bill like ole Desperado Bill,
Says, right on, Desperado Bill.

Railroad Bill went out west,
Met ole Jesse James, thought he had him best;
But Jesse laid ole Railroad Bill.

Honey babe, honey babe, can't you never hear?
I wants a nuther nickel to git a glass o' beer.
Dat's all right, honey babe, dat's all right.

Other still less elegant verses must be omitted.
Some conception of popular standards of conduct and
dress, social life and the home may be gained from the
song.

LOOKIN' FOR THAT BULLY OF THIS TOWN

In most communities there will be one or more
notorious characters among the Negroes. Often these
are widely known throughout the State, and they are
familiar names to the police. Sometimes they are
known for the most part to the Negroes. Such characters, noted for their rowdyism and recklessness,
sometimes with a criminal record, are usually called
"bullies." To be sure, "Stagolee," "Railroad Bill,"
"Eddy Jones," and the others, were "bullies," but
they were special cases. The song "I'm Lookin for

That Bully of This Town" represents a more general condition.   It is rich in portrayals of Negro life and thought.

> Monday I was 'rested, Tuesday I was fined,
> Sent to chain gang, done serve my time;
> Still I'm lookin' for that bully of this town.
>
> The bully, the bully, the bully can't be found;
> If I fin' that bully, goin' to lay his body down.
> I'm lookin' for that bully of this town.
>
> The police up town they're all scared;
> But if I fin' that bully, I goin' to lay his body 'way,
> For I'm lookin' for that bully of this town.
>
> I'm goin' down on Peter Street;
> If I fin' that bully, will be bloody meet,
> For I'm lookin' for that bully of this town.
>
> I went down town the other day,
> I ask ev'ybody did that bully come this way.
> I wus lookin' for that bully of this town.
>
> Oh, the guv'ner of this State offered one hundred dollars
>   reward
> To anybody's 'rested that bully boy.
> I sho lookin' for that bully of this town.
>
> Well, I found that bully on a Friday night,
> I told that bully I'se gwine to take his life;
> I found that bully of this town.
>
> I pull out my gun an' begin to fire,
> I shot that bully right through the eye;
> An' I kill that bully of this town.
>
> Now all the wimmins come to town all dressed in red.
> When they heard that bully boy was dead;
> An' it was the last of that bully of this town.

What a picture the song gives of the bully and his pursuer! The boasting braggart sees himself the hero of the whole community, but chiefly among the women. He is better than the police: they will even thank him for his valor. The governor will give him his reward. Everybody he meets he asks about the bully boy, and takes on a new swagger. The scene of the shooting, the reaching for the pistol, and the "layin-down" of the bully's body—these offer unalloyed satisfaction to the singer. Altogether it is a great song, and defies a superior picture.

EDDY JONES

Other notorious characters are sung with the same satisfaction. The characteristic pleasure and oblivion of time accompany the singing. While at work one may sing the words, whistle the tunes and visualize the picture, thus getting a richer field of vision. When alone, the Negro gets much satisfaction out of songs like those here given. Likewise such songs are sung in groups, at which times the singers talk and laugh, jeer one another, and retort, thus varying the song. "Eddy Jones" seems very similar in character to "Stagolee."

> Slow train run thru' Arkansas,
>   Carryin' Eddy Jones.
>
> Eddy died with a special in his hand,
>   Eddy Jones, Eddy Jones.
>
> Eddy Jones call for the coolin'-board,
>   Lawdy, lawdy, lawd!
>
> Eddy Jones looked 'round an' said,
>   "Man that kill'd me won't have no luck."

Ain't it sad 'bout po' Eddy bein' dead?
Eddy Jones was let down in his grave.

What did Eddy say before he died?
He said, "Nearer, My God, to Thee."

Eddy's mother she weeped a day,
Lawdy, Eddy Jones, Eddy Jones!

The singer turns to the women, if they be present, and sings:

You want me to do like Eddy Jones?
You mus' want me to lay down and die for you.

The "special" is a well-known term for the Negro's "gun," which is usually a pistol; the "44" is always the favorite. The "coolin'-board" is the death-bed, and is a common expression used to signify that one's time is at an end, that is, when he is to be on the "coolin'-board." The Negro criminal almost invariably dies at peace with God. The conception commonly found among the Negroes, and one which they cultivate, is that the criminal will always be reconciled before his death. So in this case Eddy Jones dies singing "Nearer, My God, to Thee."

JOE TURNER

In much the same way the man who has been to the chain gang or prison is looked upon with some sort of admiration at the same time that he is feared. In "Joe Turner" an ideal is hinted at. Each line is sung three times to make a stanza.

Dey tell me Joe Turner he done come,
Dey tell me Joe Turner he done come,
Oh, dey tell me Joe Turner he done come.

Come like he ain't never come befo'.

Come with that fohty links o' chain.

Tell-a me Joe Turner is my man.

CASEY JONES

A hero of less criminal intent was "Casey Jones." He is the hero of the engine and train. As will be noted, the Negro is fascinated by the train-song. He would like to be an engineer all his days. Negroes often discuss among themselves the possibility of their occupying positions on the trains; they take almost as much pride in being brakemen and subordinates. It is interesting to hear them boasting of what they would do in emergencies. The song that follows gives a favorite version of the ballad.

> Casey Jones wus engineer,
> Told his fireman not to fear.
> All he wanted was a boiler hot,
> Run in Canton 'bout four o'clock.
>
> One Sunday mornin' it wus drizzlin' rain,
> Looked down road an' saw a train.
> Fireman says, "Let's make a jump;
> Two locomotives an' dey bound to bump."
>
> Casey Jones, I know him well,
> Tole de fireman to ring de bell.
> Fireman jump an' say "Good-bye,
> Casey Jones, you're bound to die."
>
> Went on down to de depot track,
> Beggin' my honey to take me back,
> She turn 'roun' some two or three times:
> "Take you back when you learn to grind."

Womens in Kansas, all dressed in red,
Got de news dat Casey was dead.
De womens in Jackson, all dressed in black,
Said, in fact, he was a cracker-jack.

The verse about "begging his honey" is intended to portray the scene after the wreck, when the fireman, who did not stay on the engine with Casey, was out of a job. "Canton" and "Jackson" are regularly sung in Mississippi, while "Memphis" is more often sung in Tennessee.

JOSEPH MICA

Another version of the song as found in Georgia and Alabama is sung in honor of "Joseph Mica." Atlanta and Birmingham are the local places.

Joseph Mica was good engineer,
Told his fireman not to fear.
All he want is water 'n' coal,
Poke his head out, see drivers roll.

Early one mornin' look like rain,
'Round de curve come passenger train.
On powers lie ole Jim Jones,
Good ole engineer, but daid an' gone.

Left Atlanta hour behin',
Tole his fireman to make up the time.
All he want is boiler hot,
Run in there 'bout four o'clock.

BRADY

A more mixed scene is pictured in "Brady." Here, too, the women hear of the news, as, indeed, they always do; but this time they are glad of his death.

Why this is, the song does not tell. Brady, however, must have been a pretty bad fellow, for he did not stay in hell.

> Brady went to hell, but he didn't go to stay.
> Devil say, "Brady, step 'roun' dis way,
> I'm lookin' for you mos' every day."
>
> Brady, Brady, you know you done wrong,
> You come in when game was goin' on,
> An' dey laid po' Brady down.
>
> Up wid de crowbar, bus' open de do',
> Lef' him lyin' dead on pool-room flo';
> An' they laid his po' body down.
>
> Womens in Iowy dey heard de news,
> Wrote it down on ole red shoes
> Dat dey glad po' Brady wus dead.

The scene is one of a killing in a game of poker or craps. "They laid his po' body down" is the common way of saying they killed him. The expression has been met in a number of verses previously given. Just what the conclusion of the scene with the devil was, the Negro singer does not seem to know.

FRANK AND JESSE JAMES

While there are still many song fragments current about the notorious Jesse James, the only song found which was in any way complete is as follows:

> O mother, I'm dreaming; O mother, I'm dreaming,
> O mother, I'm dreaming 'bout Frank and Jesse James.
>
> Jesse James had a wife, she mourned all her life,
> Jesse James's children cried for bread.

Went up on the wall, thought I heard a call,
Thought I heard a call 'bout Frank an' Jesse James.

THE NEGRO BUM

"The Negro Bum" is the name of a short song that is a good exposition of the feelings of the vagrant.

I wus goin' down the railroad, hungry an' wanted to eat'
I ask white lady for some bread an' meat.
She give me bread an' coffee, an' treated me mighty kin';
If I could git them good handouts, I'd quit work, bum all the time.

Well the railroad completed, the cars upon the track.
Yonder comes two dirty hobos with grip-sacks on dere backs;
One look like my brother, the other my brother-in-law.
They walk all the way from Mississippi to the State of Arkansas.

ONE MO' ROUNDER GONE

The term "rounder" is applied not only to men, but to women also. In general, the interpretation is that of a worthless and wandering person who prides himself on being idle. It is also a term of fellowship. In the songs that follow, the chorus "One mo' rounder gone" will be found to express fitting sentiment to the accompanying scenes. The song by that name gives a repetition of the burial scenes and general feeling which was caused by the death of a girl. Its unusual feature lies in the fact that the song applies to a girl. The modern version with the automobile has not been found.

Rubber-tired buggy, double-seated hack,
Well, it carried po' Delia to graveyard, failed to bring her back.
Lawdy, one mo' rounder gone.

Delia's mother weep, Delia's mother mourn;
She wouldn't have taken it so hard if po' girl had died
at home.
Well, one mo' ole rounder gone.

Yes, some give a nickel, some give a dime,
I didn't give nary red cent, fo' she was no friend of mine.
Well, it's one mo' rounder gone.

I'M A NATU'AL BOHN EASTMAN

The Negroes have appropriate names for many of their typical characters, the meaning of which is difficult to explain. "Eastman," "rounder," "creeper," and other characters, have their own peculiar characteristics. The "Eastman" is kept fat by the women among whom he is a favorite. The "creeper" watches his chance to get admittance into a home, unknown to the husband. The "Natu'al-Bohn Eastman" gives a view of his opinion of himself, with adopted forms of burlesque.

I went down to New Orleans
To buy my wife a sewin'-machine.
The needle broke an' she couldn't sew;
I'm a natu'al-bohn Eastman, for she tole me so.

I'm a Eastman, how do you know?
I'm a natu'al-bohn Eastman, for she tole me so.

Well, they call me a Eastman if I walk around;
They call me a Eastman if I leave the town.
I got it writ on the tail o' my shirt,
I'm a natu'al-bohn Eastman, don't have to work.

Oh, I'm a Eastman on the road again,
For I'm a Eastman on the road again.

Wake up, ole rounder, it's time to go,
I think I heard dat whistle blow.
You step out, let work-ox step in;
You're a natu'al-bohn Eastman, you can come agin.

Carry me down to the station-house do';
Find nuther Eastman an' let me know.

Wake up, ole rounder, you sleep too late,
Money-makin' man done pass yo' gate.
You step out, let money-makin' man step in;
You a natu'al-bohn Eastman, you can come agin.

BAD-LAN' STONE

The Negro loves to boast of being a "bad man."
"I bin a bad man in my day," says the older fellow to
the boys about him.   Much the same sentiment is here
sung as that in the songs just given.

I was bohn in a mighty bad lan',
For my name is Bad-Lan' Stone.
Well, I want all you coons fer to understan',
I am dangerous wid my licker on.

You may bring all yo' guns from de battleship,
I make a coon climb a tree.
Don't you never dare slight my repertation,
Or I'll break up this jamberee.

Well, well, I wus bohn in a mighty bad lan',
For my name—name—is Bad-Man Stone.

In his volume Talley gives several rhymes which
are similarly descriptive of the "bad man," such as
"The Rascal" (p. 106) and "Strong Hands" (p. 167).
Two others are as follows:

WILD NEGRO BILL
(Talley, p. 94)

I'se wild Nigger Bill
Frum Redpepper Hill.
I never did wo'k, an' I never will.

I'se done killed de boss.
I'se knocked down de hoss.
I eats up raw goose widout apple sauce!

I'se Run-a-way Bill,
I knows dey mought kill;
But ole Mosser hain't cotch me, an' he never will!

LOOKING FOR A FIGHT
(Talley, p. 118)

I went down town de yudder night,
A-raisin' san' an' a-wantin' a fight.
Had a forty-dollar razzer, an' a gatlin' gun,
Fer to shoot dem niggers down one by one.

YOU MAY LEAVE, BUT THIS WILL BRING YOU BACK

It will be seen that the Negro loves to sing of trials in court, arrest, idleness, crime, and bravado. The tramp and the "rounder," the "Eastman" and the "creeper" are but typical extremes. The notorious characters sung are the objective specimens of the common spirit of self-feeling. Now comes the song with the personal boast and the reckless brag. Mixed with it all is the happy-go-lucky sense of don't-care and humor. It is a great philosophy of life the Negro has.

Satisfied, tickled to death,
Got a bottle o' whiskey on my shelf.
You may leave, but this will bring you back.

Satisfied, satisfied,
Got my honey by my side.
You may leave, but this will bring you back.

An' I'm jus' frum the country come to town,
A too-loo-shaker from my head on down.
You may leave, but this will bring you back.

THIS MORNIN', THIS EVENIN', SO SOON

What does it matter to him if he has been in serious trouble? Is not the jail about as good as home, the chain gang as good as his everyday life? He will get enough to eat and a place to sleep. The Negro sings with characteristic humor, "This Mornin', This Evenin', So Soon," and mingles his scenes in such a way that the singer enjoys them all.

Went up town wid my hat in my han' dis mornin',
Went up town wid my hat in my han'.
"Good mornin', jedge, done killed my man,"
This mornin', this evenin', so soon.

"I didn't quite kill him, but I fixed him so, this mornin';
I didn't quite kill him but I fixed him so
He won't bodder wid me no mo'."
This mornin', this evenin', so soon.

All I want is my strong hand-out, this mornin',
All I want is my strong hand-out;
It will make me strong and stout.
This mornin', this evenin', so soon.

Other couplets are sung after the style of the verses just given:

When you kill a chicken, save me the feet,
When you think I'm workin', I'm walkin' the street.

When you kill a chicken, save me the whang,
When you think I'm workin', I ain't doin' a thing.

'Tain't no use a me workin' so,
'Cause I ain't goin' ter work no mo'.

I'm goin' back to Tennessee,
Where dem wimmins git stuck on me,
This mornin', this evenin', so soon.

BRER RABBIT

With the same chorus the Negroes of the Carolinas
sing some verses about Brer Rabbit. While they are
not the purely original creation of Negro song, they
are very appropriate, and easily please the Negro's
fancy. These verses consist, as above, of various
repetitions, three of which follow:

O Brer Rabbit! you look mighty good this mornin',
O Brer Rabbit! you look mighty good.
Yes, by God! you better take to de wood,
    This mornin', this evenin', so soon.

O Brer Rabbit! yo' ears mighty long, this mornin',
O Brer Rabbit! yo' ears mighty long.
Yes, by God! dey's put in wrong,
    This mornin', this evenin', so soon.

O Brer Rabbit! yo' tail mighty white, this mornin',
O Brer Rabbit! yo' tail mighty white.
Yes, by God! yer better take to flight,
    This mornin', this evenin', so soon.

EV'YBODY BIN DOWN ON ME

Doleful and gruesome verses are very much in vogue.
Repetition of lines makes a peculiar effect. The following song, which represents another phase of the

wantonness and simplicity of the Negro, is sung at length.   Each stanza is made to contain six lines by repeating each line three times.

> Ev'y since I lef' dat country farm,
>   Ev'ybody bin down on me.
>
> I killed a man, killed a man,
>   Nobody to pay my fine.
>
> I went down to de railroad,
>   Could not find a frien'.
>
> When I git up de road,
>   Wonder who'll pay my fine.
>
> Long as I make my nine a week,
>   'Round yo' bedside I goin' to creep.

NOBODY'S BIZNESS BUT MINE

Repeated much in the same way is the song "Nobody's Bizness but Mine."   The sentiment is somewhat similar to the song " 'Tain't Nobody's Bizness but My Own," but is more careless and care-free.   The chorus, which is repeated after each stanza or omitted at will, is as follows:

> Georgia Luke, how do you do?
> Do lak I use ter, God knows!
> Do lak I use ter, God knows!

And in the stanzas the third or chorus line is repeated four times, thus doubling their length.

> Goin' to my shack,
>   Ain't comin' back.
> Nobody's bizness but mine.

Git up on my bunk,
Look in my trunk,
Count my silver an' my gold.

If you don't believe I'm fine,
Git me behin' a pine.
Treat you lak a lady, God knows!

Goin' back up No'th,
Goin' pull my britches off,
Goin' sleep in my long shirt-tail.

Goin' to my shack,
Goin' have hump on my back;
Nobody's bizness but mine.

Goin' be hump on my back:
So many chickens in de sack.
Nobody's bizness but mine.

Chickens in my sack,
Big hounds on my track,
Nobody's bizness but mine.

The above song perhaps reaches a climax of the happy and careless disposition of the vaudeville Negro. Such pictures as he paints there, he sees vividly and enjoys. There are many other verses which are sung, but which will not permit reproduction.

I'M GOIN' BACK

In much the same spirit, but with perhaps a little more recklessness, the Negro man sings:

My name is Uncle Sam,
An' I do not give a damn;
I takes a little toddy now an' then:
    I'm goin' back.

Well, some folks do say
Dat it is not a sin
If I takes a little toddy now an' then:
    I'm goin' back.

I was born in sweet ole Alabam',
An' I do not give a damn,
Where I takes a little toddy now and then:
    Well, I'm goin back.

COCAINE HABIT

The Negro singer pays his respects to the cocaine habit and whiskey. The majority of these songs are indecent in their suggestion. An example of the better verses will illustrate.

Well, the cocaine habit is mighty bad,
It kill ev'ybody I know it to have had,
    O my babe!

Well, I wake in de mornin' by the city-clock bell,
An' the niggers up town givin' cocaine hell.
    O my babe, O my babe!

I went to the drug-store, I went in a lope;
Sign on the door: "There's no mo' coke."
    O my babe, O my babe, O my babe!

ROLLIN' MILL

In the "Rollin' Mill" the singer says there's no more iron to ship to town. Sometimes he means he will not have to work because the material is exhausted, sometimes he means there will be no more chains for him, but it is most likely that he symbolizes liquor by the iron.

Rollin' mill done shut down,
Ain't shippin' no mo' iron to town.
   O babe, O babe!

If you don't believe Jumbagot's dead,
Jus' look at crepe on 'Liza's head.
   O babe, O babe!

Carried him off in hoo-doo wagon,
Brought him back wid his feet a-draggin',
   O babe, O babe!

Well, cocaine womens oughter be like me,
Drink corn whiskey, let cocaine be.
   O babe, O babe!

If you don't believe I'm right,
Let me come to see you jus' one night.
   O babe, O babe!

JULIA WATERS

In the next song the singer tells of his escape from the county gang while he was supposed to be working on the rocks. His song is almost as varied as his experiences. He sings in a monotone-like chant:

O Julia Waters! do you remember the day,
When we wus drivin' steel in ole rock querry,
I tried to git away?

'Round de mountain I went skippin',
Thru' de weeds I went flyin';
Outrun lightning-fas' mail on Georgia line.

Well, I walked up to conductor for to give him game o'
   talk.
"If you got money or ticket, I take you to New York;
If you have no money or ticket"—

"Pity me, sir, for I am po'.
Yonder come brakeman on outside,
Goin' shut up box-car do'."

I was boun' down to Louisville,
Got stuck on Louisville girl.
You bet yo' life she's out o' sight,
She wore the Louisville curl.

THOUGHT I HEARD THAT K. C. WHISTLE BLOW

Much has already been said of the Negro's attitude toward the railroad and train. His songs abound in references to the train as an agent for his desires. From "ridin' the rods" to a long-desired trip back to his sweetheart, the Negro is the frequent patron of the train. Some years ago the agents for some of the Western business concerns offered attractive inducements to Negroes to migrate for permanent work. These agents went throughout the South, securing large numbers of laborers. Many a family disposed of their goods for a trifle in order to accept the flattering terms offered, for they thought that in the new environment they would soon become wealthy and prosperous. The history of their experience is well known. They were carried out, given poor treatment, with no money and often not enough to eat. It is needless to say that all who could obtain money enough and escape came back to their old homes. Some of the most interesting and pathetic stories told by the Negroes are those of adventure and privation incurred in their efforts to return home. Many of them are humorous. The following song represents one of these laborers waiting at the station for the train to carry him back "where he come frum." The song is pathetic in its appeal.

Thought I heard that K. C. whistle blow,
Oh, I thought I heard that K. C. whistle blow!

Blow lak she never blow befo',
Lawd, she blow lak she never blow befo'!

Wish to God some ole train would run,
Carry me back where I come frum.

Out in the wide worl' alone.

Take me back to sweet ole Birmingham.

Baby-honey, come an' go with me.

Ev'ybody down on us.

(Whistle blows)

Thought I heard whistle when it blow,
Blow lak she ain't goin' blow no mo'.

(Train has come, now moves away)

Good-bye, baby, call it gone.

Fireman, put in a little mo' coal.

Fireman, well, we're livin' high.

Yonder comes that easy-goin' man o' mine.

Ain't no use you tryin' send me roun',
I got 'nuf money to pay my fine.

Out in this wide worl' to roam,
Ain't got no place to call my home.

K. C.

Still another version of the song represents a lone
laborer working near the railroad and watching the

trains go by. He has not the money, nor can he get away, but he longs to go home. As he works, he pictures these scenes, imagines himself on board the train going back to the "Sunny South, where sun shines on his baby's house." Or as a train comes from his home, he imagines that some of his friends have come to see him. He sings:

> Well, I thought I heard that K. C. whistle blow,
> Blow lak she never blow befo'.
>
> I believe my woman's on that train,
> O babe! I believe my woman's on that train.
>
> She comin' back from sweet ole Alabam',
> She comin' to see her lovin' man.
>
> Fireman, put in a little mo' coal;
> Run dat train in some lonesome hole.

L. & N.

A song of the same origin, and very much like the "K. C.," is another called "L. & N." Instead of "L. & N.," other roads may be designated. This Negro man labors with the hope that he will soon go home again. By "home" he means the community where he knows the most people. It is a song of the wanderer, and repeats much the same sentiment as that found in many of the songs under that class. This song and the one just given are sung to the "Frisco Rag-time," or train-song music described in Chapter V. The train is heard running, the wheels distinctly roar as they cross the joints of rail, the whistle blows between each verse, and the bell rings anon for the crossing.

Just as sho as train run through L. & N. yard,
I'm boun' to go home if I have to ride de rod.

So good-bye, little girl, I'm scared to call yo' name;
Good-bye, little girl! I'm scared to call yo' name.

Now, my mamma's dead, an' my sweet ole popper, too;
An' I got no one fer to carry my trouble to.

An' if I wus to die, little girl, so far 'way from home,
The folks, honey, for miles 'round would mourn.

Now, kiss yo' man, an' tell yo' man good-bye;
Please kiss yo' man, an' tell yo' man good-bye!

I'm goin' tell my mommer, whenever I git home,
How people treated me 'way off from home.

DON'T NEVER GIT ONE WOMAN ON YOUR MIND
(Knife-Song)

Very much like the railroad-song is the knife-song, which has also been described previously. Sometimes the two are combined; and with the blowing of the whistle, the ringing of the bell, and the "talkin'" of the knife as it goes back and forth over the strings, the "music physicianer" has a wonderful production. Many songs are sung to this music. In the following song the verses consist of either a single line repeated or a rhyming couplet. Two lines are sung in harmony with the running of the knife over the strings of the guitar, while the refrain, "Lawd, lawd, lawd!" wherever found is sung to the "talking" of the knife. The other two lines are sung to the picking of the guitar, as in ordinary cases.

'Fo' long, honey, 'fo' long, honey,
'Fo' long, honey, 'fo' long, honey;
    L-a-w-d, l-a-w-d, l-a-w-d!
'Fo' long, honey, 'fo' long, honey,
'Fo' long, honey, 'fo' long, honey;
    L-a-w-d, l-a-w-d, l-a-w-d!

Don't never git one woman on yo' min',
Keep you in trouble all yo' time.
    L-a-w-d, l-a-w-d, l-a-w-d!
Don't never git one woman on yo' min',
Keep you in trouble all yo' time.
    L-a-w-d, l-a-w-d, l-a-w-d!

Don't never let yo' baby have her way;
Keep you in trouble all yo' day.

Don't never take one woman for yo' frien';
When you out 'nuther man in.

I hate to hear my honey call my name;
Call me so lonesome an' so sad.

I got de blues an' can't be satisfied;
Brown-skin woman cause of it all.

That woman will be the death o' me,
Some girl will be the death o' me.

Honey, come an' go with me.
When I'm gone what yer gwine ter say?

Sung like the first stanza given, are many "one-verse" songs. Nor are they less attractive. The insertion of the chorus line takes away any monotony. Besides, the knife adds zest.

I'm goin' 'way, won't be long,
I'm goin' 'way, won't be long;
    L-a-w-d, l-a-w-d, l-a-w-d!

Went up town to give my troubles away,
Went up town to give my troubles away;
   L-a-w-d, l-a-w-d, l-a-w-d!

Too good a man to be slided down.

Slide me down—I'll slow-slide up agin.

Baby, you always on my min'.

The girl I love's the girl I crave to see.

Baby, do you ever think of me?

Baby, what have I done to you?

Wonder whar my honey stay las' night.

Got a baby, don't care whar she goes.

I goin' pack my grip, git further down de road.

Gwine to leave if I haf' ter ride de rod.

Ridin' de rod ain't no easy job.

GIVE ME A LITTLE BUTTERMILK

The Negro nearly always sings when he dances.
Many of his songs are easily converted into dance
songs, but some are especially adaptable to the rhythm
and swing of the dance, although their themes are
often very irrelevant. The instrument is more incentive to the dance than the song, but would be far
less effective without the singing.

Give me a little buttermilk, ma'am,
Give me a little buttermilk, ma'am,
Give me a little buttermilk, ma'am,
Please give me a little buttermilk, ma'am.

Ain't had none so long, so long,
Ain't had none so long, so long,
Ain't had none so long, so long,
Oh, I ain't had none so long!

The repetition is not unpleasant, but adds whatever of charm there is to the line. The singer continues—

Cow in de bottom done gone dry.

Sister got so she won't churn.

Goin' to tell auntie 'fo' long.

GREASY GREENS

But buttermilk is not more attractive than "greasy greens." In this remarkable song the Negroes dance with merriment, each final line being suitable to the "s-w-i-n-g c-o-r-n-e-r" of the dance. The picture, while not exactly elegant, is at least a strong one.

Mamma goin' to cook some,
Mamma goin' to cook some,
Mamma goin' to cook some—
  Greasy greens!

How I love them,
How I love them,
How I love them—
  Greasy greens!

Mamma goin' ter boil them—
  Greasy greens!

Sister goin' pick them—
  Greasy greens!

I goin' eat them—
  Greasy greens!

LOST JOHN

Still other dance songs are composed of single lines repeated without variation. The single song often has only three or four verses. These are repeated as long as that particular song is wanted for the dance, then another will be taken up.

Lost John, lost John, lost John.
Lost John, lost John, lost John.

Lost John, lost John, lost John.
Help me to look for lost John.

Lost John done gone away,
Help me to look for lost John.

Still I ain't bother yet,
Still I ain't bother none.

Sun is goin' down,
Sun is goin' down.

I goin' 'way some day,
Yes, I goin' 'way some day.

I'm goin' 'way to stay,
Still I'm goin' 'way to stay.

Come an' go with me,
O yes! come an' go with me.

I got a honey here,
Yes, I got a honey here.

Goin' away to leave you,
Well, I goin' 'way to leave you.

LILLY

This song, sometimes called respectively "Pauly," "Frankie," "Lilly," has many versions both among the whites and the Negroes.[1] It is the story of a murder and the conviction of the murderer. The pathos is typical, and re-echoes the sentiment of other Negro songs. The scene is Atlanta, one singer says; another says Memphis. The reader will recognize verses common to Negro songs in general. The song is an unusually strong portrayal of Negro life and thought.

> Lilly was a good girl evy'body knows;
> Spent a hundred dollars to buy her father suit o' clothes.
> Her man certainly got to treat her right.
>
> She went to Bell Street, bought a bottle of beer;
> "Good mornin', bar-keeper, has my lovin' man been here?
> My man certainly got to treat me right."
>
> "It is Sunday an' I ain't goin' to tell you no lie,
> He wus standin' over there jus' an hour ago."
> "My man certainly got to treat me right."
>
> She went down to First Avenue, to pawn-broker.
> "Good mornin', kind lady, what will you have?"
> "I want to git a fohty-fo' gun, for
> All I got's done gone."
>
> He say to the lady, "It's against my law
> To rent any woman forty-fo' smokin' gun,
> For all you got'll be daid an' gone."
>
> She went to the alley, dogs begin to bark,
> Saw her lovin' man standin' in de dark,
> Laid his po' body down.

---

[1] See Cox, J. H., *Folk Songs of the South*, Harvard University Press, 1924. for several of these.

"Turn me over, Lilly, turn me over slow,
May be las' time, I don't know,
All you got's daid an' gone."

She sent for the doctors—doctors all did come.
Sometimes they walk, sometimes they run;
An' it's one mo' rounder gone.

They picked up Pauly, carried him to infirmary.
He told the doctors he's a gamblin man;
An' it's one mo' rounder gone.

Newsboys come runnin' to tell de mother de news.
She said to the lads, "That can't be true,
I seed my son 'bout an hour ago.

"Come here, John, an' git yo' hat;
Go down the street an' see where my son is at.
Is he gone, is he gone?"

The policemen all dressed in blue,
Dey come down de street by two an' two.
One mo' rounder gone.

"Lucy, git yo' bonnet!   Johnnie, git yo' hat!
Go down on Bell Street an' see where my son is at.
Is he gone, is he gone?"

Sunday she got 'rested, Tuesday she was fined.
Wednesday she pleaded for all-life trial,
An' it's all she's got done gone.

Lilly said to jailer, "How can it be?
Feed all prisoners, won't feed me.
Lawd, have mercy on yo' soul!"

Jailer said to Lilly, "I tell you what to do—
Go back in yo' dark cell an ' take a good sleep!"
An' it's all she's got done gone.

She said to the jailer, "How can I sleep?
All 'round my bedside lovin' Paul do creep;
It's all I got's gone."

The wimmins in Atlanta, dey heard de news,
Run excursions with new red shoes;
An' it's one mo' rounder done gone.

Some give a nickel, some give a dime,
Some didn't give nary red copper cent;
An' it's one mo' rounder gone.

Well, it's fohty-dollar hearse, an' rubber-tire hack,
Carry po' Paul to cemetery, but fail to bring him back;
An' it's one mo' rounder gone.

Well, they pick up Pauly, an' laid him to rest;
Preacher said de ceremony, sayin',
"Well, it's all dat you got's daid an' gone."

BABY, LET THE DEAL GO DOWN

The Negro's propensities for "shootin' craps" and gambling in general are well known. He boasts of his good and bad luck. In "Let the Deal Go Down" he gives a characteristic picture:

Baby, let the deal go down,
Baby, let the deal go down,
Baby, let the deal go down.

I gamble all over Kentucky,
Part of Georgia, too.
Everywhere I hang my hat
Is home, sweet home, to me.

I lose my watch an' lose my chain,
Lose ev'ything but my diamon' ring.
Come here, all you Birmingham scouts!
Set down yo' money on number six.

When I left Kansas City, Missouri, had three hundred
    dollars;
Soon as I struck Birmingham, put cop on me.

GET THAT MONEY

In this song, which has the same refrain line as the
preceding song, the Negro woman talks to her "man"
and tells him to go and get the money from that
"nigger up-stairs." To be sure of his safety, she asks
him what he would do if the fellow offered trouble.
This song also reflects the vaudeville adaptation.
It is sung in a sort of monotone.

"Nigger up-stairs got hundred dollars.
Some matches lyin' on mantelpiece,
Lamp standin' right side of 'em.
Now I want you to be sho an' git dat money.

"When you git dat money,
I'll be down in big skin game."
Baby, let the deal go down.

"Suppose dat nigger start sumpin'?"
"I got my pistol in my right pocket."
"Be sho an' git dat money; an' when you git it, give me
    the wink."
Baby, let the deal go down.

Ev'y since I bin a gam'lin' man,
I bin a skippin' an' a-dodgin' in the lan'.

ODD FELLOWS HALL

Odd Fellows Hall, in most Negro communities, is
a general meeting place. So it happens often that
informal meetings like the one here mentioned are
held.

I went up to Odd Fellows Hall,
Had a good time, dat was all,
Hats an' cuffs all lyin' on de flo',
I bet six bits—all I had;
Nigger bet seven—made me mad.
To dat coon I could not help but say:

"Git off my money, don't you hit my money,
'Cause I'm a nigger, don't cuts no figger.
I'm gamblin' for my Sady—she's a lady;
I'm a hustlin' coon, that's what I am."

I GOT MINE

A version of the once-popular song "I Got Mine"
has been adapted by the Negro and is sung with
hilarity.

I got mine, boys, I got mine!
Some o' them got six long months,
Some o' them paid their fine.
With balls and chains all 'round my legs,
    I got mine.

I went down to a nigger crap game,
Really was against my will.
Lose ev'ything I had but bran' new dollar bill.
Well, a five-dollar bet was lyin' on de flo',
An' the nigger's point was nine.
When the cops come in—
    Well, I got mine.

When they brought them chains 'round,
How them niggers' eyes did shine.
With balls and chains all 'round their legs—
    Like I got mine.

FALSE ALARM

Very much like the above is a scene given in a col-
loquy which may have been between two Negroes,

but more likely between four. They are playing a game; and, being in constant fear of being apprehended, they hear sounds that do not exist. They picture it with humor.

Quit, stop, I say! Don't you hear?
Some one's at that do!
O Lord, have mercy! They've got us at las'.

Why don't you niggers stop all that fuss?
If you wusn't shootin' craps they'd think so.
Now you done giv' ev'ything away.

Why don't you open that do'?
Well, if you want it open, yo'd better
Come and open it yo'self.

Say, you niggers, you better stop jumpin' out.
Guess I better go out that window myself.
An' there was nobody at the door.

YOU SHALL BE FREE

No one appreciates more than himself the ridiculous predicaments in which the Negro often gets. His wit is quick, his repartee is effective. What a description he gives of himself and his environment, mingled with absurdities, in the following song!

Nigger be nigger, whatever he do:
Tie red ribbon 'round toe of his shoe,
Jerk his vest on over his coat,
Snatch his britches up 'round his throat,
Singin' high-stepper, Lawd, you shall be free.

Great big nigger, settin' on log,
One eye on trigger, one eye on hog.
Gun said "blop!" hog said "sip!"
An' he jumped on de hog wid all his grip,
Singin' high-stepper, Lawd, you shall be free.

Shout to glory, Lawd, you shall be free!
Shout to glory, Lawd, you shall be free!
Shout, mourner, Lawd, you shall be free!
Shout when de good Lawd set you free!

I went down to hog-eye town,
Dey sot me down to table;
I et so much dat hog-eye grease,
Till de grease run out my nabel.
Run long home, Miss Hog-eye,
Singin' high-stepper, Lawd, you shall be free.

Nigger an' rooster had a fight,
Rooster knock nigger clean out o' sight,
Nigger say "Rooster, dat's all right,
Meet you at hen-house do' tomorrow night,
Singin' high-stepper, Lawd, you shall be free."

Two barrels apples, three barrels cheese;
When I git to heaven, goin' shout on my knees.
Shout to glory, Lawd, you shall be free,
Shout to glory, mourner, you shall be free.

With the crokus sack you shall be free,
With the crokus sack you shall be free.
Shout to glory, Lawd, you shall be free.
When de good Lawd set you free.

A nigger went up town actin' a hoss;
De jedge he found him ten an' cost.
Shout, mourner, you shall be free,
When de good Lawd shall set you free!

PANS O' BISCUIT

For simplicity and exuberance of expression combined one ought to see a crowd of small Negroes singing the following verses. With mouths open and teeth shining, bodies swaying, they make a most incomparable scene.

> Settin' in de wily woods,
>   Settin' on a seven.
> Throwed 'im in a feather bed,
>   Swore he'd gone to heaven.

> Pans o' biscuit, bowls o' gravy,
> Slice pertater pie,
>   Kill a nigger dead.

> Had a sweet pertater
>   Roastin' in de san';
> Saw my mother comin'—
>   How I burnt my hand!

WHEN DE BAND BEGINS TO PLAY

In the song "When the Band Begins to Play" the Negro is at his best in clownish portrayal of unusual scenes. The chorus, always sung after each stanza, serves to unify the song, while the two-line refrain gives a hilarity to the singing.

> When de ban' begins to play,
> When de ban' begins to play,
> When de ban' begins to play.

> See dat mule a-comin', ain't got half a load.
> If you think he unruly mule, give him all de road.
> Whoa, mule, whoa! Whoa dere, I say!
> Keep yo' seat, Miss Liza Jane! Hold on to de sleigh!

Musketer fly high, musketer fly low;
If I git my foot on him, he won't fly no mo';
Well, it's whoa, mule, whoa!   Whoa dere, I say!
Keep yo' seat, Miss Liza Jane!   Hold on to de sleigh!

Had ole banjo one time, strings made out o' twine;
All song I could sing was "Wish dat Gal was Mine!"
An' it's whoa, mule, whoa!   Whoa dere, I say, *etc.*

Each of the following stanzas (sung with emphasis and pause as if four short lines), is closed with the "whoa-mule" refrain, while the original chorus, "When the band begins to play," follows each stanza.

If you want to see dat mule kick,
If you want to hear him holler,
Tie a knot in his tail,
An' poke his head through a collar.

Went runnin' down to turkey-roose,
Fell down on his knees;
Liked to killed hisself a-laughin'
'Cause he heard a turkey sneeze.

Ole Massa bought a yaller gal,
Brought her from de South.
He wrapped her hair so mazen tight,
She could not shut her mouth.

He taken her down to blacksmith shop,
To have her mouth cut small.
She made a whoop, she made a squall,
Den swallowed shop an' all.

On Sat'day night he stole a sheep,
On Sunday he was taken.
Monday was his trial day,
Tuesday he hung like bac'n.

Keep yo' seat, Miss Liza Jane!
Don't act jes' lak a fool.
Ain't got time to kiss you,
'Cause I'm tendin' to dis mule.

Ole Massa he raise a cow,
He knowed de day she was bohn.
Hit took a jay-bird seventeen years
To fly from ho'n to ho'n.

Ole Massa raised ole gray mule,
He knowed de day he wus born.
Ev'y tooth in his head
Would hold a barrel o' corn.

Ole Massa had little ole mule,
Name was Simon Slick.
Dey tied a knot in his tail,
Oh, how dat thing did kick!

Ole Mistus raised a little black hen,
Black as any crow;
She laid three eggs ev'y day,
On Sunday she laid fo'.

"When the Band Begins to Play" is full of animal
lore. These stanzas or variations of them are sung by
the Negroes all over the South. In this connection
it might be stated that Talley's work contains at
least sixty songs or rhymes which may be classed under
animal lore. Interesting variations of some of the
above stanzas are found in his work, two of which are
as follows:

FRIGHTENED AWAY FROM A CHICKEN ROOST
(Talley, p. 95)

I went down to de hen-house on my knees,
An' I thought I heard dat chicken sneeze.

You'd oughter seed dis Nigger a-gittin' 'way frum dere,
But 'twusn't nothin' but a rooster sayin' his prayer.
How I wish dat rooster's prayer would en',
Den perhaps I mought eat dat ole gray hen.

SIMON SLICK'S MULE
(Talley p. 47)

Dere wus a liddle kickin' man,
His name wus Simon Slick.
He had a mule wid cherry eyes;
Oh, how dat mule could kick.

SHE ROLL DEM TWO WHITE EYES

As in the religious songs of the Negro, so in his
social folk songs, he quickly adapts new songs to his
own environment. The music does not change as
much as in the case of the spirituals. The song
itself often becomes amusing because of its paraphrases. "Goo-goo Eyes" was sung as much among
the Negroes as among the whites. The Negroes
have improvised more than a score of verses, some
of which may be given.

Nex' day when show wus gone,
His baby threw him down.
She say to him, "I'll have you pinched
If you lay 'roun dis town."
Now, let me tell my tale of woe.

Well, de fust time I seed my brother-in-law,
He had some chickens for sale.
De nex' time I seed my brother-in-law,
He wus laid up in Collins jail.
Den he rolled dem two white eyes.

Jus' because he had them thirty days,
He thought he had to lay in jail de res' of his days.
He's de bes' dey is, an' dey need him in de biz,
Well, jus' because he had them thirty days.

Of all de beastes in de woods,
I'd rather be a tick;
I'd climb up 'roun' my true love's neck,
An' there I'd stick,
Jus' to see her roll dem snow-white eyes.

Let me tell you 'bout a cheap sport —
Was on a Sunday morn;
Put five cents in missionary box,
Took out fo' cents for change.
Well, wan't he cheap! well, wan't he cheap!

Well, I would not marry black gal,
Tell you de reason why:
Ev'y time she comb her head,
She make dem goo-goo eyes.
Well, she roll dem two white eyes.

CLIMBIN' UP THE GOLDEN STAIRS

This song is thoroughly mixed with the old spirituals and bears a slight resemblance to "In the Evening by the Moonlight." The result is a song without individuality.

Don't you hear them bells a-ringin'?
    How sweet, I do declare!
Don't you hear them darkies singin',
    Climbin' up the golden stairs?

Oh, Peter was so wicked,
    Climbin' up the golden stairs;
When I asked him for a ticket,
    Climbin' up the golden stairs.

If you think he is a fool,
    Climbin' up the golden stairs;
He will treat you mighty rude,
    Climbin' up the golden stairs.

CARVE 'IM TO DE HEART

"Carve Dat 'Possum" smacks with good times for the Negro. His recipe is quite appetizing. This is a well-known song, and much quoted.

Well, 'possum meat's so nice an' sweet,
    Carve 'im to de heart;
You'll always find hit good ter eat.
    Carve 'im to de heart.

Carve dat 'possum,
Carve dat 'possum, chillun.
Carve dat 'possum,
Oh, carve 'im to de heart.

My ole dog treed, I went to see,
    Carve 'im to de heart;
Dar wus a 'possum in dat tree.
    Carve 'im to de heart.

I went up dar to fetch 'im down,
    Carve 'im to de heart.
I bus' 'im open agin de groun',
    Carve 'im to de heart.

De way ter cook de 'possum nice,
    Carve 'im to de heart,
Fust parbile 'im, stir 'im twice,
    Carve 'im to de heart.

Den lay sweet taters in de pan,
    Carve 'im to de heart;
Nuthin' beats dat in de lan'.
    Carve 'im to de heart.

Talley gives the words and music of a slightly different version of this song.

AN OPOSSUM HUNT
(Talley, p. 23)

'Possum meat is good an' sweet
I always finds it good to eat.
My dog tree, I went to see.
A great big 'possum up dat tree.
I retch up an' pull him in,
Den dat ole 'possum 'gin to grin.

I tuck him home an' dressed him off,
Dat night I laid him in de fros'.
De way I cooked dat 'possum sound,
I fust parboiled, den baked him brown.
I put sweet taters in de pan,
'Twus de bigges' eatin' in de lan'.

CROSS–EYED SALLY

The Negro's tendency to put everything into song is well illustrated by the following monotone song. The singer appeared to be making it as he sang, all the while picking his guitar in the regular way; but he repeated it in the exact words except for the usual variations in dialect. This he could do as often as required. The song is one of many stories which the Negroes devise to tell of their adventures. It tells of varied life and custom, it hints at undercurrents of Negro thought, it tells again of woman in her relation to man, it gives splendid insight into Negro characteristics in the role of the clown who has mixed his thought, wit, bits of song and burlesque with the crude jokes he has heard.

Had ole gal one time, name was Cross-eyed Sally.
She was the blackest gal in Paradise Alley.
She had liver lips an' kidney feet.
Didn't know she was so black
Till I took a fire-coal one morning
An' make a white mark on her face.
An' I didn't know she was so cross-eyed
Till one morning she come up to me an' say:
"Look here, boy, I want to eat!"
I tole her if she had anything
She had better go to eatin' it,
I never had nuthin'.
It hurt my gal so bad when I tole her this
That she cried; an' in crying she so cross-eyed
Till the tears run down her back!

Thought I felt sorry for my girl, an'
I taken her up to ole massa's home dat day;
An' we seen a heap o' chickens—
All sorts an' all sizes.
An' I tole her to hole quiet till dat night
When we go up an' see what we could do
To dem chickens.

So we looked all 'round de house
An' we couldn't find nothin'.
We looked in de trees an' yard
An' couldn't find nuthin'.
So my girl got oneasy, thought
Dere was no chickens 'round dere.
'Long 'bout 'leven or twelve 'clock dat night
I heard ole rooster crow in hollow
Back of de hen-house. I says,
"Look here, girl' dere's chickens here."
He couldn't set up an' not crow
For midnight nor mornin' neither.

So me 'n' her goes down, an'
Chickens was settin' 'way up in cedar tree.
She say to me, "How in worl' you goin' git
Dem chickens out'n dat high tree?"
I tole her I can clam jes good
As they can fly, I can clam
Jes as good as they can fly.
So up de tree I went like anything else
Wid sharp claws—cat or squirrel—
Clam jes fas' as please.
So I seen all sorts o' chickens:
Bootlegs, Shanghais, Plymouth Rock;
An' found some ole freezlins.
She say to me, "I doan know how in de worl'
De freezlin' git up dere."
An' I say, "Nor me, neither.   He ain't got 'nuf feathers
To fly over a rail, much less up in a tree."
I say, "He must a clam tree lak I did."

I reached 'round an' got ev'ry kind o' rock
But flint rock.   But dem ole Plymouth Rock hens
Kind er rocks I'm talkin' 'bout.
I got ever' kind er eyes I seen but buckeye;
An' reason I didn't git dat was a cedar tree.
But Shanghai pullets kind o' eye I talkin' 'bout.
I got ever' kind o' freeze I seen but de weather,
An' it was hot when I went up dere.   But
Freezlin' chicken what I'm talkin 'bout.
An' I got ever' kind o' leg I seen but thousand leg,
An' dey tells me dat's a worm, an' I didn't need him.
Bootlegged roosters—dem's de kind o' legs I got.
My girl say, "You better make haste
An' come down 'way frum up'n dat tree."
I say, "Why?"   She say, "I'm gittin' oneasy down here."
I say, "'Bout what?"   She say, "Somebody may come
An' ketch you up dat tree, an' if dey do,
Times sho will be hard wid you."
I say, "Wait a minit!   Here's sumpin.   I don't know

Whether it's a bird or a chicken." I say,
"He mighty little, but he got feathers on.
I ketchin' ev'rything what got feathers on him."
Come to find out it wus little ole banter rooster.
I grabbed him an' jobbed into my sack.
I says, "Look out, girl, here dey comes."
She says, "Naw, don't throw dem chickens down here.
You may break or bruise or kill some uv them."
She say, "How in de worl' you goin'
Git down dat tree wid all dem chickens?"
I wus settin' out on big lim'. I goes out
To de body of de tree, then I slap my sack
In my mouth. You oughter seen me
Slidin' down dat tree. You oughter seen me
Slidin' down dat tree. We struck right out
Through de woods fer home. I had
Chickens enuf to las' a whole week!

But let me tell you what a jet-black gal
Will do, especially if she's cross-eyed like mine.
When de chickens give out de gal give out too.
She quit me nex mornin'. I got up
Lookin' fer my gal. She's done gone.
Her name was Lulu, but we called her Cross-eyed Sally.
So I looked fer Lulu all that day,
But could not find her nowhere.
So I foun' her de nex' evenin'. You know I tole you
She was so black I could take a fire-coal
An' make a white mark on her face. Well,
She was settin' up courtin' a great big nigger
Twice as black as she wus.
He look jes precise lak black calf
Lookin' through crack of whitewashed fence.
Reason he look dat way was, he had on
One o' dese deep turn-down collars; but
When he put it on he didn't turn it down,
He turn it up, settin' 'way up to his years.
He look lak horse wid blin' bridle on.
So I goes up an says, "Good evenin', Lulu."

She wouldn't say a word.
I says, "How are you, mister?"   An'
He wouldn't say a word neither.
I goes out-doors an' gits me a brick.
"Say!   How do you do, mister?"
He wouldn't say a word.   I drawed back
Wid my brick.   I knocked him in de head,
An' 'bout dat time I thought I killed him dead.
I reached up an' got my hat an' hollered,
"Good-bye, Miss Lulu, I'm gone—I'm gone."

CHAPTER VIII

THE WORK SONGS OF THE NEGRO

If the Negro singer in his religious zeal is appealing, the Negro laborer, singing while he works, working while he sings, physically forgetful of routine, is scarcely less characteristic of something indefinable in the Negro's spiritual make-up. The tendency of the Negro to sing has been observed many times. With the workman it is intensified, and while he may not sing as much as of yore, he is still a great singer. Whoever has seen, in the Spring-time, a score of Negro laborers chopping cotton in the fields to a chant, making rhythm, motion and clink of hoe harmonize; whoever has heard, in the autumn, a company of cotton pickers singing the morning challenge to the day and uniting in song and chorus at the setting of the sun and weighing time, will not soon forget the scene. The Negroes still work and sing; they sing while going to and coming from the fields, while driving teams and performing sundry tasks of the day. And the plowman has been known to sing again and again his song until his mule waited for the accustomed voice before swinging into the steady walk for the day. In town and country, in the city and at the camps, every class of workers finds a song a good supplement to work. The railroad and section gangs, the contractors, "hands," the mining groups and convict camps all echo with the sound of shovel and pick and song. The more efficient the song leader is, the better work will the company do; hence the singer is valued as a good workman.

As motion and music with the Negro go hand in hand, so the motion of work calls forth the song, while the song, in turn, strengthens the movements of the workers. The roustabout is willing to do almost any kind of work of short duration; he is likely to sing through his work. With song and jest these laborers rush through great feats of labor and appear to enjoy it. Sometimes the singers seem to set the ship in motion by the rhythm of their work and song,—songs of the moment, perhaps. From the woman at the wash-tub to the leader of a group, from the child to the older Negroes, song is a natural accompaniment of work. The kind of song is often determined by the nature of the work and the number of workmen. Songs are improvised at will, under the influence of work. The themes vary with the thoughts of the workmen or with the suggestions of the occasion. In general, however, work songs are not unlike the average Negro song, and are taken at random from the experiences of everyday life. The Negro sings his flowing consciousness into expression. Like the other songs, the work-songs give a keen insight into the Negro's real self.

Obviously, there may be many classes of work songs. In the first place, when the nature of the work is such that no rhythmic movements have to be executed, the worker will sing any song that occurs to him. Often it is a single phrase or verse, perhaps suggested by the work, which he sings over and over. Other songs qualify as work songs because their themes are primarily work themes. Such songs are especially interesting as portrayals of the relation of the worker to his work, his fellow-laborers, and his employer. Still others, because of their rhythmic qualities, are more suited to work that requires regular or rhythmic movement on the part of a worker or group of workers. Strict classification is, of course, impossible, but the songs will be presented in these three general groups.

The first six songs given below are not primarily work songs, but they are especially suited to the moods of the worker. As the Negro goes about his work, thinking of his money and of his "baby," it is no wonder that the following song appeals to him.

BABY'S IN MEMPHIS

Baby's in Memphis layin' around.
Baby's in Memphis layin' around.
Baby's in Memphis layin' around.
Waitin' for de dollah I done found, I done found;
Waitin' for de dollah I done found.

And, very likely, his "baby" gets the dollar. The Negro says that the woman's face is on the dollar because she always gets it away from the man. Still he maintains that there is a limit, and sings further:

I pawn my watch an' I pawn my chain.
Well, I pawn my watch an' I pawn my chain.
I pawn my watch an' I pawn my chain,
An' I pawn ev'ything but my gol' diamon' ring, gol'
    diamon' ring;
An' I ain't goin' to pawn it, my baby, my baby!

JAY GOOZE

The Negro's fondness for the railroad has been noted. "Ridin' de rods" is not only a heroic deed, but an engaging pastime. The work of the railroad stands out as one of the most prominent fields of labor for the Negro. The following verses about Jay Gould are favorites with Negro railroad workers.

> Jay Gooze said-a befo' he died,
> Two mo' roads he wanter ride.
> Ef dere's nuthin' else, goin' ride de rods,
> Goin' to leave all de coppers in de han's of God.

> Jay Gooze said-a befo' he died,
> "Fix de cars so de bums can't ride.
> Ef dey ride, let 'em ride de rods
> An' trust dey lives in de han's o' God."

SATISFIED

The origin of the following jingle is uncertain, but it is admirably suited to the happy-go-lucky mood of the laborer when he is pleased with himself and his work.

> Rich folks worries 'bout trouble,
> Po' folks worry 'bout wealth.
> I don't worry 'bout nuthin';
> All I want's my health.

> Six long months have passed
> Since I have slept in bed.
> I ain't eat a square meal o' vittles in three long weeks
> Money thinks I'm dead.

> But I'm satisfied.
> O yes! I'm satisfied.

> Some one stole a chicken in our neighborhood,
> They 'rested me on suspicion, it was understood.
> They carried me 'fo' de jury—how guilty I did flee.
> 'Cause my name was signed at de head, de jury said
> was me.

I THOUGHT I HAD A FRIEND

As a lonely worker plods along he sometimes becomes philosophical. The Negro often sings his thoughts in a sort of monotone as he works. Perhaps that is how this bit of song originated.

> I thought I had a friend was true;
> Done found out friends wont do.
> It seems to me so awful shame,
> You git confuse over such small thing.

IT'S MOVIN' DAY

For some reason, "Movin' Day" appeals to the Negro worker. Perhaps it is because the song has a swing which fits into his movements, or it may be that the theme is suited to his mood when he is working.

> It breaks my heart to see my baby part,
> And then be left behind,
> An then be left alone, By-bye, my baby!   By-bye!
>
> Pack up my trunk, pack up my trunk an' steal away,
> Pack up your trunk, pack up your trunk an' steal away,
> Oh, it's me an' my darlin' goin' steal away from home.
>
> It's movin' day, it's movin' day,
> I'm natchel-bohn git away,
> I spin ev'y cent—go camp in a tent,
> Lord, it's movin' day!
>
> Well, I jus' can't help from lovin' that baby o' mine,
> I'm crazy 'bout that brown-skin baby o' mine.
>
> I got no use for sleep, I ain't got no use for sleep,
> I hate to feel it upon me creep;
> When I am sleepy, I goes to bed;
> When I am dead, be a long time dead.

WORKMEN'S JINGLES

There are many short songs which the workmen employ. Sometimes they are stanzas from other songs. It is here that full opportunity is given for singing a great number of songs. Fragments of song are easily recalled, and sung again to new circumstances or to the regular kind of work. Most of the rhymes thus sung have their indecent counterpart, and both versions are often sung. Some of the fragments follow.

> Sister Mary, Aunt Jane,
> Whyn't you come along?   Ain't it a shame?
>
> Rabbit on de main line, Coon turn de switches,
> Bull-frog jump from bank to bank.
> Look out!   You tear yo' britches!
>
> If Johnnie was a tumble-bug an' John wus his brother,
> Wouldn't they have a jolly time a-tumblin' together?
>
> That's my brown-skin papa, better leave him alone,
> Because I'll kill you befo' day in the morn.
>
> You cause me to weep, you cause me to mourn,
> You cause me to leave my happy home.
>
> I lef' my home one cold an' rainy day,
> God knows if I ever git back again!
>
> I loved the men befo' my man died,
> Lord, I loved the men befo' my man died.
>
> The day I lef' my mother's house
> Is the day I lef' my home.

GRADE SONG

The "Grade Song" is one of the most typical of all Negro songs. Here may be seen the humor and wit of the Negro workman, and his relation to the "boss." In this song he epitomizes the events of the camp and of the day. It breathes the recklessness of the wanton workman, and shows much of the trend of common thought. It gives the attitude of the Negro and the reply of the "captain" as they are conceived by the workman. No better picture of the Negro workman can be found than that which is reflected in the verses that follow.

> Well, I tole my captain my feet wus cold,
> "Po' water on fire, let wheelers roll!"
>
> Told my captain my han's wus cold.
> "God damn yo' hands, let the wheelers roll!"
>
> Well, captain, captain, you mus' be blin';
> Look at yo' watch!   See ain't it quittin' time?
>
> Well, captain, captain, how can it be?
> Whistles keep a-blowin', you keep a-workin' me.
>
> Well, captain, captain, you mus' be blin';
> Keep a-hollerin' at me, skinners damn nigh flyin'.
>
> Well, I hear mighty rumblin' at water-trough;
> Well, it mus' be my captain an' water boss.
>
> Well, de captain an' walker raise Cain all day;
> Well, captain take a stick, run walker away.
>
> Wasn't dat ter'ble time—so dey all did say—
> When cap'n take hick'ry stick an' run walker away?

Well, I hear mighty rumblin' up in de sky,
Mus' be my Lord go passin' by.

Well, dey makin' dem wheelers on de Western plan,
Dey mos' too heavy for light-weight man.

"Skinner, skinner, you know yo' rule,
Den go to de stable an' curry yo' mule.

"Well, curry yo' mule an' rub yo' hoss,
An' leave yo' trouble wid de stable boss."

Well, if I had my weight in lime,
I'd whip my captain till I went stone-blind.

Well, captain, captain, didn't you say
You wouldn't work me in rain all day?

Well, you can't do me like you do po' Shine,
You take Shine's money, but you can't take mine.

Well, de boats up de river an' dey won't come down,
Well, I believe, on my soul, dat dey's water-boun'.

Well, pay-day comes, and dey done paid off,
I got mo' money dan de walkin' boss.

Well, I got up on level, look as far's I can,
Nuthin' wus a-comin but a big captain.

Well, I went to my dinner at twelve o'clock,
I looked on table; "fohty-fo's" was out.

Get up in mornin' when ding-dong rings,
Look at table—see same damn things.

Oh, Captain Redman, he's mighty damn mean,
I think he come from New Orleans.

The Negro's attitude toward his "captain" is especially distinct. The song represents the kind of conversation the Negroes have at the white man's expense. What does it matter to the "boss" if hands and feet are cold, or if the laborers must work in the rain all day? "On with the work!" is the only reply that the Negro claims is given him. More than anything, the laborer is loath to work a single moment over time. He waits for the minute and stops in the midst of his work, if he be free to do so. If he is restrained, his frown and restlessness show what he is thinking about. Sometimes he works in silence, then bursts out

> You hurt my feelin's, but I won't let on—

then back to silence, resenting the fact that he is worked beyond the time when whistles blow. It is then that he thinks the captain is "mighty damn mean." But the Negro also thinks his captain has great powers, and often boasts of him to other workmen. So in this case his captain gets the better of the fight and runs the "walker" away; but, according to the Negro's conception of things, it must have been a great fight. However, the general tone of the song is one of complaint. The Negro is complaining of his victuals, and shows at the same time his humor. By "forty-fours" he means peas. The combination of scenes with the characteristic imagery makes an unusually typical song.

AIN'T IT HARD TO BE A NIGGER?

Another favorite of the workman, which reveals something of the attitude of the Negro toward the white man, but which the white man rarely has the privilege of hearing, is as follows:

Ain't it hard, ain't it hard,
Ain't it hard, to be a nigger, nigger, nigger?
Ain't it hard, ain't it hard?
For you can't git yo' money when it's due.

Well, it make no difference,
     How you make out yo' time;
White man sho bring a
     Nigger out behin'.

Nigger an' white man
     Playin' seven-up;
Nigger win de money—
     Skeered to pick 'em up.

If a nigger git 'rested,
     An' can't pay his fine,
They sho send him out
     To the county gang.

A nigger went to a white man,
     An' asked him for work;
White man told nigger;
     Yes, git out o' yo' shirt.

Nigger got out o' his shirt
     An' went to work;
When pay-day come,
     White man say he ain't work 'nuf.

If you work all the week,
     An' work all the time,
White man sho to bring
     Nigger out behin'.

PICK-AND-SHOVEL SONG

The "Pick-and-Shovel Song" that follows has many
features of the "Grade Song," and shows the repetition

of form and matter that is so common in all Negro songs. "Holding his head," "going crazy," "killing him dead," and "licker" are common themes.

> Run here, mama! run here, mama!
> Run here an' hold my head, O Lord!
> Run here an' hold my head!
>
> This ole hammer, this ole hammer,
> Lord, it's 'bout to kill me dead, O Lord!
> Lord, it's 'bout to kill me dead.
>
> I'm goin' crazy, I'm goin' crazy,
> Well, corn whiskey gone an' kill me dead, O Lord!
> Corn whiskey gone an' kill me dead.
>
> O Lord, captain, O Lord, captain!
> I don't know what to do, O Lord!
> I don't know what to do.
>
> O Lord, captain, O Lord, captain!
> Well, it's captain, didn't you say, O Lord!
> You wouldn't work me in the rain all day?
>
> Honey baby, honey baby,
> Honey, don't let the bar-room close, O Lord!
> Honey, don't let the bar-room close!
>
> Honey mine, honey mine,
> If de licker's all gone, let me know, O Lord!
> If de licker's all gone, let me know.
>
> My honey babe, my honey babe,
> If you have any good things, save me some, O Lord!
> If you have any good things, save me some.

IF YOU DON'T LIKE THE WAY I WORK

The theme of this song is exactly suited to the sulky mood of a young Negro laborer.

If you don't like the way I work, jus' pay me off.
I want to speak one luvin' word before I go:
I know you think I'm pow'ful easy, but I ain't so sof';
I can git another job an' be my boss.

For they ain't goin' to be no rine,
I'll talk bizness to you some other time,
Watermelon good an' sweet,
Seed's only thing I don't eat,
You can judge from that ain't goin' to be no rine.

LAWDY, LAWDY, LAWDY!

The reckless disposition of the railroad worker is
again reflected in the favorite song of the gang:

Me 'n' my pahdner an' two 'r three mo'
Goin' raise hell 'round pay-cah do'—pay-cah do'.
Goin' ter raise hell 'round pay-cah do!
Lawdy, Lawdy, Lawdy!

It is an interesting spectacle to watch a score of Negro
laborers file into the pay-car to receive their pay. The
eager manner in which they wait, the peculiar expression on each man's face as he enters and returns,
the putting of the money into his pocket and the plans
for spending it, these are all reflected in the typical
scene. In the verse just given, the Negro is represented as being impatient, and threatens to do violence
to the paymaster; or he is boisterous with the knowledge that he will soon have money, and "raise hell"
among his fellows while the crowd waits. Such a
scene is a common one, although most of the rowdyism
is fun.

A HINT TO THE WISE

The suggestiveness in the following stanza is remarkable. The singer prides himself on being a "bad

man," and intends that "a hint to the wise" should be understood as he tells of his former partner. The "sprawlin'" man and the grave are suggestive of the common experiences which may arise among the workmen.

> Don't you remember one mornin'
> In June, about eight o'clock,
> My pahdner fell sprawlin'?
> Dey carried him to his grave—
> I ain't goin' to say how he died.

WELL, SHE ASK ME IN DE PARLOR[1]

While the theme of this song is that of the lover, it is suited, in its technique, to pulling, striking, digging, or any work that calls for long and rhythmic movements of the body. Each line has its regular cæsural pause, at which a stroke is finished and signified by the undertone of the palatal "whuk." The scenes presented in the song are graphic in contrast to the burning sun or the drizzling rain in which the Negro works. The girl and the parlor, the invitation inside, the cool fan, and the affections of the woman for the lover, are vividly portrayed. The dramatic touch in which the refusal brings forth the despair of the "dark-eyed man" touches a characteristic chord; but as usual, the Negro comes out victorious without giving further details. Happily works the dusky figure while he and his companion sing:

Well, she ask me—whuk—in de parlor—whuk,

An' she cooled me—whuk—wid her fan—whuk,

[1] Compare "She Hugged Me and Kissed Me," p. 131, Talley, *Negro Folk Rhymes.*

An' she whispered—whuk—to her mother—whuk,

"Mamma, I love that—whuk—dark-eyed man—whuk."

Well, I ask her—whuk—mother for her—whuk,

An' she said she—whuk—was too young—whuk.

Lord, I wish'd I—whuk—never had seen her,—whuk

An' I wish'd she—whuk—never been bohn—whuk.

Well, I led her—whuk—to the altar—whuk,

An' de preacher—whuk—give his comman'—whuk.

An' she swore by—whuk—God that made her,—whuk

That she never—whuk—love 'nuther man—whuk.

The rhythm of the workers may easily be seen from the metrical scheme of the lines. The cæsural pause is long enough for the laborer to begin a new stroke, and may well be represented by the triseme. There is much freedom in the use of syllables and words in harmony with a single motion. The meter is a common one for the work-song. Sometimes the expression is varied from "whuk" to various kinds of grunts. Sometimes the sound in inarticulate, while again it is only a breath.

THE DAY I LEF' MY HOME

In the next song "huh" is pronounced with a nasal twang, and has almost the sound of "huch." It serves its purpose, and is no more than the expression of the Negro's surplus breath. Here the labor perhaps suggests the home and mother. A spider is seen. And the Negro immediately puts it into his song, then goes gack to his musings on the routine of his daily work.

> The day I lef'—huh—my mother's hous'—huh
> Was the day I lef'—huh—my home—huh.
> O bitin' spider,—huh—don't bite me—huh!
> O bitin' spider,—huh—lawdy, don't bite me!

EARLY IN DE MORNIN'

The next song is that of the mining or railroad camp laborer. Sometimes the pause in the lines is one of silence, and the thought works out the rhythm.

> Early in de mornin',—honey, I'm goin' rise,
> Yes, early in de mornin',—honey, I'm goin' rise,
> Goin' have pick an' shovel—right by my side.
>
> Goin' take my pick an' shovel—goin' deep down in mine.
> I'm goin' where de sun—don't never shine.
>
> Well, I woke up this mornin'—couldn't keep from cryin',
> For thinkin' about—that babe o' mine.
>
> Well, I woke up this mornin',—grindin' on my mind.
> Goin' to grind, honey,—if I go stone-blind.

UNDER THE RAIL

"Under the Rail" expresses the sentiment of the worker, at the same time that it makes a rhythmical work-song. "Lawdy, lawdy, lawdy!" sings the section-hand.

> Under the rail, under the tie,
> Under the rail, under the tie,
> Under the rail, under the tie,
> Whar' yo' dollah lie,
> Whar' yo' dollah lie, whar' yo' dollah lie.

HO–HO

Often the work song is little more than a collection and combination of words and phrases for regular rhythm. A single reference will likely constitute each stanza. Dinner and quitting-time, coming and going and the work of the moment, are the thoughts of the following song. In this case the pause is toward the end of the line, and of longer duration. It may be filled with a word of exclamation, but ordinarily is indicated by the closing of the lips only.

> Ain't it dinner?—ho, ho!
> Ain't it dinner?—tell me so!
>
> Goin' to leave you! Let's go!
> Won't you tell me? Why so!
>
> If I leave you—ho, ho!
> Please don't leave me! Why so?
>
> Well, let's go! I'm right.
> Well, let's go! I'm right.
>
> Good-bye! I'm gone.
> Good-bye! I'm gone.
>
> To the bottom,—ho, ho!
> To the bottom,—ho, ho!

BABY MINE

In the next song, instead of the usual two parts of the line with successive repetitions, there are three, in which the third part almost equals in time the full length of the other two. The designations "baby," "woman," "gal," "girl," are but the ordinary names used in songs and conversation.

If I had it—you could get it,
    B-a-b-y m-i-n-e.

I ain't got it,—an' you can't git it.
    Woman o' mine.

Lord, I'm goin'—away to leave,
    Gal o' mine.

If you mus' go an' leave me,—don't go now,
    My man.

Well, I goin' cross the water,—to my long happy home,
    Poor girl!

I aint got no money,—but will have some,
    Pay-day.

RAISE THE IRON

The foreman of the gang cries out, "Can't you line 'em a little bit?" The leader replies in the affirmative. He then sets the standard, and they all pull together for the desired work. The formula is a good one.

Brother Rabbit, Brother Bear,
Can't you line them just a hair?
Shake the iron, um-uh!

Down the railroad, um-uh!
Well, raise the iron, um-uh!
Raise the iron, um-uh!

Well, is you got it, um-uh!
Well, raise the iron, um-uh!
Raise the iron, um-uh!

Throw the iron, um-uh!
Throw the iron—throw it away!

The real work-song, and that from which many of the Negro songs originally sprang, is the work-song phrase. The formulas by which they "pull together" are often simple expressions of word or phrase originated in communal work. The inventiveness of the Negro working in concert with his fellows is unusually marked. Consequently there is an unlimited number of "heave-a-horas" in his song vocabulary. The "yo-ho" theory may well be applied to the origin of the work-song phrase. Each group of workmen has its leader: the signals are given by him, and the leading part is always sung by him. In the majority of the work-phrases he is the sole singer. Sometimes he resigns to another member of the group, or the several members are designated as leaders in a particular kind of work. A leader ordinarily has at his command several score of appropriate phrases. Not infrequently the act of the moment is put into sound and becomes the work-song; again the natural sound arising from the work may often become the rhythmic force.

GANG-SONGS

Before giving examples that are typical of the exclamations of song in general, the prevalent method of work may be illustrated by typical verses. The rhythm may be obtained from the scansion. A leader waits for the company to pull or push. He says, "Is you ready?" After a slight pause, a second man answers, "Ready!" and the leader continues,

Joe—pick 'em up—he—heavy, pick 'em up,
Joe—he—heavy, pick 'em up,

and so on until the work is finished. Again, he and

his companions are expected to pull a large weight on the rope. They line up with hands holding, ready for the pull. The leader then shouts, "Willie!" they pull out on the first syllable and on the second syllable get the new hold. The leader repeats "Willie" with the same process. He then finishes the rhythm for the hardest pull of the three with "Willie—bully—Willie," in which the double pull is given with one hold on the first "Willie," the new hold on the "bully," and the second pull on the last "Willie." The leader then continues with as many of the periodic phrases as is necessary, using various names to suit his fancy.

Willie! Willie! Willie—bully—Willie!

Mandy! Mandy! Mandy—bully—Mandy!

Janie! Janie! Janie—bully—Janie!

Haul it! haul it! haul it—bully—haul it!

Tear 'em up! tear 'em up! tear 'em up,—bully—tear 'em up!

Thus he sings "Susie," "Patty," "Lizzie," and other names which come to mind. Again, a very similar method, and one that may represent the general habit of using the shorter phrases, is the following. The work may be pulling, pushing, or lifting. The first half of the line serves to give the signal and impetus to the pull; the second is the return stroke.

Won't you pick 'em up—in heaven?

Won't you haul 'em—in heaven?

HEAVE-A-HORAS

The shorter phrases are used in exactly the same way. They will be repeated more often. The tendency is to use the longer expressions when they are more suited to the task at hand, though long and short are freely interchanged. The Negro easily makes a long one out of several short ones. One line may illustrate the time rhythm that is characteristic of them all. In general, the long foot or syllable corresponds to a high note, and the short foot to a lower one. While they pull or work, the leader cries out "Come on, menses!" And while the "menses" come, they work as a machine. The leader repeats this as often as he works, or until he likes another phrase better. As a rule, the leader will use a single phrase an average of ten or fifteen times before passing to another. The examples that follow will indicate the free range which they cover and the ease with which the Negro composes them. It will be seen that there are no strict essentials which must belong to the song: the fitting words may be the invention of the moment. The harmony of the group of the Negroes working on the bridge, the house, the railroad, at the warehouse, or in the mine, is typified by the union of the many simple work-song phrases. They may be studied for themselves. Each line constitutes an entire work-song phrase, complete in itself.

> Hey—slip—slide him—a—slip—slide him.
> Ev'ybody bow down an' put yo' han's to it.
> Come an' go wid me—come an' go wid me.
> Heavy—heavy—heavy—heavy—hank—back.
> All right—all right.
> Draw—back-a—draw—back.

Tear 'em up-a—tear 'em up.
Come hard agin it so.
Break it, boys, break it.
Hike, hike, hike—back.
Come on here.
What's a matter—fagged out?
What's a matter'—white-eyed?
What's a matter—monkey got you?
Haul it—haul it back.
Here—yeah—here, you.
Turn—turn it—turn her on.
Let's turn 'em over.
Turn it one mo' time.
How about it?
Knock down on it.
Up high wid it, men.
Get up—get it up—any way to git it up.
Yonder she go.
Put yo' nugs on it.
Lay yo' hands on it.
Put 'im up on it.
Get up, Mary,
Hello—hello—hello!
Yang 'em—Yang 'em.
Hy, Captain, too heavy here.
Hold it, boys, till I come.
Now, let's go, bullies.
Hold—hold—hold.
Once—more—boys.
Little—lower—down.
'Way—up—'way—up.
Go ahead—go ahead.
H-e-y—h-e-y—h-e-y.
Draw—back—on it.
Do—fare—you—well.
Here—you—tight—white—eye.
Jump—up—jump—now.
Get—up—dere—last—down.
Ev'y—quack—d-o-w-n.

Bow—down—back—up—back—off.
Whack—man—a-l-l.
P-r-i-z-e—em.
Hit—'em—hit—'em—high.
Whoa—Reuben.
Whoa—head—pull 'em—a—little—over—there.
Git back on de right side now.
Drive—drive—drive.
Pull 'em over jus' a hair.
Jack 'em up, men.

Many of these exclamations in time become connected, and make more distinct songs. The songs that are given in couplets are of this type. Each couplet represents, as a rule, four parts, each line two divisions, each division a single phrase like those just given. The process is a natural one. The technique is often not as clearly noticeable as in the following railroad phrase:

Ole aunt Dinah—has a garden—
On one side—is sweet pertaters—
On other side—good ripe termaters,
      H-o-l-d—h-o-l-d!

A single glance, however, shows that each line is naturally divided into two periods, each of which makes an effective work-phrase. So in the following:

H-i-g-h-t, red bird flyin' 'round here,
Monkey sho gwine git somebody;
See 'im wid his tail turned up.
      H-o-l-d—h-o-l-d!

I broke down on de beam so long,
Till I done lost de use o' my right arm.

Come on, menses, let's pick up the iron,
Ain't it heavy all de time?

Up to my lips, down let her slips,
Where many quarts an' gallons go.

In the same way each particular kind of work may
suggest a special form of the phrase or verse. The
Negroes loading the vessels, as they rush past each
other with the freight and jeer at each other, sing,
"Git out of de way dere!" "Git 'cross de way!" "Git
to yo' place!" "Talk to me-e!" "Oh, yes! time ain't
long!" "O-o-h cross over, young man!" "O-o me-
babe!" and other exclamations differing only slightly
from the common laborer's phrases. The Negro
specializes his songs whenever he desires. Their
flexibility and his imagery and taste are not discordant.

With the Negro, then, song helps work and work
helps song. Whether he sings to unburden his soul
of feelings which threaten to overwhelm him, whether
he sings to keep his mind off his work, or whether he
sings to "help him with his work," his creations are
evidence enough that he is a real artist.

CHAPTER IX

IMAGERY, STYLE, AND POETIC EFFORT

A Story-teller. The Negro's skill as a story-teller is well known. He has unusual power to project dramatic scenes into his story and to portray the more ordinary pictures with becoming contrast. One listens to the Negro story-teller and sees what he tells about. The songs of the Negro embody this ability to a large degree; much has already been said concerning the Negro's visualization. The concreteness of the pictures and the vividness of his imagination make his songs a reality. The songs and verses which have been given show better than any discussion the mental imagery of the Negro. Every line stands for its own striking imagery. Nevertheless an effort will be made to review some of the most characteristic examples as they are found in his songs. No attempt will be made to enumerate even a large part of the detailed illustrations; to do so would be to enumerate the great majority of words and lines that occur in the Negro songs. However, the visualization, the rhyming dynamics of his mental imagery, and the tendency toward rhymed expression will prove both interesting and instructive.

The Negro's Descriptive Art. The Negro not only sees objects and persons clearly, but he makes others see what he himself sees. His pictures stand out in bold relief; they are painted on appropriate backgrounds. The total impression, be it serious or ludicrous, is formed with unchangeable definiteness. A number of typical word-pictures are given promiscuously below. A simple experiment will show the ability of the Negro to visualize and at the same time offer pleasant entertainment. Let each stanza be taken separately and read; let the impression be formed quickly and the extent of the completeness of the mental picture ascertained with exactness. Then compare this with the actual scene described and see with what unerring power the picture has been forced upon the mind. It may well be ventured that such imagery cannot be surpassed.

> Judge an' jury all in de stan',
> Great big law books in deir han'.

> Clothes all dirty, ain't got no broom,
> Ole dirty clothes all hangin' in de room.

> Ask me to de table, thought I'd take a seat,
> First thing I seed wus big chunk o' meat.

> Carried po' bully to cemetery, people all standin' round,
> When de preacher say amen, lay po' body down.

> Policemens all dressed in blue,
> Comin' down the sidewalk two by two.

> Standin' on de corner, didn't mean no harm,
> Policeman grab me by my arm.

> Went down to country to see my frien',
> In come yaller dog burnin' the win'.

> Went to sea, sea look so wide,
> Thought about my babe, hung my head an' cried.

> Railroad Bill mighty bad man,
> Shoot dem lanterns out'n de brakeman's han'.

Went up town Friday night—went to kill a kid,
Reach my han' in my pocket—nuthin' to kill him wid.

All de wimmins come to town all dressed in red,
When dey heard dat bully was dead.

All he want is water an' coal,
Poke his head out window, see drivers roll.

I pull out my gun an' begin to fire,
Shot that bully right through the eye.

Satisfied, tickled to death,
Got a bottle of whiskey on my shelf.

Went up town wid my hat in my hand,
"Good mornin' judge, done killed my man."

Goin' have hump on my back, so many chickens in my
    sack,
Big hounds on my track, never did look back.

Well I woke up this mornin' by city clock bell,
Niggers up town givin' cocaine hell.

Carried him off on hoo-doo wagon,
Brought him back wid his feet a draggin'.

Turn me over Lilly, turn me over slow,
May be las' time, I don't know.

Said to jailer how can I sleep?
All 'round my bedside policemens creep.

Again, the reader has already formed a definite opinion
of Stagolee's appearance from

Stagolee, Stagolee, what's dat in yo' grip?
Nuthin' but my Sunday clothes, I'm goin' to take a trip.
Stagolee, Stagolee where you been so long?
I been out on battle field shootin' an' havin' fun.

And "everybody knowed when dey see Stagolee comin' to give Stagolee de road." Likewise he has the "bully" appearance when he tells his wife good-bye, when he goes out of the house with a smoking gun and when he lays the man on the floor with "dat same ole fohty-fo'."

One but needs to recall the many pictures portrayed in the spirituals to see that the Negro's imagery is even more vivid in his religious state of feeling than at other times. There is place for only a reference to them.

> Well you ought to been dere to see de sight,
> People's come runnin' both cullud an' white.

> Upon mountain Jehobah spoke,
> Out of his mouth come fire an' smoke.

> Where was Ezekiel when de church fell down?
> Down in de valley wid his head hung down.

> Ezekiel said he spied de train a comin',
> We got on board an' she never stopped runnin'.

> Sometimes I hangs my head an' cries,
> But Jesus gwine to wipe my weepin' eyes.

> Some o' dese mornin's bright an' fair,
> Gwine to hitch my wings an' try de air.

No more vivid scenes have been portrayed than the descriptions of heaven and hell. The grandeur of the golden streets and the terrors of the dark and the dismal place stand out strong and clear. The walking and talking with the Lord and with Jesus, the seeing of the angels and the eating of good things while eternal rest obtains are unmistakably bright pictures.

Likewise the description of the devil and the Lord, of the judgment and the resurrection are unequaled. If one wishes to realize the full force of the descriptions let him turn back and read them. The Negro asks:

> What's dat yonder dat I see?

and answers with truthfulness,

> Big tall angel comin' after me,

and speaks truly when he says, "Dem pooty angels I shall see," for he already sees them. So it is with the long white robes and starry crowns and golden slippers which he longs to realize in a tangible form. His natural vivid imagination is heightened by his religious fervor and excitement.

Descriptive phrases. It will be observed that the Negro's imagery is assisted in its expression by the use of suitable adjectives and phrases. A word which would ordinarily mean little or nothing if used alone becomes a concrete picture when connected with the adjective or phrase; and it is the happy combination that gives the Negro his advantages. Childlike thoughts employ adjectives that give the most direct and present description. The following phrases illustrate typical word pictures:

> Big hounds.
>
> Great big law books.
>
> Great big 'possum.
>
> Great big nigger jes black as tar.

Po' boy long way from home.

Brown-skin man.

Luvin' man o' mine.

That easy-going man o' mine.

Nowhere to lay my weary head.

Bad man, bully man, Desperado Bill.

A luvin' dime.

A bad man, bad as hell, I know.

Ole corn whiskey.

One finish' fight.

Jet-black gal.

Coolin' board.

Hoo-doo wagon.

Fallin' den.

Dyin' day.

Dancin' shoes.

You sho lookin' warm.

Boozy an' foolish 'bout her head.

Brown-skin woman, chocolate to de bone.

Listening in. There are also many auditory images and they are not less distinct and concrete than are the visual ones. The Negro hears his Lord "a-calling" to him; he hears "his Jesus" speaking to him. He hears his Lord "a-rumblin' in the sky"; he hears Gabriel blow his trumpet and he hears the tombstones bursting. He hears the sinners crying and calling and he hears the thunder rolling. He hears the angels shouting and he hears Satan stumbling. He is alert, quick, his eyes strained to gain new visions, his ears tuned to catch every sound; and he applies these to himself as well as to the future state. He sings, too,

> I'm goin' to heaven on eagle's wing,
> All don't see me goin' to hear me sing.

Could he combine sight and hearing for a more vivid picture? Again the Negro has unusual powers for picturing the sound of the running train; he hears its whistle and its bell, he hears the puffing of the engine and sees the fireman putting in the coal. He hears the ringing of the "city clock bell" and the noise of the throng of Negroes up-town. Indeed, he can *hear* as well as he can see.

> Thought I heard that K. C. whistle blow,
> Blow lak she never blow befo!
>
> Wake up, ole rounder, it's time to go,
> Thought I heard dat whistle blow.
>
> Captain, captain, how can it be,
> Whistles keep blowin', you keep a-workin' me?
>
> Heard a mighty rumblin' in de sky,
> Mus' be my Lord a passin' by.
>
> Heard a rumblin' at de water trough,
> Mus' be my captain an' water boss.

Me'n my pahdner an' two'r three mo',
Goin' raise hell 'round pay car do'.

Git up in mornin' when ding-dong rings,
Look on table, same ole things.

I hate to hear my honey call my name,
Call me so lonesome an' so sad.

I heard such a knockin' at mu do',
Such a knockin' as I never heard befo'.

Personalities. Again, the Negro visualizes persons
with accurate and vivid portrayal. Whoever is mentioned in his song stands out a distinct figure. The
place he occupies and the thoughts associated with him
give him distinctness of some sort. The partial analysis of
the religious songs showed the prominence given to
the scriptural characters. Moses and Abraham, Ezekiel and Isaiah, Peter and John, Mary and Martha,
together with the others are pictured in no uncertain
terms. Jehovah, Jesus, Lord, and the devil are the
chief personages; the Father and Son are magnified.
The angels, too, are given conspicuous places. So,
too, the sinner, the gambling and dancing man, the
hypocrite and the mourner, the preacher, brothers, and
sisters occupy prominent places in the old spirituals.
In the secular songs personages occupy less prominence
in the total of song; the Negro has no celebrities to
sing, no heroes to praise, save the notorious character.
The latter is given due prominence; he is described
and visualized with skill. But for the most part the
characters are indefinite personages depicted with
definite characteristics. The secular songs tell of the
jailer, the captain, the judge, the police, the sheriff,

the bartender, the doctor, the engineer. They sing of the eastman, the rounder, the hobo, the bum, the creeper, the bully. The lover, and the "babies" and "honeys," the father and mother, the mother-in-law, and the brother-in-law make the list almost complete. "Marster" and "Missus" occur only occasionally.

Time and Place. Time and place for the Negro have both a definite and an indefinite significance. With him long years are "as a watch in the night." There is no time unity in his songs; he may as easily shift the place of action from one locality to another as to follow its unity. However, in each picture itself, both time and place are distinct. The Negro remembers the time and the exact circumstance that his imagery paints for that moment. In the secular songs time is almost always in the past; in the religious song it is often in the future. The present is of little importance with the Negro. He sees time with his eyes closed. "Three long weeks" he visualizes, "since I et a good square meal"; "six long months since I have slept in bed." But most of the events are sung in the recent past. It is the "last week," or "last Friday night," or Tuesday, Saturday or Sunday night. "Last night and the night before," "the day I left my home," "since you been gone," "so long, so long" and similar designations are most common. "All night long" and "all day" or "all the time" and "all yo' time" are expressive of the common conception of time. The Negro thus has a general standard of designation rather than an exact measurement; but his imagery transposes each into its proper visual setting. With the religious song, time is mostly looking toward the judgment day and the time for the

sinner to die; time is "when." "What you gwine do
when de devil git yo?" certainly has the time element
and is most assuredly vivid enough for the singer, but
he has no idea when it is. It is looking backward to
the time when "the Lord done set me free" and forward to the "promised land." Further than this, there
is little designation of time. The crucifixion of Christ,
the weeping and mourning of Mary and Martha, the
drinking of the wine and the praying in the wilderness
are but emblematic of the ideal of the future pro-
jected from the past.

In the place relations, it is either hell or the utopian
future, with little of the former; or the place designated is that where a religious experience of the
singer or a saint has occurred. On the mountain, in
the valley, beyond the Jordan, at the pool, in the prison,
on the sea are historical places that lead to the vivid
conception of a moment which is suddenly transposed
into the present or future. For vividness and rapid-
ity of shifting scenes, the Negro singer is hard to
beat. Much the same is true in the secular songs
where general designations are indicated. But in-
asmuch as his earthly songs deal more with earthly
localities, there must necessarily be a difference in the
visualization of places. Here the Negro is at once in
his home and on the road; both here and there and
anywhere. "If you don't find me in Atlanta, go to
Larkey's dance; if you don't find me at Larkey's
dance, come to sweet Birmingham," and so on. There
is no Southern state in which his scenes are not laid
ad libitum. And the towns most commonly known by
the Negroes are most often sung; the Negro localizes
everything when he desires to do so. The same

ability with which he adapts and composes new songs suggests that the scene may be effectively and rapidly changed; indeed it is scarcely a time process. New Orleans, Atlanta, Birmingham and Memphis are favored cities; Arkansas, Alabama, Tennessee, Georgia, and Mississippi are the favorite states. Altogether the Negro's imagery of places is much like that of time; the place *may* be anywhere before he designates the word; when once designated, it becomes that very moment an exact concrete picture. The place matters little in the effectiveness of the picture; the circumstances of the moment make the occasion, but when once the occasion is associated with the place, that place is for the moment fixed. Again, the superlative of a heightened imagery is evident.

The Dominant Self. Feeling, emotions, and mental imagery of unusual vividness combined with the Negro's expressiveness give rise to a very natural spontaneity. If the Negro visualizes with unusual power, is it not because he puts himself into the process naturally and unreservedly? The self-feeling is strong in his pictures. The individual plays the most important part and the singer is most generally the subject or the object of the action concerning which he sings. "I" and "my" are the keynotes to the great majority of situations. Next to the first person, "you" follows prominently; but it will be seen that the second person is ordinarily only the object-relation of the first person. "You" must do something, but it is either something that "I" have done, think you ought to do, or something that you must do in order to understand what "I" now understand. One need only glance at the religious song, to get an idea of the importance of the first person in all actions.   The Negro sings:

> *I'm* goin' to heaven an' *I* don't want to stop,
> An' *I* don't want to be no stumblin' block.
>   All *my* sins done taken away.

> *I* went down in de valley to pray;
> *My* soul got happy an' *I* stayed all day.

> *I'm* goin' to ride on mornin' train,
> All don't see *me* goin' to hear *me* sing.

> *I* wouldn't be sinner, tell you the reason why;
> God might call *me* an wouldn't be ready to die.

> Ever since *my* Lord done set *me* free,
> This ole worl' been a hell to *me*.

> *I* went down in de valley, *I* fell upon *my* knees,
> *I* begged an' cried for pardon, de Lord did give *me* ease.

And so it is throughout the entire mass of religious songs.   In the secular song the first personal pronoun seems even more prominent than in the spirituals. The third person and the circumstances do not exist except as the singer sees them; as in the religious song the second person is used only in its relation to the first.   One needs only to suggest the songs themselves in order to recall the imagery of the singer.   "I'm po' boy long way from home," "I ain't gotta friend in this world," "I talk to my babe all night long," "I got up in the mornin', couldn't keep from cryin', thinkin' 'bout that brown-skin man o' mine," "I got de blues but too damn mean to cry," "I wus goin' down railroad," "I'm lookin' for de bully boy," "I'm gamblin' for my honey," "If I had listened to what my mommer said," "If I die in Arkansas," and almost innumerable similar references to the first person show that the visualization reflects the same concrete imagery that has been observed elsewhere.

Contrast and Antithesis. The colloquial style of the Negro's song language is but a reflection of his imagery. For the Negro there is largely himself and the other person. He is telling something to somebody or he is asking something or commanding and advising something. The conversational tone prevails in general throughout the songs. Thus it is that the second person assists the first person in the completion of the image. Thus in the religious songs:

> You oughter been dere to see the sight.

> What you gwine do when de devil git you?

> You better git ready, I believe.

> You may talk about me just as you please.

> Don't let this harvest pass, do you die an' go to hell.

> Mind how you walk on de cross, you' foot may slip an' yo' soul git lost.

> Lay down yo' sinful ways.

> Where are you going?

> Why does you tarry?

> You must have that true religion.

> Go an' tell it on the mountain.

There is much admonition and feeling of superiority on the part of the "I" over the "you" in the religious

songs.   In the secular songs, there is less of this spirit
and more of the inter-relation between the singer and
the person spoken to.   For instance, the atmosphere
of the following colloquies reflects the general attitude:

> You brought me here and threw me down.

> Tell yo' baby good-bye.

> If you don't want me, please don't dog me 'round.

> Ain't no use for you tryin' to send me 'round.

> You sho lookin' warm.

> You broke de heart o' many a girl, but you never will
> break dis heart o' mine.

Just as the "I" stands out in the contrast to the
"you," so the common imagery often depicts scenes
in antithesis to each other.   The contrast of scenes is
a favorite portrayal with the Negro; he thus visualizes the two at once.   Satan thought he had me,
but I broke his chains and am free at last; Satan threw
a block at the mourner and thought it would hit him,
but "the rock for hell an' me for heaven."   Again,

> You can hinder me here, *but* you *can't* hinder me dere.
> You may talk about me jus' as you please,
> *But* I goin' talk 'bout you when I git on my knees.

> When I wus a sinner I loved my distance well,
> *But* when I come to know myself was standin' over hell.

> God don't talk like a natural man,
> *But* he talk so man can understan'.

Well I may be sick an' cannot rise,
But I meet you at de station when de train comes by.

You take Shine's money, *but you can't* take mine.

Carried him to cemetery, *but failed* to bring him back.

Hattie don't love me, *but* Esther do.

Yellow girl I do despise,
But a jet black girl I can't denies.

Conditional Sentences.   Very similar to the antithesis just mentioned is that which the Negro makes with his conditional clauses. He imagines that, whereas his condition or the situation is one thing now, it would be another *if* other circumstances prevailed. Both the ideal and the unreal are expressed in the conditional sentences most common:

If I had my weight in gold
I'd have the women under my control.

If I had my weight in lime.
I'd beat my captain all the time.

If I had er died when I wus young,
I would not had dis risk to run.

If you want to go to heaven when you die,
Jus' stop yo' tongue from tellin' lies.

If you wan' to dream dem heavenly dreams,
Lay yo' head on Jordan's stream.

If I had listened to what mamma said,
I would a been at home in mamma's bed.

Descending Rhythm and Flourish.   No picture for the Negro is complete without its finishing flourish.

This may be in the nature of rhythm and music alone, or it may be the insertion of words and phrases at the end of the lines in which the imagery reaches its climax. Often the last stroke of his brush resembles the wiping off of the colors rather than an integral part of the picture. Thus Stagolee is represented as being in several positions, but after each the Negro sings, "O dat man, bad man, Stagolee done come," or some other similar phrase. So it is with Railroad Bill and the other "bullies." It would seem that the desire for harmonizing pause and imagery needs the chorus line or exclamation for its completion. The Negro tells a story and adds, "Ain't I a story-teller? Lawd! Lawd!"; he sings a song but feels that he is "sho God a songster." He dances a jig, but ends it gracefully with a "swing-corner" motion of his leg, or a sweep of arms and body. In other words, the descending rhythm is not only necessary, but also incorporates in it the tendency toward recklessness and gives polish to the final scene or thought. Take some typical choruses in the Negro songs for further illustration:

> Take yo' time, take yo' time.
> 'Tain't nobody's bizness but my own.
> Yet, I ain't bother, yet, I ain't bother yet.
> Learn me to let all women alone.
> O my babe, won't you come home?
> O me, O my, baby, what have I done?
> O my baby, O my baby, honey babe.
> Ain't goin' ter rain no mo'.
> Sorry, sorry, can't be yo' warbler any mo'.
> Stagolee done kill dat bully now.
> Wus lookin' fer Railroad Bill.
> I'm lookin' fer de bully of this town.

It's one mo' rounder gone.
My man certainly got to treat me right.
Lawd, Lawd, Lawd.
Baby, let the deal go down.
Shout to glory, Lord, you shall be free.

In the religious songs the chorus represents more unity in its relation to the main theme of the religious thought. The chorus line itself, however, is not ordinarily of kindred meaning to the individual stanzas of many of the songs. Here the chorus serves rather to assist in the music and rhythm than to assist the imagery of the song. Except for the feeling imagery, the chorus of the spirituals represents only a satisfaction gained from the sense of fitness in sound and words. The chorus is often half of the song, in which case an exception to the rule follows. For instance the Negro sees a very distinct picture in "Dere's one, dere's two, dere's three little angels."

Exclamation and Variation. What the chorus line is to the stanza, the added exclamations and interjections are to the line. The same effort at finishing the picture as it is felt by the Negro is seen in the insertion of many words at the beginning of a line or stanza and at the end. Some illustrations of this tendency have been given. The Negro sings a "one-verse" song, making the stanza consist of the line repeated four times; but it is almost imperative with him that he add at the beginning of the last repetition or at the end of all some such word as "oh," "O my," or "well." Likewise such an expression is often added at the end of the second and third lines, leaving the first and fourth free. The most common words thus used are: well, yes, and, it's, say, said, yet, Lord

babe, baby, O my babe, honey, sho God, and for.
To illustrate further:

> Standin' on de corner, didn't mean no harm.
> Policeman grab me by de arm,
> Wus lookin' for Railroad Bill.

Now in the last line he may sing either, "Wus lookin'
for Railroad Bill," or simply "Lookin' for Railroad
Bill." Again he may sing it, as indeed he does do
often, "Says he wus lookin' for Railroad Bill." In
each case the imagery is slightly different and the
Negro loves to make the variation. As has been
indicated, the skillful variation which the singer gives
to verses of his song makes his repetition pleasant
rather than tiring. In the strict sense of the word,
the Negro never repeats. Sometimes the variation
is in music and tone, sometimes it is in dialect, while
again it is in the form of the added words just given.
In the last illustration, when he sings, "Says he wus
lookin' fer Railroad Bill," the Negro sees an additional
scene of himself pleading innocent and the explanation of the policeman that he had mistaken him for
Bill. This added imagery is easily but character-
istically made by the simple insertion of the extra
words.

Onomatopoetic Words. There are fewer onomatopoetic words and lines than would be expected of the
Negro. While many of his work-song phrases arise
from the natural-sound process, there are comparatively few words that manifestly have their origin
in the sound of the object represented. However, the

Negro's imagery often combines rhythmic words into phrases that certainly imitate the sound represented in the verse.   Reference has already been made to the railroad songs with the accompanying music. This is undoubtedly one of the most effective of the natural-sound combinations.   But such songs are mostly instrumental; the words do not attempt the imitation of the train except in perhaps accidental cases and as they are combined with the music.   The slow singing of "When de train come along I meet you at de station, when de train come along" seems to contain the principal conception embodied in the sound of the train.   So, too, "Slow train run through Arkansas, carryin' Eddy Jones" is sung to the funeral chant that might perhaps be represented in the *slow train*; at least the Negro often conceives it so.   Again, in "Thought I heard dat K. C. whistle *blow, blow* lak she never *blow befo'*," the Negro clearly hears the train "blow" and puts the sound into his singing. Other efforts are:

Hear de car wheel rollin' an' a rumblin' through the lan'.

Hearse wheel rollin' an' graveyard openin'!

Rain keep a droppin'!

Lightning flashin' an' thunder rolling and roaring.

Ship's a reelin' an' a rockin'.

This ole worl's a reelin' an' a rockin'.

When the ding-dong sounds.

Rapped on do', do' was locked.

Swing an' clang an' don't get lost.

Come wid a fohty links o' chain.

She made a whoop, she made a squall.

Gun say "blop," hog say "slip."

Rhyme and Rhythm. Enough has been said concerning the characteristic verses of the Negro's songs
to indicate the nature of the dynamics of his mental
imagery. The unconscious effort toward rhyme may
almost be termed a tropism. The satisfaction derived from the visualizing, hearing, and pronouncing
of big-sounding words may be more than euphonistic;
it may be called "megaphonistic." It is not only
rhythm which the Negro seeks in his verses, but rhyme
also. The rhyme is undoubtedly one of the essentials
to rhythm. Rhyme helps motion, motion makes
harmony, and harmony completes the rhythm of his
music. Not only this, but rhyme is an essential to
the full expression of the rhythmic feeling and it
assists the imagery. Negroes remember many verses
by the rhyme rather than by the meaning; but they
must get into the swing before they can recall the song.
The successful recalling of the first line invariably
suggests the other if it be rhymed. Rhymed verses
are essentially pleasure-giving to the singer. Besides, he often creates unusual pictures because his
effort at rhyme has led him to introduce a word not
logically connected with the sense. Some of the
characteristics of the Negro's song and verse may
serve to illustrate further the natural dynamics of his
imagery.

In view of the Negro's unconscious effort at

pleasure-giving expressions and his conscious attempts to make fastidious rhymes, it is not surprising to find many of his verses devoted more to sound than to meaning. In general, the verses which are the most extreme in their sacrifice of sense for the rhyme, may be divided into two groups: those which are, from the beginning, nothing more than efforts at rhyme, regardless of particular meaning, and those which have the first line containing an appropriate thought, with the second line simply finishing the rhyme regardless of the resultant meaning. It would be well to review the most typical rhymes with a view to their special features; they are too numerous to repeat at this point. However, the following rhymed couplets will illustrate these characteristics. When one notes the sense and rhymes in the following lines and remembers that they are inserted along with other verses which have no similar meaning, the effort toward a satisfying rhyme will be apparent. These should be compared, of course, with similar examples among other folk and among children.

> Went down to the country to see my friend,
> In come yaller dog burnin' the wind.

> I'm goin' to Happy Holler,
> Where I can make a dollar.
> Don't care if I don't make a dollar,
> So I wear my shirt an' collar.

> Women in Kansas all dressed in red,
> Come to town when dey heard Casey wus dead.

> When you kill a chicken save me the feet.
> When you think I'm workin' I'm walkin' the street.

> Whilst you're sittin' on your seat,
> Let me tell you something that's sweet.

In the next examples it will be observed that the first line of the couplet constitutes an original part of the song; it has sense and is logically connected with the other stanzas. But a single line is not enough; it must be rhymed. The favorite song "On a Hog" has the line "I didn't come here to be nobody's dog," and this, with the others is ordinarily repeated three times for a stanza. While one Negro was singing this, another who was standing by interrupted by saying that he knew another verse to the song. He then added: "I didn't come here to be nobody's dog, Jus' come here to git off dat hog." The verse was accepted as a better one. Thus it is with many others. For example, in

> If I had a listened to what my mama said,
> *I would a been at home in mama's bed,*

the original verses were, "If I had-a listened to what my mommer said, I wouldn't a been here to-day." The rhyme was made from the first line and easily displaced the earlier line. So again, in the one-verse song of the "K. C." song, the Negro has boarded the train and it moves only too slowly for him. He says, "Fireman, put in a little mo' coal," and "Fireman, ain't we livin' high?" The time comes when a rhyme is wanted and the Negro has added the needed line:

> Fireman, put in a little mo' coal,
> Run this ole engine in some lonesome hole.
> Fireman, ain't we livin' high?
> See them trees a passin' by?

Metric License. Such are the characteristics of the Negro's rhymes. It will be expected that he is not particular about the meter of his verse. Long lines are coördinate with short ones and long words or phrases scanned exactly as the shorter words. This may be called a prolonged rhyme, in which the Negro's imagery sees the rhyming element before he pronounces the final syllables. Accordingly his versatile prosody permits him to extend the line at will. Note the following lines, comparing the short and long verses metrically:

> Some give you a nickel, some give you a dime.
> I ain't goin' to give you a red copper cent for you ain't
> no girl o' mine.

> I begged the judge to lower my baby's fine,
> He said the judge done fined her an' the clerk done wrote
> it down.

> I love my babe an' wouldn't put her out of doors.
> I'd love to see her kill a kid wid fohty-dollar suit o'
> clothes.

> Goin' to buy me railroad of my own,
> Ain't goin' to let nobody ride but the chocolate to the
> bone.

> Went to de sea, sea look so wide,
> Thought about my babe, hung my head an' cried.

> Stagolee was a bully man' an ev'ybody knowed
> When dey seed Stagolee a comin' to give Stagolee de road.

> Six long months have passed
>   Since I have slept in bed.
> I ain't et a square meal o' vittels in three long weeks;
>   Money thinks I'm dead.

Captain, captain, you mus' be blin'!
Look at yo' watch an' see ain't it quittin' time.

The Negro thus employs synizesis in its freest usage. He not only makes two syllables count for one in the metrical unit, but he freely crowds more than one word into a single time measure.

The same flexibility of verse and imagery leads to the free omission of pronouns and conjunctions. Asyndeton is most marked in the habitual omission of the first personal pronoun and of common connectives, but it is not restricted to any words. Indeed nouns and verbs, adjectives and pronouns are often expressed only in their context; so the prepositions and sign of the infinitive are regularly omitted. Typical asyndeton may be illustrated by a few characteristic examples. The majority of the songs have for their subject the first person. Yet almost ninety per cent of the subject pronouns are thus omitted in common colloquial song. Note the application further in the songs themselves; so it is with other omissions. Entire phrases are abbreviated with a single word which expresses the meaning. The imagery is not weakened by this habit, but seems to be peculiarly strengthened. In the following typical illustrations of the most common forms of asyndeton the words habitually omitted are placed in parenthesis.

(I) Went up town (one) Friday night,
(I) Went to kill a kid.
(I) Reach my hand into my pocket,
(There was) Nuthin' to kill him wid.

(I) Went to de window an' peeped in,
(There was) Somebody in my fallin' den.

I ('ve) got a husband, (an') sweetheart, too;
(If) Husband don't love me, (my) sweetheart do.

I'm goin' back to (the) Sunny South,
Where (the) sun shines on my honey's house.

I wish some ole train would run,
(To) Carry me back where I come frum.

I wish that ole engineer was dead,
(That) Brought me away from my home.

Central, gimme long distance phone,
(I want to) Talk to my baby all night long.

(I'm a) Good ole boy, jus' ain't treated right.

Vowel Rhymes. As one would naturally expect, rhyme has mainly to do with vowels rather than with the entire word. The Negro tends to pronounce many words with final consonants silent. The final letters of a word need not affect his rhyme if the vowels be similar. A glance at the rhymed words in the Negro's verse shows the same license here as in other features of his song. It is true that a great many words are skillfully and accurately rhymed; they are naturally fitted to the sound of words with which they are intended to rhyme. Such words as *sight* and *white*, *snares* and *prayers*, *pole* and *roll*, *track* and *back*, *sure* and *pure*, *clay* and *stay*, *side* and *wide*, *spoke* and and *smoke*, *road* and *load*, *sky* and *nigh*, *cries* and *eyes*, *go* and *blow*, *fall* and *wall*, *shout* and *out*, *shake* and *quake*, *letter* and *better*, *sold* and *told*, *glad* and *had*, *slain* and *stain*, *race* and *place*, *out* and *about*, *night* and *sight*, *use* and *confuse*, and scores of others are rhymed together with no unusual features save that of the context. More irregular are the words in the following list. The words in each line have the same value for sound in rhyme.

stop—block—top
young—run
redeemed—stream—dreams
laugh—last—path—past
mourned—throne—gone—stone
sing—train—wing—ring—vain
valley—happy
long—on—Lord—strong—song
along—no one—alone—own—foam—down—home—
    bone—done
name—shame—chain
first—earth—birth
more—before—so—know—sure (sho)—door—go—floor
nine—shine—behind—mind—divine
time—mind—line—sign—nine
seen—sin
hell—wealth—farewell—well—tell
son—run—from
late—shake—gate
man—lamb—hand—understand—land
mourn—gone—horn—done
talk—fault
shoes—pool—goose
cares—fears—prayers
Christ—advice—twice—life—wife
fixed—tricks
while—child—beguiled—hide—strife
long—phone
friend—thin—wind
clock—locked
South—house
doors—clothes
back—like—track.

So also regularly rhymed together are,

>   world—girl
>   fine—time
>   hollow—dollar
>   dime—mine
>   side—five
>   nine—time—kind
>   sport—coat
>   found—down
>   shirt—work
>   whang—thing
>   North—off
>   wagon—dragging
>   yard—rod
>   come—run

Many of the groups of words in the foregoing list have no common rhyme values when pronounced correctly, but the Negro singer gives them exactly the shading or intonation needed to complete his rhyme. The listener is rarely ever aware of clashing sounds or forced rhymes, so skillfully does the singer harmonize his words.

Thus it appears that in the songs of the Negro one of the elemental drives is the pleasure obtained from the construction of rhythmic rhymes. Great as his descriptive powers are, they are secondary. In fact, a striking descriptive phrase often finds expression only because the Negro stumbled upon it in his quest for rhyme. He omits words and even phrases in order that he might have the satisfaction of bringing rhymed words into proper relationship. He stretches short lines and speeds through long ones in order to come out in perfect time with the pat of his foot or the rhythm of his guitar. He assigns the same rhyme value to words of vastly different sound value; and he even makes jingles of lines that are positively lacking in sense connection. It is true that he has many verses which are not rhymed, but it is also very likely true that such verses are unstable and will undergo various transformations until some singer chances upon a satisfactory rhyme. If the new verse combines sense and rhyme, well and good. If the sense does not adjust itself, so much the worse for it. Rhyme and rhythm must survive.

SELECT BIBLIOGRAPHY OF NEGRO FOLK SONGS

BOOKS

ALLEN, W. F., and others, *Slave Songs of the United States*. New York, 1867. Words and music of 136 songs are given.

ARMSTRONG, M. F., *Hampton and Its Students*. New York, 1874. Fifty plantation songs.

Cox, J. H., *Folk Songs of the South*. Harvard University Press, 1924. Most of these songs are songs of the whites of the mountains, but they are particularly valuable in that they throw light on the origin of many Negro songs.

FENNER, T. P., *Religious Folk Songs of the American Negro*. Hampton Institute Press, 1924. (Arranged in 1909 by the Musical Directors of Hampton Normal and Industrial Institute from the original edition by Thomas P. Fenner. Reprinted in 1924.) This volume contains the words and music of 153 religious songs.

FENNER, T. P., and RATHBUN, F. G., *Cabin and Plantation Songs*. New York, 1891. Old Negro plantation songs with music.

HARRIS, JOEL CHANDLER, *Uncle Remus, His Songs and Sayings*. New York, 1880. Nine songs.

HARRIS, JOEL CHANDLER, *Uncle Remus and His Friends*. New York, 1892. Sixteen songs.

HOBSON, ANNE, *In Old Alabama*. New York, 1903. Ten dialect stories and songs.

KENNEDY, R. EMMETT, *Black Cameos*. Albert & Charles Boni, New York, 1924. A collection of twenty-eight stories, mostly humorous, with songs interwoven. The words and music of seventeen songs are given.

KREHBIEL, H. E., *Afro-American Folk Songs*. G. Schirmer, New York and London, 1914. A careful study of Negro folk songs from the point of view of the skilled musician. Songs and music from Africa and other sources are analyzed and compared with American Negro productions. The music of sixty or more songs and dance airs is given.

MARSH, J. B. T., *The Story of the Jubilee Singers*. Boston, 1880. An account of the Jubilee Singers, with their songs.

PETERSON, C. G., *Creole Songs from New Orleans*. New Orleans, 1902.

PIKE, G. D., *The Jubilee Singers*. Boston and New York, 1873. Sixty-one religious songs.

TALLEY, THOMAS, W., *Negro Folk Rhymes*. Macmillan, New York, 1922. This volume contains about 350 rhymes and songs and a study of the origin, development, and characteristics of Negro rhymes. Besides a general index of songs, a comparative index is included.

WORK, JOHN WESLEY, *Folk Song of the American Negro*. Fisk University Press, Nashville, 1915. The words of fifty-five songs and music of nine, together with a study of the origin and growth of certain songs.

PERIODICALS

BACKUS, E. M., "Negro Songs from Georgia," *Journal of American Folk Lore*, vol. 10, pp. 116, 202, 216; vol. 11, pp. 22, 60. Six religious songs.

BACKUS, E. M., "Christmas Carols from Georgia," *Journal of American Folk Lore*, vol. 12, p. 272. Two songs.

BARTON, W. E., "Hymns of Negroes," *New England Magazine*, vol. 19, pp. 669 et seq., 706 et seq. A number of songs with some musical notation and discussion.

BERGEN, MRS. F. D., "On the Eastern Shore," *Journal of American Folk Lore*, vol. 2, pp. 296-298. Two fragments, with a brief discussion of the Negroes of the eastern shore of Maryland.

BROWN, J. M., "Songs of the Slave," *Lippincotts*, vol. 2, pp. 617-623. Several songs with brief comments.

CABLE, GEORGE W., "Creole Slave Songs," *Century*, vol. 31, pp. 807-828. Twelve songs with some fragments, music of seven.

CLARKE, MARY ALMSTED, "Song Games of Negro Children in Virginia," *Journal of American Folk Lore*, vol. 3, pp. 288-290. Nine song games and rhymes.

GARNETT, L. A., "Spirituals," *Outlook*, vol. 130, p. 589. Three religious songs. However, they appear to have been polished considerably by the writer.

HASKELL, M. A., "Negro Spirituals," *Century*, vol. 36, pp. 577 et seq. About ten songs with music.

HIGGINSON, T. W., "Hymns of Negroes," *Atlantic Monthly*, vol. 19, pp. 685 et seq. Thirty-six religious and two secular songs, with musical notation.

LEMMERMAN, K., "Improvised Negro Songs," *New Republic*, vol. 13, pp. 214-215. Six religious songs or improvised fragments.

LOMAX, J. A., "Self-pity in Negro Folk Song," *Nation*, vol. 105, pp. 141-145. About twenty songs, some new, others quoted from Perrow and Odum, with discussion.

"Negro Hymn of Day of Judgment," *Journal of American Folk Lore*, vol. 9, p. 210. One religious song.

ODUM, ANNA K., "Negro Folk Songs from Tennessee," *Journal of American Folk Lore*, vol. 27, pp. 255-265. Twenty-one religious and four secular songs.

ODUM, HOWARD W., "Religious Folk Songs of the Southern Negroes," *Journal of Religious Psychology and Education*, vol. 3, pp. 265-365. About one hundred songs.

ODUM, HOWARD W., "Folk Song and Folk Poetry as Found in the Secular Songs of the Southern Negroes," *Journal of American Folk Lore*, vol. 24, pp. 255-294; 351-396. About 120 songs.

PERKINS, A. E., "Spirituals from the Far South," *Journal of American Folk Lore*, vol. 35, pp. 223-249. Forty-seven songs.

PERROW, E. C., "Songs and Rhymes from the South," *Journal of American Folk Lore*, vol. 25, pp. 137-155; vol. 26, pp. 123-173; vol. 28, pp. 129-190. A general collection containing 118 Negro songs, mostly secular.

REDFEARN, S. F., "Songs from Georgia," *Journal of American Folk Lore*, vol. 34, pp. 121-124. One secular and three religious songs.

SPEERS, M. W. F., "Negro Songs and Folk Lore," *Journal of American Folk Lore*, vol. 23, pp. 435-439. One religious and one secular song.

STEWARD, T. G., "Negro Imagery," *New Republic*, vol. 12, p. 248. One religious improvisation, with discussion.

THANET, OCTAVE, "Cradle Songs of Negroes in North Carolina," *Journal of American Folk Lore*, vol. 7, p. 310. Two lullabies.

TRUITT, FLORENCE, "Songs from Kentucky," *Journal of American Folk Lore*, vol. 36, pp. 376-379. Four white songs, one of which contains several verses often found in Negro songs.

WEBB, W. P., "Notes on Folk Lore of Texas," *Journal of American Folk Lore*, vol. 28, pp. 290-299. Five secular songs.

INDEX TO SONGS

RELIGIOUS SONGS

SOCIAL SONGS